The im-
Possibility

of

INTERRELIGIOUS
DIALOGUE

The im-Possibility

of

INTERRELIGIOUS DIALOGUE

Catherine Cornille

A Herder & Herder Book
The Crossroad Publishing Company
New York

The Crossroad Publishing Company
16 Penn Plaza – 481 Eighth Avenue, Suite 1550
New York, NY 10001

Printed in the United States of America

The text of this book is set in 11.5/16 Sabon.
The display face is News Gothic.

Library of Congress Cataloging-in-Publication Data
Cornille, C. (Catherine)
     The im-possibility of interreligious dialogue / Catherine
  Cornille.
        p.   cm.
     "A Herder & Herder Book."
     Includes bibliographical references (p.   ) and index.
     ISBN-13: 978-0-8245-2464-7 (alk. paper)
     ISBN-10: 0-8245-2464-0 (alk. paper)
     1. Religions – Relations. 2. Dialogue – Religious aspects.
  I. Title.   II. Title: Impossibility of interreligious dialogue.
  III. Title: Possibility of interreligious dialogue.
  BL410.C675 2008
  201'.5 – dc22
                                                    2008007661

1   2   3   4   5   6   7   8   9   10   12   11   10   09   08

For Jeff

CONTENTS

Contents

Contents

ACKNOWLEDGMENTS

This reflection on the challenges of interreligious dialogue for religious traditions in general, and Christianity in particular, is the fruit of almost two decades of engagement in dialogue with other religions, mainly Hinduism and Buddhism, both in Asia and in the West. I wish to thank my partners in dialogue, too many to mention, for opening my mind and heart to the many ways in which truth manifests itself in the teachings and practices of other religions, and for prompting a desire to find ways in which that truth can be brought to bear upon my own Christian tradition. Among the many Christians directly involved in interreligious dialogue, I wish to thank my fellow members of the Voies de l'Orient (Brussels) for their unwavering dedication to the cause of dialogue between Christianity and the religions of Asia, and for including me in their efforts. Through the years, their example of true openness to other religions and faithful commitment to their own has nourished my belief in the importance and possibility of a genuine and constructive dialogue between religions.

I began this study of the conditions for the possibility of interreligious dialogue about ten years ago, on the occasion of a conference on God in Global Dialogue at the University of Lund, Sweden. I would like to thank those friends and colleagues who have responded to various versions or different chapters of this work:[1] Werner Jeanrond, David Tracy,

James Heisig, Joseph O'Leary, Gavin D'Costa, Paul Knitter, Francis Clooney, John Makransky, Ruth Langer, John Berthrong, Valeer Neckebrouck, Emilio Platti, Tariq Ramadan, Norman Solomon, Maria Clara Bingemer, Michael Fitzgerald, and Anthony Kelly. Their interest and encouragement have convinced me of the importance of this project and of seeing it through to its completion. A special thanks also to my gifted student and research assistant, Michelle Hubele, for her helpful and enthusiastic reading of the finished manuscript.

But most of all, I wish to thank my husband, Jeffrey Bloechl. Not only did he temporarily set aside his own writing in order to allow me to finish this book without too much disturbance to our family life, but he also read through each chapter, discreetly changing words and phrases, and transforming the often faltering language of a non-native speaker into more elegant prose. Through the years of working on this book, Jeff has been my constant dialogue partner, offering critical feedback, valuable insight, as well as moral and intellectual support. It is for all these reasons, and many more, that I dedicate this book, with love, to Jeff.

INTRODUCTION

The idea of dialogue between religions has become as familiar as it is perplexing. In a world of close encounters between members of different religions, interreligious dialogue presents itself as an essential feature of peaceful coexistence and as a promise for religious growth. The dialogue between religions has taken various forms, from meetings between religious leaders in a common display of solidarity and friendship to collaboration between members of different religions in grassroots projects, and from intense discussion and debate between religious scholars to interreligious prayer and spiritual exchange. Recent times have witnessed the emergence of numerous organizations dedicated to the promotion of dialogue, from international movements to local ones, and from interfaith organizations to confessional ones. Some dialogue meetings include members from many different religions, while others concentrate on only a few traditions. Some deal with spiritual practice or ethical concerns, while others focus on theoretical matters of religious belief and doctrine. Scholarly as well as popular journals have emerged in order to advance interreligious dialogue in general and between particular religious traditions. In these cases, peaceful exchange and productive collaboration between members of different religions are generally regarded, if not as realizable goals, then as ideals to which all religions are held to strive.

While interreligious dialogue has thus become a programmatic notion, it can hardly be said that all religions are by nature inclined to constructive communication and exchange with other religious traditions. As the history of religions amply bears out, the encounter between members of different religions leads to tension and violence more often than to peaceful coexistence and collaboration, and the existence of other religious traditions is often regarded as a source of religious disturbance or at best indifference rather than as an occasion for mutual enrichment. Most religions tend to self-sufficiency rather than to mutual dependency and to something approaching inner complacency rather than to active interest in the other. To the degree that this is so, it stands to reason — if one needs a reason for what is everywhere evident — that the relationship between individuals belonging to different religions is thus often governed by mutual fear and aversion rather than by friendship and attraction, and by feelings of superiority and condescension rather than by mutual respect. Though rarely the sole reason for conflict, religious beliefs have often enough been used — even lent themselves — to the task of justifying or intensifying aggression toward others. The very urgency with which religions are called to engage in peaceful and constructive conversation may in fact signal a certain religious reticence, if not resistance, to dialogue.

Interreligious dialogue is, simply put, a challenge for most religious traditions. Scholars engaged in the dialogue between religions have proposed varying lists of conditions for fruitful dialogue.[1] Some focus on necessary social and political conditions (freedom of religion, separation of church and state), whereas others emphasize essential psychological attitudes and dispositions necessary for genuine conversation and exchange.

While such external circumstances are indeed necessary, it seems to me that the main obstacle for dialogue lies not so much outside as within religious traditions. As such, I wish to focus here on the conditions for dialogue as they pertain to the very self-understanding of religious traditions.

Any identification of the essential conditions for the possibility of dialogue between religions will of course depend on what one conceives to be its meaning and purpose. At the most basic level, dialogue between religions may be regarded as an exchange of information, and as a means to mutual understanding and tolerance. In that case, the conditions for dialogue coincide largely with those which apply to all forms of intercultural and interreligious hermeneutics.[2] However, beyond this accumulation of facts about the other, dialogue may also include the possibility of learning from the other religion. Here dialogue becomes part of a continuous religious pursuit of truth. It consists of an open and constructive exchange between individuals belonging to different religious traditions, oriented to the possibility of change and growth. This notion of dialogue may include not only verbal exchange, but also serious engagement with the texts and teachings of another religion. It may focus on questions of doctrine, practice, or organization. But it presupposes some level of identification with a particular religious tradition. Needless to say, this generally involves identification with a particular school or sect within a larger religion. And indeed, most dialogue takes place not between Islam and Christianity, but between Shi'ites and Methodists, or between members of a particular Sufi order and those of an order within the Roman Catholic Church. The inner relationship of a particular domination or sect, not to mention one's own personal understanding of it, to a more embracing tradition will be a constant and unavoidable complication of any reflection on dialogue as such.

◆ ◆ ◆

If dialogue is to include the possibility of change and growth, not only of the individuals involved, but also of the religions themselves, then certain essential conditions are to be fulfilled. In this book, I frame these conditions for a constructive and enriching dialogue between religions in terms of a series of virtues that, however, point to deeper doctrinal and epistemological demands. A first condition for genuine dialogue is *doctrinal or epistemic humility.* Any possibility of change or growth indeed presupposes recognition of one's own fallibility and imperfection. Doctrinal humility thus entails a certain degree of admission of the finite and limited ways in which the ultimate truth has been grasped and expressed within one's own religious teachings, practices, and/or institutional forms.

A second condition for a meaningful and constructive dialogue between religions is *commitment* to a particular religious tradition. Whereas this may seem evident, dialogue often creates a delicate or unstable balance between openness to the other religion and commitment to one's own. A profound engagement with the teachings of other religions may well lead to a questioning of the truth of one's own tradition. But interreligious dialogue, if it is truly interreligious, nonetheless requires that its interlocutors remain rooted in the particular religious community from which and for which they speak. It is this investment in the truth of a particular tradition that distinguishes dialogue from New Age syncretism. Dialogue requires both partners to share willingly not only the contents but also the truth of their own respective beliefs and to bring the fruits of the dialogue back to their own religious traditions.

And this requires a sense of commitment to and care for the tradition.

A third condition for dialogue is *interconnection,* or the belief that the teachings and practices of the other religion are in some way related to or relevant for one's own religious tradition. Interreligious dialogue necessarily requires some meeting point where religions may find one another and engage in a meaningful conversation. As a matter of aim or goal, this may involve a shared commitment to certain social or political causes, or a shared reaction to external challenges (secularism, globalization). But the belief that the teachings and practices of other religions may in some way derive from or point to one's own conception of ultimate reality provides a particularly powerful motivation, if not a condition for dialogue.

Moving from conditions relating mainly to one's own tradition to those involving the other, genuine dialogue also presupposes the possibility of understanding the other religion as other. This fourth condition for dialogue involves the ability to gain not only an intellectual but also an experiential understanding of the other. Whereas knowledge of facts and concepts represents an important dimension of dialogue, a fuller understanding of the religious other must include some grasp of the religious meaning of particular teachings and their impact on the life of believers. This point must be made more boldly: it is only to the degree that one is able to resonate with the religious meaning of particular teachings and practices of the other religion that they may have an impact upon one's own religious tradition. As such, dialogue requires an important exercise of *empathy.*

When all of these necessary conditions for dialogue are fulfilled, the possibility for genuine dialogue still demands ultimately the recognition of other religions as potential sources of genuine and distinctive truth. Any a priori rejection of truth in other religions in general, or in certain religions in particular severely limits and perhaps even aborts any chance of productive dialogue such as I have defined it. Whereas the actual presence of truth need not — and in most cases cannot — be determined beforehand, only a belief in the possibility of discovering distinctive truth in the other religion renders dialogue not only possible, but also necessary. *Hospitality* to the authentic truth of the other thus forms the sole sufficient condition for dialogue.

◆ ◆ ◆

It is clear that each of these conditions represents a challenge for most religious traditions and for individuals engaged in interreligious dialogue. Though some religions may be more attuned to certain conditions than others, fulfillment of all of the conditions requires a certain hermeneutical effort and creativity, a reinterpretation of traditional teachings or a mobilization of latent resources hidden within one's own religious texts and teachings. As the field of modern hermeneutics has taught us, the meaning of religious texts is multivalent and polysemic, and therefore subject to a continuous process of reinterpretation. Religious symbols and concepts that at one time and context were used to insist on the superiority and uniqueness of one's own religion may in a different context become the basis for openness and receptivity toward the truth of the other religion. Of course, this cannot mean that religious symbols and texts are infinitely open or unlimited by rules of interpretation. But it does suggest that the possibility (or impossibility) of interreligious dialogue is less a matter of the hard and fast teachings of a particular religion than of the hermeneutical principles that may be brought to bear on its self-understanding.

Even though these conditions — if sound — may be applicable to any religious tradition, I here focus mainly on the degree to which they may come to be fulfilled within Christianity. There seems to exist a certain ambivalence and suspicion about the Christian involvement in dialogue, both from within and from outside the tradition. Even though Christians have been actively involved in many initiatives for dialogue, these initiatives are often regarded as covert forms of proselytizing. And church authorities have themselves at times been less than univocal in their commitment to dialogue. Within the past fifty years, the Roman Catholic Church has created a special Secretariat for non-Christians (1964), changed its name to the Pontifical Council for Interreligious Dialogue (1988), folded it back into the Pontifical Council for Cultures (2006), and subsequently reinstated it. This is enough to remind us of the volatile nature of interreligious dialogue and of the need to firmly ground such dialogue within the very self-understanding of a religious tradition. In the past half a century, a rich body of theological reflection has developed around the Christian relationship to other religious traditions that have been classified as pluralist, inclusivist, and exclusivist in their respective approaches to the question of salvation, or as replacement, fulfillment, mutuality, and acceptance models in their attitude to religious truth. It is evident that each of these positions has a direct bearing on the conditions for dialogue, and I draw extensively from the work of Christian theologians of religions to illustrate or test particular conditions. However, my work does not so much seek to instill itself among the existing paradigms as to offer a new lens from which to reflect on the challenges and possibilities of religious plurality and dialogue, not only for Christianity, but also — hopefully — for other religious traditions.

This book is neither an apology for dialogue, nor a glorification of the Christian role in it. It does not judge the truth of religions according to their capacity for dialogue. On the contrary, it recognizes the epistemic priority for believers of faith and revelation over any external demands or expectations. For this reason, it also proposes that if dialogue is to be possible, it must find its deepest reasons and motivations within the self-understanding of religious traditions themselves. Only thus will dialogue become an internal necessity rather than an external obligation.

CHAPTER ONE

HUMILITY

We need not be afraid of making them proud, because love of truth is always accompanied by humility. Real genius is nothing else but the virtue of humility in the domain of thought. — SIMONE WEIL[1]

The impulse to dialogue arises from the desire to learn, to increase one's understanding of the other, of oneself, or of the truth. It thus presupposes humble awareness of the limitation of one's own understanding and experience and of the possibility of change and growth. Contemporary language and everyday speech have come to associate the term "humility" with modesty, with a reluctance to accept rightfully deserved distinction and recognition. Humility may also be understood, however, in a more radical sense to denote a genuine acknowledgment of the limitation and imperfection of one's insights and accomplishments, as indeed of all human realization and self-expression.[2] In dialogue, it is such a humble awareness of the finite and partial nature of one's own understanding that drives one from the same to the other, from complacency to an active search for growth in the truth.

Dialogue between religions requires at least two forms of humility in each participant or agent. Most evidently, it demands humility toward other traditions. This involves recognition of the limitation of one's knowledge and understanding of the other. The study of religions has borne witness to the ways in which religious knowledge is related to power, and in which representations of the other may become distorted through religious and cultural prejudices. Every religious tradition represents a complex whole of beliefs and practices, philosophical schools and sectarian developments that no single individual can pretend to master. At this level, humility toward the other is a matter of necessary cognitive vigilance: one must always guard against imposing one's own categories of understanding upon the other and indeed remain open to constant correction and growth in one's knowledge of the other tradition.

However, dialogue between religions requires humility not only toward the other religion, but also toward — or rather about — one's own religious tradition. Openness and receptivity toward the truth of the other religion presupposes humble recognition of the constant limitation and therefore endless perfectibility of one's own religious understanding of the truth. This also includes recognition of the partial and finite nature of the ways in which ultimate truth has been grasped and expressed in the teachings and practices of one's own tradition. Such humility about one's own religious teachings and practices may be called epistemic or doctrinal humility.

One cannot deny that the attitude of doctrinal humility runs against the grain of most religious self-understanding. Most religious traditions regard themselves as the ultimate if not the sole repository of truth, as the highest path to salvation or the most efficacious means to liberation.[3] It is this belief in the absolute and final truth of one's own teachings and practices that prevents one from listening to, let alone learning from other religious traditions. If the fullness of truth is already expressed within one's own beliefs and practices, then other traditions can only be regarded as deficient and wrong, or at best as a partial and pale reflection of what one already knows. Of course, one may still engage other traditions as a sign of benevolent tolerance or perhaps out of a willingness to collaborate peacefully in a pluralistic society. Yet without doctrinal humility, there seems little prospect for mutual religious transformation or growth.

Even though the attitude of humility about one's own teachings and practices does not come naturally to most religious traditions, they may still harbor resources by which to develop it. We shall here focus on possible resources for the cultivation of doctrinal humility embedded within Christianity. The most evident location from which to retrieve such humility would be the rich Christian tradition of explicit reflection on the category of humility. Humility indeed plays a central role within Christian spirituality, as in most spiritual traditions. It is regarded as the path to the ultimate experience of God, as well as an expression of that experience. While spiritual humility may offer some basis for a greater openness toward other religions, it does not unequivocally lead to doctrinal humility. Such humility about Christian doctrines may thus require a certain hermeneutical effort and focus on Christian teachings that recognize a difference or distance between the ultimate truth and the forms of its expression within the tradition.

Though it is a condition for dialogue, doctrinal humility may also come about as a result of dialogue with other religions. As Raimon Panikkar, one of the pioneers of modern interreligious dialogue, points out:

In the dialogue we are reminded constantly of our temporality, our contingency, our own constitutive limitations.

Humility is not primarily a moral virtue, but an ontological one; it is the awareness of the place of my ego,
the truthfulness of accepting my real situation, namely,
that I am a situated being, a vision's angle on the real, an
existence.[4]

Not only does the confrontation with different worldviews and
religious paths enhance awareness of the contingency and historical conditioning of one's own understanding of the truth,
but dialogue with other religions may also deepen one's very
understanding of humility.

CHRISTIAN HUMILITY AND DIALOGUE

Christianity is not generally considered to be a humble religion. On the contrary, the Christian tradition is more likely to
be associated with arrogance and triumphalism than with an
attitude of humility. Yet the virtue of humility has formed the
heart of Christian spiritual and moral life from the very beginning. Anthony of the Desert referred to humility as "the first of
all virtues,"[5] and Augustine considered it to be "the sum total
of the medicine required to cure us."[6] St. Benedict, the founder
of the Western monastic tradition, speaks of the spiritual path
as an ascent through twelve steps of humility. And humility is
also a central theme in the works of most Christian mystical
writers, from Gregory the Great to the anonymous author of
The Cloud of Unknowing, and from Teresa of Avila to the spiritual correspondence between Jeanne de Chantal and Francis
de Sales. Even in times when the virtue of humility may seem
to have been virtually eclipsed by Christian imperialism and
church power, it continued to inform the work of great theologians such as Thomas Aquinas and founders of new spiritual

traditions such as Ignatius of Loyola. And although humility has become antithetical to the modern emphasis on human autonomy and individual excellence, it still figures prominently in the work of important contemporary Christian thinkers such as Simone Weil and Jean-Louis Chrétien.

With the help of these thinkers, we will explore the meaning and role of humility in the Christian tradition and its relationship to doctrine. Does the spiritual understanding of humility also imply doctrinal humility? And to that extent does the Christian discipline of humility lend itself to the cultivation of openness and dialogue with other religious traditions? An immediate focal point for this latter question may be found in Bernard of Clairvaux's classic *The Twelve Steps of Humility and Pride.*[7]

Spiritual Humility

The Christian understanding of humility is fundamentally grounded in a Christian faith relationship to God. It is the belief in a creator-God, source of all goodness and truth, that reduces to naught all tendencies to self-glorification and pride. Contemplating the absolute, one is intensely aware of one's own dependency and insignificance as a human being. And the experience of God presupposes the eradication of all human pride and sense of self-sufficiency. Christian definitions of humility therefore emphasize the insignificance and worthlessness of the human being in the face of ultimate reality. For Benedict, humility means confessing and truly believing oneself "lower and of less account than all others"[8] and for Bernard it animates "that thorough self-examination which makes a man contemptible in his own sight."[9] Modern Christian writers are equally stark on this point. In the middle of the twentieth century, Simone Weil stated:

13

Humility consists in knowing that in what we call "I" there is no source of energy by which we can rise. Everything without exception which is of value in me comes from somewhere other than myself, not as a gift, but as a loan which must be ceaselessly renewed. Everything without exception in me is absolutely valueless; and, among the gifts which have come to me from elsewhere, everything which I appropriate becomes valueless immediately I do so.[10]

In the face of the absolute, all human accomplishment seems insignificant and all human endeavors futile, even obtrusive. The Christian notion of humility thus emphasizes the radical and total worthlessness of the human person, not in comparison with any worldly or human agency, but in an absolute sense, or in relation to God.

This emphasis on humility appears to set Christianity apart not only from the Greek and Roman cultures in which it was formed, but also from secular life in general. Augustine already anticipated an immense challenge "to persuade the proud of how great is the virtue of humility, which raises us, not by a quite human arrogance, but by divine grace, above all the earthly dignities that totter on this shifting scene."[11] And Brian Daley points out:

Christian humility seems to be one of those few central categories of faith that biblical religion does not draw from the wider store of human wisdom and that therefore will always appear paradoxical, dangerous, and nonsensical to the secular mind. For this very reason, humility seems to be one of the categories that distinguish Christian love and Christian goodness from a love and

14

goodness not illumined by faith. It is one of our basic ways of responding in faith to the Christian mystery.[12]

Though at odds with secular culture, the concept of humility is firmly grounded in biblical anthropology. The tension between the call to radical obedience and humble surrender to God, and the temptation to succumb to one's own will and judgment and thirst for greatness, informs the whole biblical narrative, from the account of the Fall in the book of Genesis to Paul's admonition to the Corinthians: "What have you that you did not receive? If you then received it, why do you boast as if it was not a gift?" (1 Cor. 4:7). Pride is regarded in the Bible as the beginning of all sin and humility as the expression of our true nature. The importance of humility is, if anything, still more prominent in the example and teaching of Jesus Christ. For Christians, Jesus is the very embodiment of humility: his birth occurs in the humblest of circumstances, he lived a humble life of total surrender to the will of God, and then submitted himself to the ultimate humiliation of death on the Cross. Humility already made its way fully into the metaphysics of the Incarnation in the early Christology of the Fathers, for whom Jesus Christ embodies the self-humbling God, a God whose self-emptying (*kenosis*) is expressed in the divine become flesh. But it is already stated in Paul's letter to the Philippians (2:6–8), which points to the example of Christ, who "did not count equality with God a thing to be grasped, but emptied himself, taking the form of a servant, being born in the likeness of men. And being found in human form he humbled himself and became obedient unto death, even death on a cross." Of course, Jesus not only embodies humility, but also teaches it. Humility is the very first of the virtues to be extolled in the Beatitudes: "Blessed are the poor in spirit, for theirs is the kingdom of heaven" (Matt. 5:3).[13] And in one of the few appeals to the example of his own life, Jesus states, "Learn from me, for I am gentle and lowly in heart, and you will find rest for your souls" (Matt. 11:29). More indirect references to the importance of humility may be found in Jesus' reversal of worldly convention, as when he says that "many that are first will be last, and the last first" (Matt. 19:30), or when he refers to the Kingdom of God as "the smallest of seeds" that becomes "the greatest of shrubs" (Matt. 13:31).

Perhaps it was inevitable that Christian spirituality would be organized around the notion of humility. The process defined itself first within the context of monastic spirituality. The Rule of St. Benedict (eighth century), a virtual blueprint for much of Western monastic life, associates progress in spiritual growth with an ascent through various steps of humility:

> And the ladder erected is our life in this world, which for the humble of heart is raised up by the Lord unto heaven. Now the sides of the ladder are our body and soul, into which sides our divine vocation has fitted various degrees of humility and discipline which we have to climb.[14]

For Benedict, humility begins with "guarding against evil desires" and ends with full manifestation of humility in mind, speech, and posture. In his own version of *The Steps of Humility,* Bernard (twelfth century) retraces Benedict's steps in reverse order, carefully analyzing the process by which the soul becomes entangled in ever deepening states of pride. Each of the steps of pride is described with great psychological and spiritual insight and has served as a guideline for monks throughout the ages. Both Benedict and Bernard believed that only monastics could attain the highest levels of humility, since these are so precarious as to require submission to the guidance of a superior.

The ultimate end of the spiritual discipline of humility is divinization, the experience of union with God. This is plainly stated in the words of Gregory the Great: "Let the humble, therefore, be told that in abasing themselves, they rise to the likeness of God."[15] Various images have been used within the Christian spiritual tradition to express this paradox. Meister Eckhart, for example, uses the image of valleys and heights to refer to the concurrence of humiliation and divinization:

> the highest heights of exaltation lie precisely in the lowest depths of humiliation; for the deeper the valleys go, the loftier the heights that rise above them; the deeper the well, the higher too: for depth and height are the same thing.[16]

It is through completely abasing oneself, through eradicating all sense of pride and self-esteem, that one attains human perfection. Since pride is regarded as the origin of sin, humility leads to a state of spiritual and moral purity. The author of *The Cloud of Unknowing* states that if a person attains perfect humility "he will not sin, and afterwards, only a little."[17] Humility thus leads to a transformation of the individual into the image and instrument of God. It is also the source of true greatness since, as Chrétien remarks, "that which is too great for human beings to achieve, God can only accomplish through those who are humble, for they do not lean on their own powers."[18]

While a certain degree of humility can likely be attained through human effort and understanding, complete or perfect humility is believed to be a gift from God (lest humility itself lead to pride). Within Christian spirituality, a distinction is often made between "acquired" and "infused" humility (Aquinas), between "cognitive" and "connative" humility (Bernard), or between "imperfect" and "perfect" humility (*The Cloud of Unknowing*). Whereas imperfect humility contains a sense of helplessness and despair arising from a strong awareness of the human condition of wretchedness and sin, perfect humility leads to the highest joy, peace, and detachment from the world. No longer concerned with praise or blame from others, one achieves the positive freedom of authentic creatureliness, and with it the peace described by Thomas à Kempis:

> Humble people are always at peace, even when they are put to shame, because they trust in God and not in the world. So if you wish to reach the height of perfection, never think of yourself as being virtuous until you know sincerely in your heart that you are the least of all.[19]

As the fruit of the experience of God, humility has often come to function within the Christian tradition as the basis for distinguishing genuine from false experiences of God, or experiences of God from experiences of the devil. Teresa of Avila observes that an experience of the devil "leaves disquiet behind it, and very little humility, and does not do much to prepare the soul for the effects which are produced when it comes from God."[20] And John of the Cross states that while divine visions and experiences "cause the mildness of humility and the love of God," diabolical visions "produce spiritual dryness in one's communion with God and an inclination to self-esteem."[21]

Though the pursuit of perfect humility is generally seen to be a distinctly monastic endeavor, humility is also identified as a key virtue in the life of all believers. Thomas Aquinas regarded humility as "foundation of the spiritual edifice" and accorded it pride of place among the other virtues since "it expels pride, which God resists, and makes man submissive and ever open to receive the influx of Divine grace."[22] No doubt influenced by Aristotle, he identifies humility with self-control, and indeed with true self-knowledge:

> Humility consists essentially in the appetite, insofar as one restrains the impetuosity of the soul, lest it tend inordinately toward great things. But it has its rule in knowledge, namely, that a man must not esteem himself above what he is. And the principle of each of these elements is the reverence one has toward God.[23]

Notice that in this case self-knowledge and reverence for God entail not complete renunciation of all desires (as is the case in monastic life) but attunement to one's natural talents and gifts. For Aquinas, humility also contains an interpersonal dimension: it entails subjecting oneself to God and to all there is of God in others.[24]

One of the distinctive characteristics of Christian humility is its Christocentric nature. Not only is Christ the ultimate example of humility,[25] but humility is also understood as participation in the life of Christ. This is particularly evident in Jesuit spirituality, where the stages or degrees of humility, cultivated during the second week of *Spiritual Exercises,* culminate in the experience of union with Jesus Christ. While the first degree of humility relates the person as creature to God and the second degree brings about detachment from the world, the third and most perfect kind of humility consists of identification with the particularities of the life of Jesus:

> If we suppose the first and the second kind attained, then whenever the praise and glory of the Divine Majesty

would be equally served, in order to imitate and be in reality more like Christ our Lord, I desire and choose poverty with Christ poor, rather than riches; insults with Christ loaded with them, rather than honors; I desire to be accounted as worthless and a fool for Christ, rather than to be esteemed as wise and prudent in this world. So Christ was treated before me.[26]

Thus humility is here not an end in itself, but a means to oneness with Christ. This points to the relational — and indeed affective — dimension of Christian humility.

Another characteristic of Christian humility is its unattainable or eschatological nature. Though Jesus Christ represents the example and focal point of Christian humility, it is believed that no one can ever attain the fullness of humility that Christ represents. Only in Jesus Christ, the unique Son of God and divine incarnation, was the perfection of humility fully realized. Herein lies what Chrétien calls "the Christian paradox according to which only God is humble."[27] While humans may attain moments of genuine humility and enjoy glimpses of the fruit of that experience, perfect humility cannot be attained as a permanent state in this life. Whereas this may seem discouraging or de-motivating to some, it may also, as Chrétien suggests, inspire praise and even rejoicing before a God who is always more humble than we are. Moreover, it may be conducive to a deepening of humility by "renouncing the vain idea of a maximum state of humility to which our efforts might lead us."[28] Christians are thus held to remain humble about their very humility.

Spiritual Humility and Dialogue

While the Christian understanding of humility revolves in the first place around the relationship between the individual believer and God, the teaching and practice of humility may also be seen to contain direct or indirect implications for the relationship with members of other religions. Rather than the notion of humility itself, it is the concept of truth associated with the practice of humility that may suggest greater openness and receptivity toward the teachings of other religions. We shall focus our attention on *The Steps of Humility* by Bernard of Clairvaux in which, as Rémi Brague has put it, the link between humility and truth receives the "unprecedented breadth that has led it to persist in the history of Christian spirituality."[29] In Bernard's approach, the twelve steps of humility indeed culminate in the three steps of truth. Humility is the "toil," whereas truth is the "fruit of the toil";[30] the twelfth step of the former is equally the first step of the latter, with two more to follow.[31] In order, the three are: truth about self, truth about the other, and truth about God. What are these truths that are the fruit of humility, and what might they imply for dialogue? It is obvious that Bernard himself was not considering the implications of his teachings for the relationship with other religious traditions. Insofar as the pursuit of truth is the ultimate goal of the practice of humility and the practice of dialogue, however, insights gained by one may come to inspire the other.

The understanding of humility as the expression of ultimate self-knowledge is a constant theme in Christian spiritual writings. Still writing in the vein of monastic spiritual discipline, the anonymous author of *The Cloud of Unknowing* defines humility as "a true knowledge and experience of yourself as you are, a wretch, filth, far worse than nothing."[32] And likewise in *The Imitation of Christ,* Thomas à Kempis states that "nothing is so beneficial as a true understanding of ourselves, which produces wholesome self-contempt. Always think kindly of others, while holding yourself as nothing; this is true wisdom and leads to perfection."[33] This is, in the estimation of Jean-Louis Chrétien, "the distinctively Christian and thus paradoxical response to the injunction 'know thyself.' "[34] Bernard, for his part, focuses at length on the confluence of ignorance and pride. It is pride, "love of your own excellence," that leads to ignorance, or that "dims the mind and overshadows the truth in such a way that...you can no longer see yourself as you are actually or potentially; but you either fancy that you are or hope you will become such as you would love to be."[35] Now, this pride is usually generated by focusing on the weaknesses of others and developing a high self-esteem by comparison. Inevitably, then, one's relationship to others comes to be governed by feelings of envy (second step of pride), by constant focus on one's own excellence and forgetfulness of sin (third step of pride), leading to attempts to be better than others (fifth step of pride) and to be recognized as such (sixth step of pride), through demands or expectation to be first (seventh step of pride) and then, if necessary, self-justification (eighth step of pride) all the way to hypocritical forms of confession (ninth step of pride). In the end, pride thus distorts one's image of oneself and of the other. This has been evident in the encounter between religions. Concern with securing the sense of superiority of one's own religion has often led to misrepresentation of both one's own religion and the other, resulting in a comparison between an idealized image of one's own religion and a caricatured image of the other. An example of deliberate distortion may be found in the some of the images of Mohammed that circulated in the Christian world during the Middle Ages. It hardly needs to be said that this sort of distortion is generally motivated by a desire to argue for the superiority of one's own tradition. Within this atmosphere, the admonition of Thomas à Kempis to "think kindly of others, while holding yourself as nothing"[36] might represent a helpful corrective to the more natural religious inclination to the reverse.[37]

Bernard does on occasion directly address the implications of pride for dialogue. Painting a vivid picture of the way in which a proud person engages in conversation, he states:

> He must either talk or burst.... Opinions fly around, weighty words resound. He interrupts a questioner; he answers one who does not ask. He himself posts the questions, he himself solves them, he cuts short his fellow speaker's unfinished words.... He does not care to teach you, or to learn from you what he does not know, but to know that you know that he knows.[38]

These lines can certainly be applied to some instances of the dialogue between religions, which can fall under the sway of a desire to teach and convince the other of the truth of one's own tradition, rather than a desire to learn. To be sure, such an attitude is often inspired by religious enthusiasm and zeal, which, if present on both sides, may lead to a passionate and enriching discussion. However, it may also arise from an attitude of arrogance and condescension, which rules out any form of mutuality in dialogue.

Bernard's second step of truth consists of knowledge of the other. Here, humility is said to lead to love of the other: "Truth gives love to those to whom it is revealed. But it is revealed to the humble, and so it gives love to the humble."[39] Perhaps this echoes the earlier statement by Augustine, for whom humility leads to "the most genuine kind of love for one's fellows, love without mixed motives, without conceit, without arrogance, without deceit."[40] For Bernard, too, this love is unconditional, transcending one's judgment of the other. Dialogue conducted in humility might thus be dialogue conducted in love, before and beyond the question of the other person's particular religious beliefs and practices. Humility then comes to represent not only a passive reality, an absence of pride, but also an active and dynamic force that drives one beyond oneself to encounter with the other.

But more than this, the love generated by humility also contains, according to Bernard, a cognitive dimension. It is through humility and love that one is able truly to understand the other and empathize with his or her experiences and feelings. "The merciful," Bernard states, "quickly grasp truth in their neighbors, extending their own feelings to them and conforming themselves to them through love, so that they feel their joys or troubles as their own. They are weak with the weak; they burn with the offended. They rejoice with them that do rejoice, and weep with them that weep (Rom. 12:15)."[41] It will be necessary later to reflect at length on the cognitive or epistemic possibilities and limits of empathy. But it is already clear that for Bernard genuine understanding of others requires a certain degree of humility, or freedom from preoccupation with one's own thoughts and feelings. By this time, the basis for such a conclusion has been made clear: humility facilitates understanding through love of the other and an enhanced awareness of one's own prideful ignorance. This may be what James Fodor has in mind when he argues:

> Ironically, it is the Christian virtue of humility and not the modern liberal democratic ideal of tolerance which is genuinely open to the otherness of the stranger. For

24

Christian humility cultivates a love for the particular in a way that does not negate the stranger or hide from itself its own temptations to coercion, its own lust for power, its own proclivities to sin.[42]

While tolerance often includes an attitude of indifference or even disregard for the distinctive beliefs and practices of the other (one need not understand, let alone respect, what one is willing to tolerate), genuine humility is accompanied by an attitude of interest in the other and by a self-critical awareness of the possibility of distortions in one's own understanding of the other.

Bernard's third and final step of truth involves understanding or experience of the ultimate reality itself. Having overcome "the three obstacles arising from ignorance and weakness and willfulness," one achieves "the ecstasy of contemplation."[43] While the first and second steps of truth involve for Bernard a certain degree of human effort, the highest truth is considered to be pure gift, that is to say, it is attained by the grace of God.[44] In attempting to describe his experience of the ultimate truth, Bernard resorts to paradox:

There it sees invisible things, hears unspeakable words, which it is not lawful for man to utter. They surpass all that knowledge which night sheweth unto night; but day unto day uttereth speech, and it is lawful to speak wisdom among the wise and to compare spiritual things with spiritual.[45]

In the third [step] they are caught up to the mysteries of truth and exclaim, *My secret to myself, my secret to myself.*[46]

The spiritual path of humility thus ultimately leads to an experience that cannot be expressed in words and categories. With this, Bernard's third step of truth rejoins the long Christian tradition of apophatic theology, which emphasizes the ineffability of ultimate reality. Rather than a denial or refusal of concepts and doctrines, this tradition focuses on the progressive transcendence of all finite categories in order to attain to the ultimate truth. It is precisely here that spiritual humility may become the basis for doctrinal humility, or humility about the ways in which the truth has been grasped and expressed within one's own teachings and doctrines. Since the ultimate truth is beyond our grasp, all doctrinal categories are to be regarded as at best approximate reflections of that truth. Hence, humility must also entail a certain abandonment of all preconceived knowledge of God and of all theological or doctrinal pride. It is through spiritual humility that one attains both to the realization of the ultimate and to insight into the limitation of all doctrinal formulation — and, moreover, in a relation of reciprocal confirmation. Since the ultimate reality is beyond all words, it can be reached only through an attitude of total humility. This is expressed nowhere more powerfully than in the words of Gregory the Great:

> Great, my brethren, great and sublime is the virtue of
>   humility,
> which can reach what none can teach,
> worthy to obtain what none can explain,
> worthy to conceive by the Word and of the Word
> that which it cannot set forth in its own words.[47]

This notion and its formative role in monastic life may help explain why monks have played such an important role in interreligious dialogue. Many of the early pioneers of the East-West dialogue (Henri Le Saux, Bede Griffiths, and Thomas Merton) were monks. And the inter-monastic dialogue has become one of the most enduring and fruitful forms of interreligious dialogue. Various elements may explain this. In addition to shared monastic emphasis on poverty and renunciation, silence and contemplation, other monastic values such as hospitality have been invoked to account for the importance of monastic openness to other religious traditions.[48] But it might be above all a life of immersion in the cultivation of humility that generates a greater attention and receptivity to the truth of other religions.[49] Conversely, the monastic experience of dialogue with other religions also seems to reinforce the attitude of humility about one's own tradition. Decades of deep involvement with the Hindu tradition led the British Benedictine monk Bede Griffiths to move from a strong conviction of the ultimate truth of Christian doctrines, to a view of all symbols and doctrines as mere "signs and appearances."[50] And encounter with numerous non-Christian spiritual masters led the French Benedictine Henri Le Saux to state that:

> We should simply thank God in deepest humility when we happen to meet such a saint or sage, no matter to which dharma he may outwardly belong, and be open to accept with open heart his witness and message.[51]

Spiritual Humility and Doctrine

Even though the spiritual practice of humility may thus lead to a more humble relationship to doctrine, it must be clear that the Christian virtue of humility has not always been seen to include doctrinal humility. Insofar as humility is seen to relate to doctrine, it has more often been regarded as an attitude to be adopted *toward* rather than *about* the truth of Christian doctrines. Religious teachings and doctrines in fact often function as mediators of humility. It is through submission of one's own will and intellect to the teachings of the tradition that one is said to attain to freedom from intellectual pride and autonomy. Here, humility is thus reflective of an attitude of faith that acknowledges the limitations of human reason in attaining ultimate truth and that submits itself to a particular set of authoritative teachings. The more authoritative particular teachings or doctrines are, the more unconditional the attitude of humble assent incumbent on the believer. As such, humility and absolute claims to truth may at times come to reinforce one another.

While the Christian tradition maintains a certain hierarchy of truths and acknowledges the development of doctrines, doctrinal teachings have always derived their authoritative status from their foundation in scripture. In the early church, doctrines were considered to be a direct elaboration of scriptural revelation and believed to be permanent and unchanging expressions of the truth, or propositions "which have been believed everywhere, always and by all," as one of the earliest definitions puts it.[52] When doctrinal development came to be recognized in the course of time, continuity with scripture and with the apostolic tradition remained the ultimate basis for the authority of doctrine. This is evident in John Henry Newman's famous criteria for distinguishing authentic from inauthentic doctrines: preservation of type, continuity of principles, assimilative power, early anticipation, logical sequence, preservative additions, and chronic continuance.[53] The hierarchy of truths also came to be grounded in the relationship of particular teachings to the foundation of Christian faith.[54] And the status of "infallibility" of certain teachings of the

Magisterium of the Catholic Church is said to be ultimately derived from their being "co-extensive with the deposit of revelation, which must be religiously guarded and loyally and courageously expounded."[55]

Insofar as Christian doctrines are seen to be in continuity with the ultimate truth of revelation, the proper response is thus generally conceived in terms of *obsequium religiosum,* which may be understood as an attempt "to overcome any contrary opinion I might have, and achieve a sincere assent of my mind."[56] Though the church encourages conscious and reflective endorsement of its teachings (rather than fideism) and though it recognizes the possibility of dissent with regard to some of its teachings, the ultimate goal of Christian faith consists in the attempt to conform one's will and judgment to all the doctrines of the church. In the course of Christian history, assent to the doctrines of the church has at times been regarded as a sign of humility and dissent as a lack thereof. One thinks immediately of Augustine's conception of pride as "the mother of all heretics" and his belief that "if there were no pride there would be no heretics, no schismatics, no circumcised, no worshippers of creatures or of images."[57] But one also thinks in more recent times of Bernard Lonergan's notion of the normative function of Christian doctrines and his observation that "while the unconverted may have no real apprehension of what it is to be converted, at least they have in doctrines the evidence both that there is something lacking in themselves and that they need to pray for illumination and to seek instruction."[58] In relation to Christian doctrines, humility is thus to be understood in terms of a faithful submission to the truth of particular teachings, or in terms of the recognition of one's inability to grasp the fullness of their meaning. But it is not usually seen to include humble acknowl-edgment of the partial or incomplete nature of those doctrinal formulations.

All of this seems to indicate that the Christian virtue of humility does not readily lend itself to the development of doc-trinal humility. If the same attitude of humility that denotes a recognition of dependence on the absolute is extended to an attitude of submission to doctrine, there can be little doubt that it will instill something approaching a complete assent to all the teachings of the church. Humility is indeed often mea-sured by one's assent to the ultimate truth of Catholic doctrine. This leaves little room for critical reflection on Christian claims to truth or for doctrinal humility. On the contrary, absolute claims to truth and the cultivation of humility in fact seem to reinforce one another: doctrines elicit a response of humble assent, proportional to their importance and truth, and hu-mility binds the believer to them. Interestingly, at this extreme point, humility may come to coincide with what can only be called doctrinal pride. While the attitude of pride is generally discouraged in Christianity, as in other religious traditions, it is often tolerated and at times even encouraged when directed toward one's own beliefs and practices.

There is then no mistaking that humility, when applied to doctrine, may just as well become an obstacle as a vehicle for dialogue. It seems clear that the traditional Christian no-tion of humility does not necessarily imply recognition of the incompleteness, finitude, or fallibility of Christian teachings themselves. To the degree that the attitude of humility toward the doctrines of one's own tradition tends to reinforce their ab-solute status, it is more likely to generate religious antagonism and conflict, rather than dialogue.[59] If the spiritual concept of humility itself does not automatically lead to doctrinal humility, maybe such humility can be retrieved from modern and postmodern understandings of doctrinal truth.

DOCTRINAL HUMILITY AND DIALOGUE

We have seen that the Christian notion of spiritual humility, while not necessarily conducive to dialogue, nonetheless can stimulate it. There are other theological resources and hermeneutical principles also capable of serving that purpose. One important impetus behind the emergence of a more humble attitude about doctrine within the Christian tradition has been the modern shift from a static to a more dynamic understanding of truth. Whereas classical thinking emphasizes the eternal and immutable nature of expressions of truth, modern consciousness is marked by an awareness of the historicity of all linguistic and symbolic expressions. Even though Christianity has been slow to recognize the implications of these developments for its own self-understanding, its conception of doctrine did eventually become transformed by historical consciousness. We will here focus on some of the consequences of this new understanding of the nature of doctrine for interreligious dialogue.

Resources for a humbler relation to one's own truth-claims may be found not only in particular attitudes toward doctrine, but also in certain doctrinal or religious beliefs themselves. In particular, the Christian belief in the eschatological fulfillment of truth at the end of time offers one promising basis for the development of doctrinal humility. And the tradition of apophatic theology, already alluded to above, has also become a popular resource for Christian theologians engaged in dialogue with other religious traditions.

Historical Consciousness

If by historical consciousness one means an awareness of the historical and cultural conditioning of all knowledge and understanding, then its emergence must be closely related to a series of developments in the theory of knowledge and the philosophy of language that emphasize the role of the subject and of language in all perception. Dissatisfied with the premise of an absolute standpoint or an unconditioned objectivity, modern hermeneutics has preferred to approach understanding in terms of an interplay between subject and object or between external data and the subjective processes of interpretation. Applying itself to the question of truth, hermeneutics thus tends to highlight the co-constitutive role of personal and collective history in the development of knowledge and understanding. In recent decades, this awareness of particularity has become, if anything, more acute under the influence of currents such as post-colonial theory, which suggests that epistemic principles and rules of rationality are not only historically embedded but also culturally defined. As such, all understanding and expression of the truth would be subject to continuous reinterpretation and reformulation within differing historical and cultural contexts.

The shift from a static to a more dynamic and historical conception of truth did not come easily in the Christian tradition. One has only to think of the Catholic Modernist crisis of the late nineteenth and early twentieth centuries, in which a central stake was the possibility of exposing Christian revelation to the methods of historical criticism. While some went so far as to submit the truth of revelation solely to those methods (thus marginalizing or even suspending properly theological interpretation) others responded with an exaggerated defense of the scholastic conception of doctrine strictly as a body of eternal and unchanging truths. Nonetheless, historical consciousness finally did come to play an important role in defining the official Christian understanding of doctrine in the course of the twentieth century. The fruits of this are explicit in the 1973 document of the Catholic Church *Mysterium Ecclesiae*. While reacting against doctrinal relativism, the document acknowledges the historical contingency of all expression of the truth:

> With regard to its historical condition, it must first be observed that the meaning of faith depends partly on the expressive power of language used at a certain point in time and in particular circumstances. Moreover, it sometimes happens that some dogmatic truth is first expressed incompletely (though not falsely), and at another date, when considered in a broader context of faith or human knowledge, it receives fuller and more perfect expression. (5)

Here one may thus detect a degree of what I have been calling "doctrinal humility," or humility about the way in which the ultimate truth is grasped and presented in doctrinal formulations. That said, it must be emphasized that the document rejects the idea of doctrinal indeterminacy, or the idea that we cannot know the unchanging meaning of doctrines. But it does at least recognize the contingency and limitation of human language and symbols in expounding ultimate truth, and thus also the possibility of change and growth in the understanding and expression of that truth. The effect is to have freed the truth of Christian doctrine from a strict identification with a particular formulation, in favor of a closer relation to its unfolding meaning. Here one must think of the achievement of Bernard Lonergan, whose integration of modern hermeneutics into what remains a properly theological method enabled him to state that "what is permanently true is the meaning of the dogma in the context in which it was defined."[60] The preservation of this truth, then, presupposes continuous reformulation in different historical and cultural contexts. This also applies to the notion of infallibility. As Francis Sullivan points out, "the term 'irreformable' cannot be predicated of dogmatic *statements* as such, because it is impossible to formulate a statement about revealed truth which would not be open to different and possibly better formulation."[61]

Integration of historical consciousness within Christian self-understanding has thus resulted in a greater humility, if not with regard to the meaning of doctrines, at least with regard to the way they are expressed in a particular time and culture. Perhaps this is already an opening for genuine dialogue with other religions. Recognition of the particularity of the expression of Christian faith within Western culture entails an imperative to reformulate Christian teachings into categories and symbols integral to other cultural contexts. This is an idea that even Hans Urs von Balthasar was willing to countenance, insisting that "there is therefore no cause for dismay in the idea that the truth of revelation, which was originally cast in Hellenistic concepts by the great Councils, could be equally recast in Indian or Chinese concepts."[62] The attempts at inculturation or indigenization of the Christian message in non-Western cultures often lead spontaneously to interreligious dialogue. Insofar as inculturation involves the appropriation of symbols and rituals of other traditions, it always entails some degree of informed and creative engagement with their original meaning. And this negotiation represents a form of dialogue.[63]

Historical consciousness has also led to radically new theories of doctrine, resulting in their own way in a more humble relationship to the truth of Christian doctrine. This is evident in George Lindbeck's cultural-linguistic approach to doctrine. Inspired by Wittgenstein's argument that meaning and truth are always embedded in particular language games, Lindbeck has come to understand doctrines not as a reflection of a universal and objective state of affairs, but rather as "communally authoritative rules of discourse, attitude, and action."[64] Doctrines, he thus contends, must be understood as the expression of a grammar that defines the parameters of what can be said in a particular tradition. And this suggests that different religious worldviews and sets of beliefs are parallel and distinctive cultural-linguistic attempts to come to terms with the ultimate questions of life. The truth of these systems is determined, not by their correspondence to an ontological reality, but by their internal logic and coherence.[65] Lindbeck developed this intrasystemic conception of doctrinal truth precisely in order to "oppose the boasting and sense of superiority that destroys the possibility of open and mutually enriching dialogue."[66] He believed it would allow for a desirable balance between traditional faith in the ultimate truth of one's own religious teachings and recognition of the existence of alternative worldviews and belief systems:

> To hold that a particular language is the only one that has the words and concepts that can authentically speak of the ground of being, the goal of history, and true humanity is not at all the same as denying that other religions have resources for speaking truths and referring to realities, even

35

highly important truths and realities, of which Christianity as yet knows nothing and by which it could be greatly enriched.[67]

At this point, it is worth pausing over the necessary distinction between doctrinal humility, doctrinal relativity, and doctrinal relativism. While the notion of relativity implies recognition of the historical and cultural particularity of all expressions of truth, relativism entails a radical reduction of all truth to historical and cultural contexts. Whereas doctrinal humility requires some form of acknowledgment of the relativity of religious expressions, relativism is at odds with religious self-understanding. Regardless of how much religions are willing and able to concede in terms of the particularity of their historical expressions, all religions maintain a certain degree of ontological and/or universal truth for their teachings and practices. As such, in order to serve as a religious resource for openness and dialogue, the notion of doctrinal humility should remain clear of any confusion with doctrinal relativism.

Eschatology

Of all Christian teachings, belief in the eschatological fulfillment of all goodness and truth at the end of times offers the most natural and compelling foundation for the development of doctrinal humility. The Christian notion of eschatology expresses on the one hand the Christian hope in the ultimate fulfillment of the Kingdom of God while it points, on the other hand, to the humble awareness of the partial and imperfect nature of any historical realization of the Kingdom. The latter has been rendered in terms of the notion of "eschatological proviso," representing a permanent reminder of the conditioned

and provisional nature of all historical understanding and realization. This notion of the temporality and imperfection of
historical realities may be applied to personal accomplishment,
human reason, as well as historical institutions. It thus constitutes a firm theological basis for the development of doctrinal
humility.

An eschatological understanding of the realization of truth
is clearly expressed in various official documents of the Catholic Church. The Vatican II Dogmatic Constitution on Divine
Revelation (*Dei Verbum*), for example, states:

> The Tradition that comes from the apostles makes prog-
> ress in the Church, with the help of the Holy Spirit. There
> is a growth in insight into the realities and words that
> are being passed on.... Thus, as the centuries go by, the
> Church is always advancing toward the plenitude of di-
> vine truth, until eventually the words of God are fulfilled
> in her. (8)

In this text, the church itself humbly recognizes the historicity
of its own understanding of the truth and embraces the possibility of continuous growth. The implications of this view
for interreligious dialogue are evident in the Vatican document
Dialogue and Proclamation, which states:

> The fullness of truth received in Jesus Christ does not give
> individual Christians the guarantee that they have grasped
> that truth fully. In the last analysis truth is not a thing we
> possess but a person by whom we must allow ourselves to
> be possessed. This is an unending process. While keeping
> their identity intact, Christians must be prepared to learn
> and to receive from and through others the positive values
> of their tradition. (49)

This text thus roots the impulse to dialogue in a vital conception of doctrine as unending growth in the truth. In that sense, a realization of limits becomes an inspiration to progress, and indeed openness to learning still more from other religious traditions.

Besides its application to Christian understanding of the truth, the notion of eschatology also applies more generally to the conception of the historical church and its relationship to the Kingdom of God. This dimension of Christian eschatology is particularly relevant for dialogue since much of the Christian triumphalism and arrogance toward other religious traditions have derived from a tendency to identify the historical church with the Kingdom of God. Recent documents of the Catholic Church have been especially attentive to this distinction. *Redemptoris Missio,* for example, refers to the historical church as the "seed, sign and instrument"[68] and as "straining toward its eschatological fullness."[69] This document also stresses the importance of dialogue with other religions and of humility in dialogue. It calls upon all those engaged in dialogue to "be consistent with their own religious traditions and convictions, and be open to understanding those of the other party without pretense or close-mindedness, but with truth, humility and frankness, knowing that dialogue can enrich each side."[70]

It is thus not surprising that Christian theologians engaged in dialogue with other religions and in the development of a theology of religions have eagerly appropriated this notion of eschatology as the basis for a greater theological openness and receptivity. Jacques Dupuis, for example, writes:

There is, perhaps, nothing which provides interreligious dialogue with such a deep theological basis, and such a

true motivation, as the conviction that in spite of the differences by which they are distinguished, the members of
different religious traditions, co-members of the Reign of
God in history, are traveling together toward the fullness
of the Reign of God, toward the new humanity willed by
God for the end of time, of which they are called to be
co-creators with God.[71]

While Dupuis recognizes a privileged role for Christian revelation and the church, all religions are here regarded as oriented
toward an ultimate state of realization that is beyond any
one particular religion. Pressing the limits of Christian self-
understanding further, some theologians have even come to
deny any privileged role to Christian revelation in the Kingdom
of God. Paul Knitter, for example, suggests that "the Reign
of God can be seen as an economy of grace genuinely different from the one made known through the Word incarnate in
Jesus (in whom, of course, the Spirit was also active)."[72] This
is evidently meant to secure recognition of the equality of all
religions in dialogue.[73]

The humility derived from the eschatological orientation of
Christianity expresses itself not only as a principle of critique
and vigilance against claiming absolute truth for historical
categories of understanding, but also as a dynamic power of
change and growth. It is the Christian belief in the Holy Spirit as
the power and presence of God in the world, guiding humanity
toward its fulfillment in the Kingdom, that both reminds Christians of the partial or limited nature of their understanding or
realization of the truth and impels them to a continuous pursuit
of the fullness of truth. In *The Meeting of Religions and the
Trinity*, Gavin D'Costa thus argues that this belief in the Holy
Spirit "precludes any triumphalist understanding of the Spirit's

presence, for it does not elevate to an Archimedian point either the practices or the articulations of the church, but shows the constant need to re-engage and re-present the gospel under the guidance of the Spirit."[74] Because of its eschatological nature, the Kingdom of God is to be actively pursued by Christians in history. Taking all of this together, eschatology saves Christianity from simple resignation to the relativity of all truth and from indifference toward the truth of other religious traditions. While a humble understanding of the provisional, relative, and historical nature of truth provides a necessary condition for dialogue, it is faith and hope in the possibility of growth and of progressive understanding of the truth that constitutes the dynamic impulse to engage the world and other religions.

Apophatic Theology

We have already pointed to the Christian tradition of negative theology as a ready resource for humility and dialogue. Here, we shall merely remind ourselves of its role in the cultivation of doctrinal humility. This is particularly evident in the works of Nicholas of Cusa. In *On Learned Ignorance,* Cusanus directly points to the relationship between humility and knowledge of the ultimate truth. He argues that since God is beyond all comprehension, the humble realization of one's own ignorance is in fact the highest form of learning:

> The greatest and profoundest mysteries of God, although hidden to the wise, are revealed by faith in Jesus to the little ones and the humble walking in the world. . . . Since God is not knowable in this world, where reason, opinion and teachings lead us, by means of symbols, from the better known to the unknown, God is known only where persuadings leave off and faith enters in. Through faith

we are rapt in simplicity so that, while in a body incorpo-
really, because in spirit, and in the world not in a worldly
manner but celestially, we may incomprehensibly contem-
plate Christ above all reason and intelligence, in the third
heaven of the simplest intellectuality. Therefore, we also
see that because of the immensity of his excellence, he
cannot be comprehended.[75]

Just as only humility leads to an experience of ultimate reality,
that experience itself reinforces awareness of the limitations of
human concepts and categories in expressing ultimate reality.
This attitude of doctrinal humility coincided with a remarkable
openness — for his age — toward other religious traditions.
Nicholas of Cusa is also at times regarded as the forefather
of modern Christian theology of religions.[76] While maintaining a strong belief in the ultimacy and superiority of Christian
teachings, Cusanus regarded other religions as willed by God,
who "sent the different nations different prophets and teach-
ers, some at one time and others at another."[77] The different
religions were seen to be different ritual expressions of one universal faith. In the present context, there is no immediate need
to determine whether it was Cusanus's conception of truth that
led to his uncommon openness to other religions, or for that
matter whether his recognition of other religions reinforced his
understanding of the ineffability of truth. But there is certainly
an evident theological relationship between the two.

In more recent times, negative theology has become more
consciously used as a basis for openness and dialogue between religions. In the pluralism of John Hick, the distinction
between ultimate reality itself and the religious understanding of this reality is developed in a manner that supports
the idea of a divine truth and its revelation from beyond

the Christian tradition. For Hick, this transcendence establishes the ultimate equivalence of all religions. Pointing to the fact that all religious traditions make the distinction between "the Godhead in its own infinite depths beyond human experience and comprehension" and "the Godhead as finitely experienced by humanity," he concludes in quasi-Kantian fashion that all religious conceptions of the ultimate reality may be regarded as "different phenomenal experiences of the one divine noumenon."[78] One easily recognizes the pluralist line of reasoning: insofar as the differences between religious conceptions are determined by particular historical and cultural circumstances, no religious tradition is entitled to claim superiority for its own conception of the ultimate reality or its own set of religious beliefs and practices. Needless to say, this may be regarded as an expression of radical doctrinal humility, since it responds first of all to an awareness of the fundamental and essential limitation of all religious language and doctrinal formulations. But Hick's position may also be seen to lean toward doctrinal relativism, which moves beyond the self-understanding of most religions.

While focus on the transcendence of ultimate truth may thus lead to radical doctrinal humility bordering on relativism, it may also lead to more moderate and theologically coherent conceptions of humility. Most Christian theologians engaged in dialogue with other religions in fact implicitly or explicitly point to the ineffability of ultimate reality as the basis for dialogue or as the ultimate goal of all religious dialogue. Michael Barnes, for example, states that a theology of dialogue always starts from the humble realization or reminder that "wherever Christian deliberation on the mystery of the self-revealing God starts, there is more to be said; wherever it ends, there will always be other routes back to the beginning, there to start again."[79]

A Note on Rahner's Anonymous Christianity

One of the more paradoxical theological expressions of Christian humility may be found in Karl Rahner's concept of "anonymous Christianity." Coined in order to come to terms with the possibility of salvation outside of Christianity as understood from within a Christian theological framework, this expression has provoked significant critique, both from within and from outside the Christian tradition. While many have thought it to express a blatant Christian arrogance and triumphalism, Rahner himself referred to it as an expression of "the greatest humility" on the part of Christianity:

> Non-Christians may think it presumption for the Christian to judge everything that is sound or restored (by being sanctified) to be the fruit in every man of the grace of his Christ, and to interpret it as anonymous Christianity; they may think it presumption for the Christian to regard the non-Christian as a Christian who has yet to come to himself reflectively. But the Christian cannot renounce this "presumption," which is really the source of the greatest humility for both himself and for the Church. For it is a profound admission of the fact that God is greater than man and the Church. The Church will go out to meet the non-Christian of tomorrow with the attitude expressed by St. Paul when he said: What therefore you do not know and yet worship (and yet *worship!*) that I proclaim to you (Acts 17:23). On such a basis one can be tolerant, humble, and yet firm toward all non-Christian religions.[80]

For Rahner, the humility contained in the expression "anonymous Christianity" follows from the fact that God transcends human imagination and any alleged Christian monopoly on

understanding God. Divine truth and revelation may thus become manifest in other religions — though these other religions
do need Christian revelation in order to attain genuine consciousness of that truth. Rahner's conception of humility thus
appears to remain qualified by Christian claims to superiority and has consequently rarely been embraced by theologians
involved in interreligious dialogue.

Yet it is possible to understand Rahner's phrase in a different
way. Perhaps the expression may also indicate an awareness of
the fact that all conceptions of the other are always to some
degree determined by one's own particular and limited set
of presuppositions. After all, Rahner always emphasized that
the expression was explicitly and self-consciously confessional,
used only for Christians to come to terms with the possibility
of salvation beyond the confines of the Christian tradition.
He also willingly and gratefully accepted the possibility that
Buddhists might refer to him as an "anonymous Buddhist."
From this perspective, the notion of "anonymous Christianity"
would represent one of any number of expressions signifying
a humble awareness of the historical and conceptual particularity of all religious perceptions of the other. Though this
may not necessarily lead to an open and reciprocal dialogue, it
does reflect a healthy epistemological realism that constitutes
a necessary stepping stone in the dialogue between religions.

DIALOGUE ON HUMILITY

Humility in Other Religions

Humility plays a central role not only in Christianity, but in
most religious traditions.[81] It is of utmost importance in theistic religions, where humble submission to the will of God

defines the very heart of the traditions. In the formative period of Judaism, humility was considered to be the principal
virtue and the basis for all other virtues. It is described in the
Torah as an expression of human created nature and as the
proper means to salvation. Rabbinic texts speak of "those who
dwell in dust" (Isa. 26:19) as the humble who will be raised
on the last day,[82] and of the eschatological reversal of pride
and humility: "I saw an upside down world, what is [exalted]
on high is down [humble] below, and what is [humble] below
is [exalted] on high."[83] Humble submission to the Torah and
its concrete injunctions constitutes the fundamental religious
attitude that infuses the daily life of observant Jews. As for
the Muslim tradition, the importance of humble submission
of one's own will to the will of God may be found in the rich
etymology of the term *Islam* itself, which is said to mean "surrender," or the peace that results from the attitude of surrender
to God. In addition to obedience to the Koran and to the divine
law (*shari'a*), the spiritual tradition of Islam speaks of the need
for total self-annihilation (*fana*) on the path to the ultimate
experience of God. Other theistic traditions, or strands within
religions, also regard humble surrender to the divine reality as
the ultimate expression of and path to salvation or liberation.
Within devotional Hinduism, the final liberation from endless
transmigration is believed to be attained through the attitude
of humble surrender to God (*prapatti*). This attitude is based
on the conviction, advocated in the philosophy of Rāmānuja
and the Vaishnava tradition, that everything has its ultimate
source or cause in Brahman and that everything is thus radically and permanently dependent on Brahman for its existence.
Humility is then believed to actualize one's own true nature in
relationship to God.[84]

But the virtue of humility is far from absent in religions that do not advocate belief in a personal God. Even if the term "humility" is not explicitly used, Buddhism as well as the nondualistic traditions of Hinduism are similarly oriented toward the annihilation of pride. In both traditions, the ultimate source of pride is located in ignorance, or in a false sense of self. Humility thus here coincides with an experience of the true self (*ātman*) in Hinduism or no-self (*anātman*) in Buddhism.

Finally, humility also forms a central theme and indeed a constant refrain in the *Tao Te Ching,* one of the foundational scriptures of Taoism. Arrogance, pride, and conceit are here regarded as the ultimate barrier, not only to personal spiritual growth, but also to social peace and harmony. While the *Chuang Tze* uses the method of ridicule to expose pride, the *Tao Te Ching* dedicates various aphorisms and warnings to the importance of humility and of keeping a low profile:

> He who shows himself is not conscious;
> He who considers himself right is not illustrious;
> He who brags will have no merit;
> He who boasts will not endure. (XXIV and XXII)[85]

This serves to illustrate that humility plays an important, if not a central role in most religious traditions, both theistic and nontheistic. Perhaps it is clearest in the master-disciple relationship, which in virtually all spiritual traditions is oriented toward the annihilation of the ego and the surrender of pride. As such, humility may be regarded as a distinctly religious, rather than a specifically Christian virtue.

That said, it is nonetheless evident that the specific understanding of the origin and nature of pride, as well as the particular disciplines for cultivating humility, differ from one religion to the next. Whereas theistic religions understand humility in relational terms, nontheistic traditions conceive of humility in terms of the complete annihilation of the conventional understanding of the self. Some religions attribute the origin of pride to an external power, or to inherent human nature, while others regard it as a deviation from an original state of perfect humility and knowledge. And while some religions emphasize human effort, others appeal more to divine grace in order to overcome pride. The differences between these various conceptions of pride and humility may shed light on the irreducible particularity of each religion. But they may also come to function as a basis for fruitful dialogue.

Such dialogue may come to enrich the Christian tradition in a variety of ways. Awareness of the universal importance of humility in religious traditions may lead to a revaluation of humility or a rediscovery of its importance in religious and spiritual life. The virtue of humility has often been regarded as an outdated and even oppressive feature of Christianity, where, to be sure, it has been at times distorted and abused. Not only is it seen as antithetical to the modern emphasis on autonomy and love of personal excellence, but it has also been the object of both philosophical suspicion and feminist critique.[86] Nietzsche, for example, regarded the Christian emphasis on humility as a typical instance of the glorification of slave morality, as the transformation of a weakness into a virtue.[87] Humility, he contends, is no more than a Christian exhortation of "pusillanimity," contemptible timidity or lack of courage. Feminists, on the other hand, are alert to the fact that humility has often been regarded within the Christian tradition as a typically feminine virtue. The model of Christian humility in the Bible is the figure of the virgin Mary, who unquestioningly accepts her fate. This has often led to an identification of humility with female subservience and with a call for women to accept their "humble" role in society and in the church. As such, the Christian virtue of humility has been used — consciously or not — to justify and preserve the patriarchal structures of the church. These critiques involve a conception of humility as a predominantly moral virtue, regulating worldly ambition and attitudes toward others. One of the functions of dialogue may be to reinstate religious humility in its proper place as a primarily spiritual virtue, as an expression of human self-understanding in relation to God, rather than in relation to others or to any worldly conception of dignity and worth. Mary's example of humble submission in the Magnificat is a response to a message from God, rather than to a directive issued by men. Properly understood, Christian humility is always derived from and oriented toward an experience of God. While a careful attention to Christian spiritual literature may in itself bring home this fact, dialogue with other religions and the realization of the universal importance of humility in spiritual life may inspire a renewed attention to its indispensable role and its proper meaning in Christian spiritual life and practice.

Humility in the Buddhist-Christian Dialogue

Beyond a revaluation of the general importance of humility in the spiritual life of Christian men and women, dialogue with other religions may also shed light on particular dimensions of humility that are less in evidence in Christian teaching and practice. I will limit myself here to the understanding of humility in the Christian dialogue with Buddhism. Buddhism offers not only a radically different ontological basis for understanding humility, but also a rich diversity of spiritual practices that may promise to enhance the Christian discipline of humility.

It must first of all be pointed out that within Buddhism, the term "humility" is scarcely in use, for the obvious but easily overlooked reason that it presupposes a self that must be humbled. Buddhist teachings deny the existence of a permanent, abiding self, as well as of a personal creator God. Buddhism, however, does regard pride as one of the main causes of evil and suffering. According to the second of the four noble truths, pride is caused by ignorance and by attachment to the illusory idea of a permanent self or ego. In the *Dhammapada,* it is said that "The fool will desire undue reputation, precedence among monks, authority in the monasteries, honor among other families. Let both laymen and monks think, 'by myself was this done; in every work, great or small, let them refer to me.' Such is the ambition of the fool; his desires and pride increase."[88] Pride is thus related to the pursuit of desires, which according to Buddhist teaching lies at the origin of all pain and suffering. Pride is first of all itself based on a desire for recognition and honor. But it also lies at the origin of the pursuit of other desires, which will in turn reinforce one's pride and self-esteem.

The Buddhist cure for pride lies in the realization that there is no permanent and unchanging self, and that every illusion of self represents no more than a momentary or fleeting configuration of the five aggregates, or *skandhas* (form, perception, feeling, impulse, and consciousness). Insight into the absence of such an unchanging self leads to the abolition of all pride. The Buddhist notion of *anātman,* or "no-self," thus involves explicit denial of any ontological basis for pride and may thus be regarded as a direct analogue to the Christian concept of humility.

Various disciplines and techniques have developed within the Buddhist tradition to overcome or uproot pride. In the oldest scriptures of Buddhism, the Pali Canon (first century BCE), monks are encouraged to meditate on the *skandhas* with the realization that "all this body is not mine, not this am I, not mine is the soul." This, according to the text, leads to "loathing for the body, for feeling, for perception, for the aggregates, for consciousness. Feeling disgust he becomes free from passion, through freedom from passion he is emancipated, and in the emancipated one arises knowledge of his emancipation."[89] In this line, the Dalai Lama thus states that "the antidote for pride is meditation on the *skandhas*."[90] In Buddhist *Vipāsana* or insight meditation, feelings and thoughts of pride are absolved by meditating on their unsatisfactory (*dukkha*), impermanent (*anitya*), and selfless (*anatta*) nature. Rather than suppress or ignore feelings of pride or conceit, the emphasis is on letting go of those feelings by observing their transient nature. Taking up this task, Buddhist texts such as the *Visuddhimagga* (eighth century) propose a complex classification of diverse objects for meditation, depending on particular types of personality and the specific form of pride which is to be overcome. Among the forty meditation subjects, the ten kinds of foulness may be regarded as particularly effective for overcoming pride. They involve meditation on a bloated corpse, a livid one, a festering, cut-up, gnawed, and scattered one, the hacked and scattered, the bleeding, the worm-infested body, and the skeleton.[91] Buddhist monks also typically engage in deliberate acts of self-humiliation such as begging, performing menial jobs within the monastery, or engaging in scrupulous public confession of sins of pride.

While the Buddhist experience of no-self is largely a matter of wisdom and insight, it may also express itself in relationship to others. In the famous Mahāyāna Buddhist text *A Guide to the Bodhisattva Way of Life*, Shantideva suggests that pride may be overcome by the practice of "exchanging self for others":

> Creating a sense of self in respect of inferiors and others, and a sense of others in oneself, imagine envy and pride with a mind free from false notions.[92]

The exchange of self and other brings home the futility and the relativity of all feelings of pride and arrogance. Within Mahāyāna Buddhism, this practice is also rooted in the idea of the interconnection of all reality and the importance of cultivating loving compassion toward all sentient beings. In his commentary on *A Guide to the Bodhisattva Way of Life* the Dalai Lama points to the positive karmic implications of the practice of humility:

> The result of wishing to be superior to others, to be famous, will be lower rebirth as an idiot, in abject misery, with an ugly body. On the other hand, true humility, treating others as more important than oneself, will lead to our being reborn in the higher realms.[93]

In certain lay forms of Buddhism, humility is also realized and expressed through attitudes of surrender to and dependency on monks and on heavenly Buddhas and Bodhisattvas. In the Pure Land tradition, where liberation from suffering is attributed to the saving grace of the heavenly Buddha Amida, humility takes the form of complete surrender to the saving power of Amida. This is based on the belief that all forms of religious discipline contain an element of pride and on an awareness of the fundamental human incapacity to overcome pride. Accordingly, the Pure Land ideal is embodied in the person of utter humility and simplicity (*myokonin*), who has no esteem for his or her own knowledge and power. Humility is here itself understood as a gift of divine grace.

The Buddhist notion of no-self and the Christian virtue of humility thus display certain remarkable similarities. Religious life is in both cases oriented toward the overcoming of pride and the attainment of knowledge of the true self, or no-self; the monastic traditions of the two religions have developed similar disciplines in order to cultivate humility: begging, submission to a superior and to the rule of the community, public confession of sins or transgressions against the rule, etc. And like Christianity, the Pure Land tradition of Buddhism understands humility as the result of divine grace. However, none of the foregoing changes the fact that there are also important differences between the Christian path of humility and the Buddhist practice of no-self. The Christian belief in a personal God and in a permanent relationship between the self and God marks an important difference from the corresponding Buddhist conceptions. Even in Pure Land Buddhism, no permanent ontological reality is attributed to the source of divine grace, for in the end, the heavenly Buddha Amida constitutes only one form or expression of the *Dharmakāya,* i.e., the ultimate and undifferentiated truth. In short, and appearances notwithstanding, the difference between a relational concept of humility, rooted in the notion of a true self, and the nonrelational notion of no-self must also permeate the different practices and indeed the psychological impact of spiritual experience accompanying them.

Within Christianity, humility and pride are considered as two opposite attitudes of the self in relationship to God. Pride is regarded as an expression not only of ignorance, but also of sin against God. As such, pride may lead to guilt and at times to obsessive concern with one's own sinfulness. Conversely, intense engagement in practices of self-humiliation may easily result in an attitude of pride about one's very humility. This is why Christianity has always understood perfect humility to be a gift of God and why Christians are called to remain humble about their very humility. Within Buddhism, on the other hand, humility and pride are not so much understood as opposite attitudes or dispositions of the self, but as expressions of insight and ignorance respectively. Since there is ultimately no self, there is no "one" who is humble or proud. Hence, there is less ground for feelings of guilt about one's ignorance or pride about one's humility.

These differences may offer a promising opportunity for genuine dialogue and growth. From a Christian perspective, the Buddhist focus on gaining insight into the nonsubstantiality of the self suspends and moves beneath the moral conception of humility otherwise bound to arise as soon as one begins to feel, according to the Christian tendency, guilty about one's lack of humility. Buddhist forms of meditation may thus serve to help uproot the very source of pride, so that the path of humility is perhaps clearer than it could ever be as long as one supposes an operative self, or agent. More than an antidote to overtly negative conceptions of the human person and to the despondency the latter may produce, the Buddhist practice of permanent attention to the nonsubstantiality of all forms of pride cannot but deepen the pursuit of humility. It is thus not surprising that many Christians engaged in the dialogue with Buddhism experience little conflict between the Buddhist and the Christian spiritual paths and find in Buddhist practices an occasion to enrich their own spiritual growth. Though it seems likely that the difference between affirmation and denial of an ultimate self and between the belief in and ignorance of the existence of a personal God will continue to distinguish Buddhist and Christian experience, Buddhist forms of meditation may nonetheless help Christians in their pursuit of humility by cultivating insight into the illusion of a self separate from God.

But the Buddhist correlate of Christian humility entails not only purely spiritual, but also epistemic or doctrinal connotations. Within the Mahāyāna tradition of Buddhism, the soteriologial notion of no-self is inscribed in a more general philosophy of the emptiness (*śūnyatā*) of all reality. It is especially here that the dialogue with Buddhism promises to enrich the Christian understanding of humility *as a condition for the possibility of dialogue with other religions*. Mahāyāna Buddhism is famous for its attitude of humility about all doctrinal formulations. In reaction to the early Buddhist philosophical discussions that focused on the existence of ultimate essences (*dharmas*) from which all reality was ultimately derived, Mādhyamika philosophers such as Nāgārjuna argued against the existence of any essential nature or permanent and unchanging essences in favor of the concept of emptiness (*śūnyatā*). Carried to its logical conclusion, this concept applies not only to an analysis of physical and natural essences, but to all teachings and doctrines, including the teaching of emptiness itself. Nāgārjuna writes: "The Victors have declared emptiness as the expeller of all views, but those who hold emptiness as a view they have pronounced incurable."[94] Though debate continues over whether or not this very claim should be regarded as a distinct view that promotes an ultimate truth, it is clear that Nāgārjuna's ultimate intention was freedom from any clinging to ultimate propositions and truth-claims.[95] All linguistic and doctrinal assertions were to be regarded as conventional designations, which were not to be confused with ultimate truth itself. This led to the "two-truths theory," which emphasizes the distinction between ultimate truth, which is "beyond the scope of intellection," and conventional truth, which can be grasped by the intellect.[96] While some (Mādhyamika) thinkers emphasize the radical distinction between the two truths and at times even the adverse nature of conventional truth, others (belonging to the Yogācāra tradition) recognize the possible efficacy of conventional concepts in pointing to ultimate meaning. The fact that conventional categories remain important within Buddhism is reflected in the fierce doctrinal disputes and disagreements that have been an integral part of the tradition, leading to the development of different schools, each with its own hierarchy of truths and insistence on the superiority of their own teachings. Nonetheless, the Buddhist tradition has on the whole maintained a strong sense of the provisionality and conventionality of teachings or doctrines as skillful means (*upāya*), mere rafts leading to ultimate liberation. Within Mahāyāna Buddhism, this attitude of doctrinal humility — the recognizing of the finite and limited nature of conventional teachings — is thus an integral part of the tradition.

There is no doubt that the Buddhist two-truths theory differs radically from the traditional Christian propositional understanding of the truth. Perhaps, however, it is less alien to the subtler, more fluid conceptions of truth and doctrine found along different lines in both the apophatic mystical tradition and in modern historical consciousness. We have already seen that both of these approaches recognize the transcendence or ineffability of ultimate truth and the historical contingency of all doctrinal language. It is precisely this distinction between the ultimate truth itself and its expression in finite categories that provides the ground for a humbler attitude about one's own teachings and doctrines. If these attitudes and the resources they tap into are sometimes dormant or less than fully developed in Christian consciousness, one might well expect that dialogue with a tradition such as Buddhism might awaken them and bring them to the fore. This is indeed evident in the works of John Keenan and Joseph O'Leary, two contemporary Christian theologians who have engaged in far-reaching dialogue with Mahāyāna Buddhist philosophical traditions. Using Buddhist philosophical categories in order to rethink traditional Christian religious beliefs and doctrines,[97] both Keenan and O'Leary came to emphasize the importance of humility in relation to doctrine. Keenan, for example, comes to insist that it is precisely the act of "clinging to the conceptual form even of doctrine" that "becomes an obstacle to realizing wisdom, to understanding the very content of doctrine."[98] He uses the Buddhist categories of emptiness, dependent co-arising, and the two truths in order to reveal dimensions of Christian truth that he believes have been obscured by traditional metaphysical categories. Taking his cue from those Buddhist categories and the humble attitude toward doctrine that they entail, he understands doctrinal discourse as a matter not of "identifying absolute categories," but of "skillfully using conventional theological language."[99] Something quite similar is proposed by O'Leary when he states that one of the fruits of understanding Christianity in terms of Buddhist ontology is its success in liberating us "from clinging to views, thus undoing the roots of dogmatist and fanatical fixation."[100] Far from a denial of the importance of religious and doctrinal language, he argues that "insight into the provisional and conventional character of words and concepts permits a skillful and demystified use of language in which all the discriminations of conventional discourse can be respected within the limits of their applicability."[101] This of course repeats a lesson already on record in the Buddhist tradition: the most radical humility about one's own doctrines or claims to truth need not lead to relativism or to a complete absence of concern with religious truth. After all, the different schools of Buddhism have themselves long been engaged with doctrinal disputes and the development of different systems of doctrinal classification and hierarchies of truth. The incorporation of Buddhist philosophical categories may allow Christian theologians to use traditional doctrinal categories "more lightly and adroitly,"[102] as O'Leary puts it, or with a greater degree of humility.

◆ ◆ ◆

The Christian tradition possesses a long and rich tradition of reflection on and cultivation of the virtue of humility. Even though it is mainly the spiritual virtue of humility that has been emphasized, the tradition contains ample resources for the development of a less absolute attitude toward its own conception of the truth and a more open attitude toward the possible truth of other religious traditions. Dialogue with other religious traditions has a way of reminding members of the different traditions of the particularity and the contingency of their own beliefs and practices and thus of enhancing doctrinal humility. But the process of dialogue with certain religions and the reinterpretation of one's own beliefs through the framework of the other may also enhance awareness of the tension between conventional and absolute truth and bring about a sense of humility about the former.

It is clear that openness to dialogue with other religions is directly related to the degree of humility about one's own religious traditions. The more attached one is to the absolute truth of one's own religious doctrines and practices, the less inclined one will be to engage the teachings of other religions in a spirit of openness and receptivity. Christian theologians concerned with the dialogue with other religions have thus sought to develop doctrinal humility in a variety of ways, especially through emphasis on eschatology and the difference between the historical church and the Kingdom of God, and on negative theology and the distinction between the ultimate truth itself and the ways in which it may be grasped in human symbols and categories. These are the theological resources within Christianity that lend themselves most readily to the development of doctrinal humility, and of course they need not apply to non-Christian self-understanding. Other traditions no doubt develop doctrinal humility along quite different lines. In the end, then, dialogue does call on each to discover and cultivate resources for humility about claims to truth within its own set of teachings and practices.

While humility represents a necessary condition for dialogue, it is certainly not the only one, nor for that matter a sufficient one. On its own, humility may still entail a dismissal of the teachings and practices of other religious traditions, either due to a general attitude of relativism in which all religious expressions of the truth are reduced to their historical and cultural contexts, or due to a belief that one's own religion still remains the only legitimate — if imperfect — expression of the truth. The possibility of dialogue also requires a continued commitment to the truth of one's own tradition, a belief that other religions are in some way relevant to one's own tradition, faith in the possibility of understanding the other, and last, but especially important, a recognition that the teachings of other religious traditions may contain elements of truth relevant to one's own religious development and growth. It will be necessary to address these other conditions in turn, and with the close attention they command.

CHAPTER TWO

COMMITMENT

Interreligious dialogue in the full sense of the term involves engagement between religions, or between individuals insofar as they confess adherence to their particular religious tradition. This does not necessarily entail a full compliance with every single aspect of the tradition, and still less a dogmatic insistence that what one holds must in any case be upheld without qualification. But it does presuppose commitment to a particular worldview and belief system and a willingness to attest to its truth and validity in dialogue with other worldviews and belief systems.

One of the challenges facing interreligious dialogue from within is the lurking sense of incompatibility between firm commitment to a particular religious tradition and openness to other religions. The history of religions seems to indicate that — exceptions notwithstanding — strong religious commitment coincides with religious intolerance, while attitudes of openness toward the truth of other religions somehow go together with a looser relationship to the truth of one's own tradition. Interreligious dialogue has often come to be conducted by individuals who find themselves on the margins of their own respective traditions, whether by necessity or by choice. This marginality may impose itself upon individuals as a result of attitudes of self-sufficiency and superiority that often characterize the mainstream self-understanding within religious traditions. Insofar as religions lay claim to possessing the absolute truth or the ultimate means to salvation, dialogue cannot but be regarded as a form of redundancy or a threat. While a certain degree of collaboration and mutual under-standing may be allowed, the more radical forms of dialogue oriented toward the possibility of transformation and growth are rarely conducted by individuals who find themselves in the center of institutional hierarchies. Religions are indeed not always ready for what transpires in dialogue.

However, the tension between religious commitment and interreligious dialogue may also be attributed to those engaged in dialogue themselves. It cannot be denied that the interest in other religions and the practice of dialogue often derives from, or leads to, a more independent stance with regard to one's own religion. While some may engage in dialogue out of a desire for mutual understanding and peaceful coexistence, others may be drawn to other religions on the basis of a reli-gious desire or a quest for truth that is seen to remain largely unfulfilled within their own religious tradition. Dialogue may itself also lead to a greater alienation from one's own religion. In-depth engagement with the beliefs and practices of another religion may at times lead to a recognition of their truth and to a questioning of the claims of one's own tradition.

While dialogue and commitment may not always go hand in hand, I wish to here argue for the importance and possibil-ity of commitment in dialogue and dialogue in commitment. Such commitment marks the difference between a genuinely interreligious and a strictly interpersonal dialogue. And the tradition also provides for individuals engaged in dialogue a solid point of departure and a critical place of return.

Continued religious commitment moreover forms the only means of moving the tradition itself forward.

TRADITION AS POINT OF DEPARTURE

The concept of tradition is often associated with conservatism and constraint, with the debilitating weight of history inhibiting innovation and change. Traditions tend to be regarded as immobile institutions, concerned primarily with the preservation of established teachings, practices, and hierarchical structures. Consequently, commitment to a particular tradition while in dialogue with another may be regarded as an undue limitation of religious options or as a hopeless attempt to transform a structure that is defined by its resistance to change. This view leads many to engage in dialogue from a position of freedom from all defined forms of religious conviction and religious identity. Some may claim a sense of belonging to two or more religious traditions while others reject all notions of religious commitment and belonging. Undoubtedly, such loosening of commitment to a particular religious tradition renders dialogue less encumbered. Yet it also involves the loss of any firm religious foundation from which to engage other religious traditions.

Dialogue without Commitment

As religious diversity has become a permanent part of the religious landscape in most parts of the world, different forms of engagement with the teachings and practices of different religions have emerged. In the West, one of the earliest attempts to fully embrace the reality of religious plurality and to integrate elements from various religious traditions occurred in the Theosophical Society founded in 1875 by Helena Blavatsky and Henry Steel Olcott. Having read some of the early translations of Hindu and Buddhist scriptures, Blavatsky and Olcott came to believe in the fundamental unity of all religions and in the importance of integrating the best of all religious traditions in the course of one's own religious or spiritual quest. Blavatsky herself published numerous books,[1] reflecting her own personal synthesis of elements from the Western esoteric tradition, Hinduism, and Buddhism. Olcott, for his part, became the champion of the Buddhist revival in Southeast Asia. Among the main characteristics of Theosophy are free enquiry into the teachings and practices of all religious traditions and active responsibility for one's own spiritual growth and realization. What we now call the New Age movement may be regarded as a late twentieth-century outgrowth of the Theosophical tradition. Though the term is somewhat disputed, "New Age" refers in general to the personal and autonomous assimilation of teachings and practices derived from different religions.[2]

Theosophy and New Age may be regarded as forms of interreligious dialogue in the broad sense of the term. They embrace what they take to be elements of truth in all religious traditions and act on a belief in the possibility and indeed necessity of growth through learning from different religions. Yet this dialogue takes place not so much between religious traditions, as between — or within — individuals belonging to no particular religious tradition. New Age is characterized by a radical rejection of all forms of traditional religious authority and by a focus on the subject as the ultimate measure of religious truth. This concept of religious autonomy appears as one evident outcome of the modern shift to the subject, and of the development of notions of freedom and an undetermined will that were formulated in Europe around the time of Descartes — notions assumed and then radicalized in the postmodern thought of free-play in which much of the New Age feels at home. In the absence of objective or natural meaning, individuals have the liberty and the responsibility to constitute their own conception of truth. This defines what sociologists of religion describe as "disembedded, desituated, or detraditionalized selves" who "consider themselves to be self-directional, authorial agents, relying on their own — inner — sources of authority, control and responsibility."[3] Within the domain of religion, it manifests itself in an aversion to any form of religious commitment or in an attitude of "believing without belonging."[4] Eschewing the heteronomy implied in submitting to an external authority, the individual self becomes the final norm. Accordingly, religious truth is measured only by the degree to which a particular teaching or practice comes to enhance one's personal sense of well-being or wholeness.

There is no denying that an avowedly autonomous search for truth and wholeness may lead to remarkable expressions of human and spiritual realization. One thinks immediately of the person and life of Mohandas Gandhi. Having rejected most of the social and ritual conventions of his original Hindu religion,[5] as well as belief in the absoluteness of any particular religion,[6] Gandhi set out on a lifetime search for truth, "no longer depending upon outside authority."[7] Rather than through any particular revelation, Gandhi believed that truth could be discovered through the consistent practice of service, nonviolence (*ahimsa*), and purity, or self-control (both physical and spiritual). To this day, he is regarded by most as one of the greatest moral and spiritual leaders in modern history. His insights, as well as those of many others who have likewise embarked on a search for truth outside of any particular religious commitment, may certainly inspire those engaged in interreligious dialogue. Yet dialogue between religions ultimately requires some degree of identification with a particular religious tradition from which one engages the other.

Even though identification with a particular religious tradition may at times seem to entail a cumbersome and unnecessary self-limitation, it may also serve as a safeguard against some of the more questionable propensities of New Age. While purely individual forms of dialogue may lead to genuine religious realization and personal integration, they also run the risk of becoming self-serving. The tendency to pick and choose from different religious traditions according to one's own taste and judgment may easily result in the indulgence of one's own personal desires and needs. In what has also been called "the religion of desire," individuals often become caught up in the restless pursuit of new experiences in one religion after the other. Each experience creates the desire, sometimes insatiable, for more and different experiences. Rather than a real meeting at a depth that yields mutual enrichment and permanent transformation, this type of purely individualistic dialogue often leads only to endless wandering.[8] Since rational or conceptual coherence is not the main concern of New Age, it also tends toward a religious "hodgepodge,"[9] or "an extraordinary mishmash of ideas, a positive ferment of ideas having little obvious connection with each other."[10] While such personal syncretism of ideas coming from different religious traditions may possess a certain relevance and coherence for the individual, there is on the whole little to no concern with the larger, that is to say shared, intelligibility of one's religious insights. This distinguishes New Age syncretism from interreligious dialogue in the full sense of the term.

A less radical form of dialogue without exclusive identification with one particular religion may be found in the phenomenon of multiple religious belonging. Here, individuals do not so much reject the authority of all established religious traditions as divide their allegiance between two and sometimes more religious traditions. This phenomenon of double or multiple religious belonging also raises questions regarding commitment and belonging in the context of interreligious dialogue.[11]

Insofar as all dialogue with other religions involves a profound immersion in the teachings and practices of the other, it may itself engender a sense of multiple religious belonging. While individuals enter the dialogue from a clearly defined religious position, the encounter with other forms of religious thought and practice may at times lead to a sense of divided allegiance, or to a loss of any sense of single commitment. This form of multiple religious belonging exhibits some of the same characteristics and limitations as mentioned with regard to New Age. If no particular religion exercises a normative religious role, then it is the individual who is left to determine what is true and valuable in the religions to which he or she may feel to belong. On the other hand, the experience of multiple religious belonging may also prove to be highly instructive for the dialogue between religions. It may not only shed a sharper light on the fault lines between religions, but it may also point to areas of religious hunger or need in which one's own religious tradition may be lacking, and which may become the focus for dialogue.

Traditions in Dialogue

Though the term "interreligious dialogue" is used for many forms of mutual engagement and collaboration between members of different religions, the defining characteristic of such dialogue is thus its grounding within concrete religious traditions. At its best, this means that participants engage in dialogue not only in their own name but also as representatives of their respective traditions, and bring to the discussion an entire storehouse of religious teachings and practices that have been tried and transmitted, purified and enriched through the ages. For believers, the tradition is both the link to the founding events and teachings of the religion and the custodian of what is of ultimate importance. It contains the stories and the thoughts of generation upon generation of people who have tried to understand, explain, and experience the truth of the traditional teachings. And it contains the history of struggle to maintain and indeed improve the purity of those teachings, and to transmit them in new forms, intelligible in different cultures and epochs. It thus represents a lens that provides focus and understanding — even if it is necessary, from time to time, to look again and reconsider, or even to step back and inspect the lens itself.

Religious commitment is generally understood as a deliberate identification with the teachings and practices of a particular tradition. It thus entails assent to the truth-claims of a particular tradition and recognition of the authority of the tradition in matters of doctrine and discipline. On closer inspection, the process of committing oneself to a particular religion generally includes both voluntary and involuntary dimensions. Many come to adopt a religious conviction through a process of socialization and education in which particular views of the world and of the meaning of life are absorbed with little or no reflection. Once committed to a particular religious tradition, many of the reasons for remaining within that religion also exceed purely rational argumentation. Yet mature religious commitment presupposes a certain degree of critical reflection on its teachings and practices and a conscious embrace of its truth. This is far from meaning that religious commitment requires unquestioning acceptance of all tenets of faith within a particular religion. Most religions allow for a certain degree of dissent and for various levels of intensity of religious commitment. Still, religious commitment is ultimately characterized by the recognition of some form of heteronomy, or religious authority beyond one's own subjective will and judgment.

Such commitment is vital for all parties involved in inter-religious dialogue. For one's interlocutor, it offers the basis for confidence that one is effectively engaged in a dialogue with a genuine religious tradition, rather than with an arbitrary in-dividual. And for the individual, it provides the strength and security that comes by appeal to the authoritative voice of the tradition, as opposed to speaking solely in one's own name. To be sure, this represents not only an opportunity but also a responsibility for those involved. In representing the tradition, one is also accountable for those in whose name one speaks, as Jürgen Moltmann points out:

> All participants must remain conscious of those for whom they and their interlocutors speak. If people deviate too far from their roots to be considered representative spokes-persons for their communities, they will never be respected in reporting back to those communities and they will even-tually end up being isolated, representing only their own opinions.[12]

This responsibility requires not only faithfulness but also a certain religious competence. While dialogue does not nec-essarily presuppose expert knowledge, it does presume the ability to speak with a certain informed confidence about the beliefs and practices of one's tradition. This explains why many believers seem to shy away from interreligious dialogue. They fear misrepresenting the tradition or being outwitted and exposed by the religious expertise of the other. However, dialogue may also become the occasion to deepen and broaden one's religious knowledge and proficiency. Confrontation with a worldview and belief system radically different from one's own often raises questions about one's own tradition — questions that one may have hitherto not recognized, let alone addressed. And the attempt to understand another religious tradition generally sheds new light on one's own, if at times only in terms of generating a deeper grasp of its particularity.

It is evident that no single individual can ever claim to represent the whole of a particular religious tradition. Every participant in dialogue belongs to a specific school or tradition, favors particular forms of religious practice, and is influenced by the thought of certain scholars or theologians. Dialogue between a Shi'ite and a Methodist will no doubt look very different from a dialogue between a Sunni Muslim and an Orthodox Christian. Perhaps this is forgotten or obscured by talk of the "Hindu-Christian dialogue" or the "Muslim-Jewish dialogue."[13] General religious categories such as "Christian" or "Buddhist" have often obscured the reality of internal diversity and dissonance within religions, while at times setting unnecessary limits on our understanding of "sameness" and "difference" across religious traditions. Members of a particular religion may often discover more (structural or formal) similarities between their own religious beliefs or attitudes and those of members of another religion than with those of individuals belonging to their own general religious tradition. Once it is understood that different traditions include some of the same diverse currents within themselves — or at least a corresponding diversity — the necessary particularity of each representative relative to his or her own tradition may become an opportunity for enhanced understanding and further dialogue.

Dialogue and Mission

If dialogue involves engaging the other from a clear and defined faith perspective, one cannot but address the question of the relationship between dialogue and mission or proclamation. This has long been the subject of discussion and debate, especially in the Christian tradition. In approaching this question from the perspective of dialogue, it becomes evident that the traditional emphasis on the distinction between dialogue and proclamation has been based on a weak understanding of dialogue. Interestingly, both church authorities and religious pluralists alike emphasize the distinction between dialogue and mission, albeit for opposite reasons. Seeking to maintain the missionary impulse of its members, the official documents of the Roman Catholic Church insist that "these two elements [dialogue and proclamation] must maintain both their intimate connection and their distinctiveness; therefore they should not be confused, manipulated or regarded as identical, as though they were interchangeable."[14] While for the church the goal of dialogue is "both to discover and acknowledge the signs of Christ's presence and the working of the Spirit [in the other religion], as well as to examine more deeply her own identity and to bear witness to the fullness of revelation which she has received for the good of all,"[15] the purpose of proclamation is formulated in terms of "guiding people to explicit knowledge of what God has done for all men and women in Jesus Christ through becoming members of the Church."[16] The documents acknowledge that dialogue involves an important dimension of witnessing to one's faith, and that proclamation must be done in a spirit of openness and dialogue. But ultimately it is said that dialogue "cannot simply replace proclamation, but remains oriented towards proclamation insofar as the dynamic process of the Church's evangelizing mission reaches in it its climax and its fullness."[17]

At the other end of the spectrum one may find religious pluralists who seek to overcome all forms of what they consider religious arrogance and proselytism. For some, dialogue has come to replace mission as the proper way to relate to members of other religious traditions. In an attempt to empty the dialogue of all a priori conviction and missionary impulse, John Hick introduces a distinction between "confessional" and "truth-seeking" dialogue:

> At one extreme there is purely confessional dialogue, in which each partner witnesses to his own faith, convinced that this has absolute truth while his partner's has only relative truth. At the other extreme is truth-seeking dialogue, in which each is conscious that the transcendent Being is infinitely greater than his own limited vision of it, and in which the partners accordingly seek to share their visions in the hope that each may be helped toward a fuller awareness of the divine Reality before which they both stand.[18]

Evidently, for Hick, confessional and truth-seeking dialogue, or simply religious conviction and a genuine search for truth, cannot coexist, and so the former must be excluded from all genuine dialogue.

This debate over the relationship between dialogue and proclamation also extends to the question of the legitimacy of apologetics in dialogue. Apologetics is generally understood to involve argumentation for the truth of one's own particular beliefs in light of the other's. In the interest of maintaining harmony and friendly relationships in dialogue, Raimon Panikkar states that "we must eliminate any apologetics if we really want to meet a person from another religious tradition."[19] Over against this, Paul Griffiths has argued that "if representative intellectuals belonging to some specific religious community come to judge at a particular time that some or all of their own doctrine-expressing sentences are incompatible with some alien religious claim(s), then they should feel obliged to engage in both positive and negative apologetics vis-à-vis these alien religious claim(s) and their promulgators."[20] Rather than a blind defense of the truth of one's own beliefs (as apologetics is often wrongly understood to be), apologetics may be seen to involve a careful reasoning on the basis of the hypothetical truth of the beliefs of the other. As such, it may also lead to religious growth and transformation. In arguing for the truth of one's own religion, interreligious apologetics will ideally use the categories or terminology of the other tradition in order to clarify and compare teachings and in order to argue for the superiority of one's own. However, in the process, new dimensions of one's own beliefs may come to light, and new ways of expressing the truth of one's own tradition may be revealed.

In both debates over the relationship between dialogue and proclamation and dialogue and apologetics, dialogue tends to be limited to a process of learning about and from the other religion. This certainly constitutes an essential dimension of interreligious dialogue. However, dialogue involves a two-way process in which each partner is engaged in a process of not only informing but also convincing the other of the truth of his or her own beliefs and practices. As such, all authentic dialogue necessarily contains a missionary and apologetic dimension. The fullness of dialogue may be regarded as a form of mutual proclamation in which participants alternately adopt the roles of missionary and seeker. While seemingly contradictory, these roles may coexist in a religious attitude capable of balancing humility and conviction.

In addition to presuming a weak conception of dialogue, the sharp distinction between mission and dialogue also causes confusion and suspicion in one's interlocutor. The notion of a form of engagement with other religions that is to be distinguished from dialogue is disruptive for an open dialogue with the other. It leads to a questioning of the sincerity of one's willingness to enter into a genuine dialogue and to suspicions of a hidden agenda. In the dialogue with Hinduism, for example, Christians have been accused of merely using dialogue as a way to convert the unwary masses to the Christian faith.[21] Authentic dialogue with other religions may thus require abandoning the traditional distinctions between dialogue and mission or dialogue and apologetics and developing a more robust understanding of dialogue.

TRADITION AS PLACE OF RETURN

Commitment to a particular religious tradition offers not only a point of departure, a place or platform from which to engage in dialogue with other religious traditions, but also a place of return in which the insights and experiences gained in dialogue may be critically engaged and eventually brought to bear upon the tradition as a whole. Even from a position of firm commitment to a particular religious tradition, dialogue generally remains a personal affair, conducted between single individuals from different religious traditions or within the intimacy of one's own reflection and experience. Return to the tradition entails, among other things, exposure of one's own insights to the collective authority of the tradition. This is a dimension of dialogue that is not without tension and conflict and, in fact, is often bypassed. This can occur for one of two basic reasons. At times, individuals engaged in dialogue become estranged from their respective traditions. Or the tradition itself may be less than open and receptive to what transpires in the dialogue. Nonetheless, the ultimate goal of dialogue is growth in the truth, not only for disparate individuals who have the capacity and the luxury to engage in such dialogue, but for the tradition itself. As such, dialogue requires a deliberate commitment and faithfulness, both from individuals engaged in dialogue toward their respective traditions, and from the religious traditions toward those individuals.

Dialogue and Liminality

Even though dialogue requires grounding in a particular religious tradition, it also at times presupposes a moment or attitude of qualified, or perhaps temporary, suspension of fixed identity on the part of participants. This stage or state of separation from normative social identities and societal rules and conventions has been designated by anthropologists by the term "liminality."[22] It is typically found in traditional puberty rituals where children must separate themselves from their mother and familiar social environment and dwell alone in search for their own truth before being reintegrated within the tribe or the social group.[23] More generally, then, liminality may thus be characterized as solitary pursuit of the truth in the margins of an established tradition. It is usually associated with great openness and creativity, but also with vulnerability and danger.

In the dialogue between religions, the term "liminality" has been used by Michael Amaladoss to refer to individuals who "exist on the border between two communities and their symbolic universes, feeling at ease within both, and who experience religious solidarity with each of the two communities."[24] Though Amaladoss here thus refers in particular to the experience of double religious belonging, the term "liminality" may be extended to apply to the process of entering another religion and attempting to grasp the meaning of its beliefs and practices from within. This often requires years of study, apprenticeship with masters of the other tradition, and deep immersion in its ritual and spiritual practices. A prominent example of this in the dialogue with Islam is the figure of Louis Massignon (1883–1962). Having converted to Christianity within a Muslim context, he saw his own life as one of mediation between Islam and Christianity, of interpreting Islam for the Christian world, and of offering his own life (in a vow of *Badaliya*, or substitution) for the sake of Muslims.[25] In the dialogue with Hinduism, the experience of liminality is most readily associated with the figure of Henri Le Saux, or Abhishiktananda (1910–73). In an attempt to bring about a deep inculturation of Christianity in Hindu spiritual traditions, he spent a lifetime in search of the deepest spiritual experience of nonduality of self (*ātman*) and ultimate reality (*Brahman*) as described in the tradition of *Advaita Vedānta*, and in search of a reconciliation between this experience and Christian faith. Le Saux's contemporary and successor as guru of the Indian Benedictine ashram, Bede Griffiths (1906–93), also a Benedictine monk, became one of the great pioneers of the Christian ashram movement. In Griffiths's work, the experience of liminality received a broadly communal expression: Christian ashrams are small religious communities based on the Hindu model of a group of religious seekers living a simple life of renunciation under the guidance of a spiritual master, or guru. In addition to bringing about an inculturation of Christian spiritual life, Christian ashrams also became free havens of experimentation in the Christian dialogue with Hinduism. Hindu forms of meditation and devotion were integrated in daily life and worship, and readings from Hindu (as well as Buddhist) scriptures included in Christian worship and prayer. Thus maintaining a certain distance and independence from the official institutional structures of the church, these Christian ashrams represent virtual hearths of liminality.

In close communion with Le Saux and Griffiths, but nonetheless with a focus all his own, Raimon Panikkar (born in 1918) has dedicated his life to cultivating a theological and intellectual climate receptive to the spiritual and religious insights of Hinduism and Buddhism. Born from a Catholic mother and a Hindu father, Panikkar became a Catholic priest and theologian, always moving in the margins of both the institutional and the theological structures of the church in order to break through established ways of understanding Christian faith. Panikkar's thought expresses liminality in advancing religious and theological categories that may be regarded as neither traditionally Christian nor explicitly Hindu, but as offering a synthesis of both religious traditions.[26]

The Christian dialogue with Buddhism has been marked by such figures as well. One thinks of Hugo Enomiya-Lassalle, Vincent Shigeto Oshida, and Aloysius Pieris, each of whom has contributed greatly to a more direct and constructive engagement with the Buddhist tradition. Enomiya-Lassalle (1898–1990) was a German Jesuit who arrived as a missionary in Japan in 1929. In the attempt to inculturate Christianity in Japan, he became deeply involved in the study of Zen Buddhism, eventually regarding it as a way of purification on the spiritual path and as an important complement to traditional Christian theology and spiritual practice. Another pioneer of what we now call Christian Zen is Father Oshida (1922–2003), a Dominican priest who had converted to Christianity and attempted to achieve "a meeting at the depths" between Christianity and Zen Buddhism by integrating elements from the two traditions in the daily religious and liturgical life of his small religious community in the Japanese Alps. This sort of experimentation has become more widespread in the West, where numerous centers and courses in Christian Zen work constantly at spiritual integration.

Focusing more on the dialogue between Christianity and Theravada Buddhism in Sri Lanka, Aloysius Pieris, S.J., founded the Tulana Research Center in Colombo, where the dialogue between the two traditions is explored in religious practice, esthetic expression, and theological research. Himself a Christian theologian trained in Buddhist philosophy, Pieris has written widely on the complementarity of Buddhism and Christianity and on the need for a thoroughly inculturated Christian theology in Asia. More than many other theologians engaged in dialogue, Pieris emphasizes the importance of maintaining a focus on the poor and the marginalized in all dialogical reflection.[27]

Common to all these pioneers of interreligious dialogue is a movement to leave the security of one's established worldview and religious practices in order to allow the dialogue with the other religion to take one wherever it may lead. For many, this stage of liminality expresses itself in a continuous movement back and forth between understanding the other religion from a Christian perspective and understanding Christianity from the perspective of the other tradition. While some eventually manage to attain a stage of integration between the two traditions, others continue to struggle with an inability to reconcile Christian faith and theology with the religious principles and practices of the other tradition. The pain of this struggle is nowhere expressed with more pathos than in the writings of Abhishiktananda (Henri Le Saux). In a 1966 letter to Raimon Panikkar, he writes:

> You cannot be torn apart in the depth of your soul, as we are by this double summons (from advaitin India on the one side, and from Revelation on the other), and by this double opposition (from India and the Church, in their ritualism, their formalism and their intellectualism), without being lacerated even physically.[28]

Abhishiktananda's journal offers a powerful testimony to the experience of oscillation between moments of personal resolution of the teachings of the two traditions, and moments of doubt and despair at the realization that the Hindu and the Christian worldviews can never be brought into perfect harmony.[29] Though not a work of systematic theological reflection, it is precisely as a testimony to a life of open and uninhibited experimentation with Hindu thought and practice that it has come to represent an important source of inspiration and insight for other Christians.

Though the experience of liminality may be stronger with some than with others, it is clear that all of these pioneers of interreligious dialogue could attain to their respective experiences and insights only by removing themselves physically and/or mentally from established ways of thinking and acting. This stage or stance of liminality — of profound immersion in and experimentation with the teachings and practices of other religions — is of course not fit for everyone. Most individuals do not have the spiritual freedom, the personal courage, or the luxury, let alone the desire, to engage in prolonged and creative dialogue with other religious traditions. Such dialogue presupposes a willingness to stray from the trodden path and to doubt. Every attempt to reconcile religious traditions, to integrate elements of another religious tradition into one's own, is a process of trial and error in which some insights and experiences will be welcomed by one's own religion and others flatly rejected. This, it may fairly be said, requires a certain hardiness, or even a courage all its own. It is only when the more familiar courage that does not shy away from one's deepest convictions is coupled with another courage to experiment freely with the teachings and practices of other religions that dialogue may move forward.

Dialogue and Discernment

Interreligious dialogue in the sense that I have been developing it here is not complete without a return to the tradition from which one entered it, now offering the fruits of the dialogue to that original tradition as a whole, by way of a process of discernment that transcends individual judgment. This step in the dialogue is often particularly arduous. Religious traditions are not only large and complex, but also by nature conservative, which is to say slow in accepting change. Well aware of this, individuals engaged in dialogue may tend to keep their experiences and findings to themselves, or share them only with a select group of like-minded individuals. This, however, automatically renders dialogue a marginal activity with little or no impact on the tradition as a whole. Return to the tradition thus serves to share one's experiences and insights with individuals who are unable or unwilling to engage in profound dialogue, and to move the tradition itself forward. But it may also assist the individual involved in dialogue in the process of discernment of the fruits of dialogue. This, however, requires humility, openness, and trust, on the part of both the individual and the tradition itself.

The very idea of applying criteria of truth of one tradition to the teachings of another often meets with resistance among individuals engaged in dialogue. Within the climate of religious pluralism and a strong conception of the equality of religions that often lies at the basis of dialogue, the idea of imposing one's own norms and judgment on another religion is regarded as arrogant and presumptuous. Yet dialogue conducted by anyone who identifies with a religious tradition by definition presupposes a certain a priori assent to the truth of that tradition. The point is in the first place strictly hermeneutical: religious identity naturally entails commitment to the epistemic priority of one's own set of beliefs and practices, which function as the lens through which the world is understood and evaluated.[30] It should be clear that all individuals engaged in dialogue between religions judge the truth of the other, either implicitly or explicitly, on the basis of their own particular worldview and norms. This being the case, the notion of referring the teachings and practices of the other tradition to one's own normative judgment becomes a matter of hermeneutical necessity rather than theological triumph.

As individuals engaged in dialogue return to their respective traditions, these may in turn themselves participate in the process of discernment. The way in which traditions exercise their normative function will, of course, differ from one tradition to the next. While some religions may operate on a more communal basis of decision-making, others may be structured more hierarchically. Within the Roman Catholic tradition, one may find both a communal form of discernment, expressed in the notion of the *sensus fidelium,* or the sense of the faithful, and a more hierarchical form, represented by the teaching authority of the church. This teaching authority may include foundational texts and traditions (such as that of the Apostolic Fathers), sets of fundamental principles transmitted through the ages, or individual bearers of authority (such as the Magisterium of the Catholic Church). At its best, the teaching authority functions to bring to bear on any new insight or experience a deep and rich constellation of principles that help one to make sense of and indeed measure the truth of what one encounters in the other religion. It is in this sense that the tradition serves as an ultimate arbiter of truth, a check on an otherwise undefined flow of individual judgment and subjective taste or desire, so that the meaning of the other religion may show up without becoming an effect simply of one person's temporary and limited perspective.

Return to the tradition represents an act not only of intellectual and spiritual humility, but also of solidarity with the tradition as a whole, and with individuals who might otherwise never be able to taste the fruits of dialogue. It cannot be denied that interreligious dialogue places high demands on those directly engaged in it, requiring not only solid theological grounding within one's own tradition, but also personal openness, linguistic expertise, and a great deal of religious and spiritual imagination. If, however, dialogue really does offer the promise of religious development and spiritual growth, then those who have both the capacity and the opportunity to engage in it also have the responsibility to dedicate their results to the benefit of others and of the tradition as a whole. Bringing much of this together, Leonard Swidler frames this responsibility in terms of a dialogue that is by definition two-sided:

> Interreligious, interideological dialogue must be a two-sided dialogue, beyond the community and within it. We must be in regular dialogue with our fellow religionists, sharing with them the results of our interreligious, interideological dialogue so they too can enhance their understanding of what is held in common and where the differences truly are, for only thus can the whole community grow in knowledge and inner and outer transformation, and thereby bridge over antipathies and draw closer. In fact, if this two-sided dialogue is not maintained, the individual dialogue partners will grow in knowledge and consequently be changed, thus slowly moving away from their unchanging community and becoming a third reality, a *tertium quid* — hardly the intended integrative goal of dialogue.[31]

The risks of generating a *tertium quid* are not imaginary. Much of what occurs in interreligious dialogue often remains largely the provenance of those directly engaged in it. Books arising from the dialogue with other religions are read (or understood) mostly by individuals sharing a common interest or expertise. This may ultimately lead to a neutralization of the efforts and insights of dialogue, or else to the development of various subgroups within a religious tradition. Francis Clooney hints at this when in *Seeing through Texts* he envisions the possibility of the development of new communities of practice within the tradition, based on an individual believer's particular spiritual or ritual affinity with one or the other form of thought and prayer.[32] This may indeed lead to a genuine enrichment of the tradition, as individuals may find different ways of nourishing their particular religious and spiritual needs within their own religion. Yet insofar as the fruits of the dialogue then remain confined to select communities of believers, it may deprive the religion as a whole from the opportunity to benefit from the dialogue. Such opportunity, however, also places certain requirements upon the tradition itself.

Tradition as Obstacle or Instrument

The main obstacle for returning to the tradition and sharing the fruits of the dialogue with other believers often lies not with the individuals involved, but with the tradition itself, with its innate resistance to change. While religious traditions may overtly support and even encourage dialogue, they are generally less than receptive to the new insights arising from dialogue, especially when these might challenge established ways of thinking or acting. There is ample evidence of the latter in the history of Christian response to changes proposed by individuals engaged with the religious or cultural practices of other religions. It took no less than two centuries for the Roman Catholic Church to come to terms with the Rites controversy in China,[33] and the efforts by Roberto de Nobili to adapt Christianity to the Indian religious and cultural context was met with considerable resistance, even from within his own Jesuit congregation. This attitude, moreover, has continued until well into the twentieth century, if not into the present day. Hugo Enomiya-Lassalle's attempts to integrate elements of Zen meditation into Christian practice were rejected by Rome, and in an attempt to prevent his ashram from being absorbed by the established institutional structures of the church, Bede Griffiths affiliated it with the Benedictine order of Camaldoli. The work of theologians engaged in dialogue with other religions has often met with considerable suspicion, and even condemnation.[34] Official documents of the Catholic Church generally adopt a reactionary style and tone with regard to what is perceived as an encroachment of teachings and practices of other religious traditions on the integrity and traditional self-understanding of Christianity. This is evident in the document *Dominus Iesus*, which, though in many cases rightfully pointing to some of the dangers of relativism, displays an unmistakable attitude of defensiveness, arguing purely from tradition and scripture without recognizing the possibility of change and growth in the tradition.

All this signals a significant problem for interreligious dialogue. While faithfulness to the tradition and to its principles of discernment characterizes genuine dialogue between religions, the religions themselves are often indifferent and at times even actively resistant to the religious challenges and possibilities emerging from the dialogue. However, as Terrence Tilley has recently reminded us, openness to change and growth forms the mark of a vibrant religious tradition, and the more a tradition is committed to the truth through a process of "unrestrained communication," the wiser it is to commit to it.[35] It is thus only through the presence of an open and constructive dialogue within the tradition that individuals engaged in dialogue with other religions may feel confirmed in their own continued religious commitment, and indeed encouraged in their desire to submit the fruits of interreligious dialogue to the tradition. And it is only through such openness that the tradition itself may move forward without the loss of individuals who have dedicated their lives to the constructive dialogue with another religion.

OPENNESS IN COMMITMENT

Though dialogue between religions thus presupposes commitment, the main challenge remains that of finding a proper balance between commitment to one's own religion and openness to the other. The openness required for interreligious dialogue is often understood in radical terms as involving recognition of the equality of all religions and a willingness to convert to the other religion, if that is where the dialogue leads. If these conditions indeed define openness to other religions, then commitment and openness may be difficult to reconcile. Commitment to the truth of one religion logically excludes recognition of the equal truth of others, and religious commitment generally entails a sense of belonging that does not present itself as a priori subject to change. We shall here therefore reflect on the meaning and role of equality and conversion in the dialogue between religions and on the degree to which commitment to one religion may still allow for openness to another.

Openness and Equality

Any genuine dialogue, that is to say, any dialogue dedicated to mutual exchange of meaning and truth, requires and indeed presupposes a modicum of respect. Some individuals engaged in dialogue go so far as to argue that the exigencies of interreligious dialogue command recognition of the complete equality of all participants. Thus, for Leonard Swidler, "dialogue can take place only between equals,"[36] and Jean-Claude Basset agrees that equality is "an indispensable condition for the reciprocity of dialogue, without which difference cannot be respected."[37] Langdon Gilkey calls for "parity" or "rough parity" between religions, without which "a serious discussion of diversity and its theological meaning would not be undertaken, nor would serious and authentic dialogue between religions be possible."[38] And Paul Knitter believes that an attachment to the superiority of one's own tradition cannot but stifle any genuine interest in, understanding of, or receptivity to what is different in other religious traditions.[39]

Perhaps this insistence on abandoning all claims to superiority may be understood as a reaction to and correction for certain regrettable attitudes Christianity is known to have displayed toward other religions. Christian complicity in the history of the abuses of Western colonialism is sometimes thought to indicate an intrinsic connection between belief in the uniqueness and absoluteness of one's own belief system and the attitudes of arrogance and aggression adopted toward other religious traditions and cultures. But emphasis on the equality of all religions may also result from a confusion of theological and phenomenological approaches to religious plurality. As the historical and cultural particularity of all religious claims to superiority has become evident, some theologians have come to shy away from such claims and to admit, with Langdon Gilkey, that "no cultural logos is final and therefore universal (even one based on science); no one revelation is or can be the universal criterion for all the others (even, so we are now seeing, Christian revelation)."[40]

In the attempt to create a "level playing field" between religions, some theologians have come to either downplay or reinterpret Christian claims to uniqueness and superiority. John Hick and Paul Knitter, for example, regard the traditional Christian understanding of the uniqueness of Jesus Christ as an unintended — or at least unnecessary — development of early Christology. In their view, it came about through an (unfortunate) shift in early Christology from the use of metaphorical or love-language to the use of metaphysical categories to refer to the meaning and role of Jesus Christ in the history of salvation. While Hick thus proposes to do away with all claims to superiority and uniqueness, Knitter suggests the possibility of understanding Christ as "truly" rather than the "only" savior, arguing that such a shift in no way impairs or diminishes religious commitment.[41] He uses the image of marital love and commitment to point out that genuine commitment to one tradition does not preclude appreciating "the best and the absolute in others."[42]

Knitter's focus on dialogue and on religious equality as the basis for dialogue has certainly shed a critical light on some of the ways in which religions have suffered from a lack of recognition and respect.[43] In particular, he has called for attention to those religious voices that might otherwise be excluded from the dialogue due to cultural and linguistic circumstances. Even in a context of considerable openness, it might happen that dialogue is dominated by a single religious tradition that sets the agenda or that is most at home in the language and culture in which the dialogue takes place. Knitter thus appeals to the majority religions and cultures to allow representatives of other religions to speak in their own languages and to propose their own topics of interest and concern. As such, at minimum, the principle of equality of religions may lead to a critical consciousness of the various forms of social and racial prejudice that may color the dialogue between religions.

Yet the question is whether such respect and recognition necessarily requires affirmation of the religious equivalence or equal truth of all religions, and whether such notion of equality is even coherent or possible in the context of a dialogue between religions. Religious commitment involves assent to a certain worldview and body of teachings that would logically preclude affirmation of the equal truth of alternate religious worldviews and teachings. Not only are the religious views of different traditions at times directly opposed or mutually exclusive,[44] but the very claim to ultimacy of one religion necessarily precludes the truth of the claims of others. While many have attempted to soften or downplay such claims, they remain the foundation of the faith of most religious believers and as such can only be compromised at the peril of a genuine dialogue between religious traditions. Moreover, such claims to uniqueness and truth form the very content of the dialogue. As such, Moltmann rightly states that "a religion which has given up claiming uniqueness, one might fairly say, is of no special interest."[45] It is indeed in the meeting between strong convictions that dialogue takes place.

A favorite category that has been used by some theologians to suggest the equality or the equivalence of religions is that of "complementarity." In his book *Love Meets Wisdom*, Aloysius Pieris, for example, argues for the complementarity of the Christian concept of love and the Buddhist notion of wisdom, pointing to traces of each in both traditions.[46] And Jacques Dupuis has similarly come to use the term in order to emphasize the basic equality or equivalence of religions in their differences.[47] It is no doubt true that different religions may be regarded as complementary in some respects, but it is also true, at the same time, that that complementarity is always recognized and defined in light of one particular religion or conception of truth. As such, Dupuis ends up speaking of an "assymetrical complementarity" between Christianity and other religious traditions.[48]

In addition to the logical or theological inconsistency of affirming the equality of religions, some have pointed to the moral dubiousness of such a position. The conception of the equality of all religious and moral systems leaves little or no ground for the development of ethical norms by which the abuses or injustices of any religion may be judged and criticized. Religious equality and pluralism thus generally tends to moral relativism. Religious thinkers have often attempted to avoid this relativism by appealing to shared ethical norms (Hick), or to a shared commitment to the alleviation of social and economic injustice and suffering (Knitter). Recognizing the moral paradox entailed in the idea of a radical parity of religions, Gilkey, for his part, still emphasizes the importance of "ultimate values" and an "ultimate vision of things," as well as an "absolute commitment to this understanding of things."[49] Between equality and moral criteria, he comes to advocate a vision of the "relative absoluteness"[50] of one's own religious claims. This expression and Dupuis's "asymmetrical complementarity" both reflect an attempt to strike a balance between recognizing each religion in its own particularity, on the one hand, and the internal logic of faith and moral judgment, on the other. Taken together, they remind us of the impossibility of reconciling religious commitment with a recognition of the radical equality of religions.

However, if the notion of religious equality may not be religiously or theologically coherent, neither is it necessary for genuine dialogue to take place. Such dialogue merely requires a recognition of the presence of elements of genuine truth and value in the other religion and of the equal dignity and religious integrity of the partner in dialogue. Reacting against the dangers of religious and moral relativism, the Vatican document *Dominus Iesus* (22) states that "*Equality*, which is a presupposition of interreligious dialogue, refers to the equal personal dignity of the parties in dialogue, not to doctrinal content, nor even less to the position of Jesus Christ — who is God himself made man — in relation to the founders of the other religions." Such an elevation of a core religious belief beyond the level of beliefs articulated by other religions is not only religiously coherent, but probably also quite representative of how many religions approach the dialogue. If this is so, then true equality would have to lie in the very fact that all participants enter the dialogue convinced of the superior truth of their own beliefs and practices. It is thus, as Dupuis also points out, "in this fidelity to personal, non-negotiable convictions, honestly accepted on both sides, that the interreligious dialogue takes place 'between equals' — in their differences."[51]

Commitment and Conversion

One of the greatest conundrums facing the reality of commitment in dialogue lies in whether and how a firm commitment to one religious tradition might allow for the possibility of conversion to the other. Numerous scholars engaged in interreligious dialogue insist on the necessity of openness to such possibility for genuine dialogue to take place. Raimon Panikkar, for example, states that dialogue "must begin with my questioning myself and the relativity of my beliefs (which does not mean their relativism), accepting the challenge of a change, a conversion, and the risk of upsetting my traditional patterns."[52] And Paul Knitter argues that "dialogue without the possibility of conversion is like a sleek aircraft that can take us anywhere but is not allowed to land."[53] While David Tracy emphasizes the importance of "self-respect," which, he states, "includes, of course, a respect for, even a reverence for, one's own tradition or way," he also emphasizes that dialogue requires a "willingness to risk all in the questioning and inquiry that constitutes the dialogue itself."[54] There is no mistaking the line of thought: interreligious dialogue must take the form of freedom from attachment to religious presuppositions and openness to the possibility of being convinced by the superior truth or the more effective religious practice of the other religion. The question, however, is how such openness may be combined with an existing belief in the ultimate truth and efficacy of one's existing religious beliefs and practices? Religious conviction constitutes an integral part of one's personal identity that one normally cannot conceive of changing, especially not "by voluntary fiat" as Paul Griffiths also argues.[55] There is no reason to exclude the possibility of conversion to the other religion, or to deny the fact that such conversions do indeed take place in and through dialogue. But to require openness to the possibility of conversion as a condition for dialogue may be both unrealistic and unnecessarily limiting.

Any religious conviction consists of a complex and inscrutable mixture of voluntary and involuntary commitments and of deeply affective attachments that have come to shape one's personal identity and that one has come to assume as a second nature. It informs one's way of being, one's relationships, and the set of principles according to which one organizes and gives meaning to one's life. While religious convictions may be rationally argued and defended, their truth is ultimately grounded in an attitude of faith, in a personal surrender to a particular worldview and set of beliefs that defy purely rational argumentation. Religious beliefs and convictions are rarely experienced as a set of principles over which one has conscious control, or which one might even conceive of giving up under any circumstance. The very thought of possibly abandoning one's own religious beliefs in favor of others may thus be seen to signal an attitude of detachment that is far from representative of traditional religious faith or commitment. It must also be noted that the experience of conversion to another religion generally entails considerable personal and spiritual pain, whether distantly or at a moment of crisis. It frequently causes a rupture with one's familiar social and religious context and with cherished forms of symbolic and ritual expression. All this may explain why conversion to the other religion is in fact a rare occurrence in the dialogue between religions. Individuals engaged in dialogue may attempt to integrate the best of the other religion within their own religious life, or even at times reinterpret their own tradition according to the basic religious categories of the other — suggesting the possibility of at least some level of conversion to the worldview of the other. But radical conversion to the other religion would simply go too far and cost too much for most individuals committed to a particular religion to imagine. All of this illustrates why the possibility of conversion — though not unthinkable — cannot be made into a condition for dialogue between individuals genuinely committed to their respective traditions.

It is certainly true that dialogue presupposes openness to the possibility of change. As Lesslie Newbigin put it succinctly, "A person whose mind is incapable of being changed is incapable of genuine dialogue."[56] The changes occurring through dialogue may take a variety of different forms, ranging from the integration of ritual forms and religious categories that may come to enrich the tradition, all the way to at least the possibility of a radical reinterpretation of traditional beliefs and practices through the hermeneutical framework of the other tradition. They may include self-critique or a shift in one's traditional self-understanding. Within Christianity, the possibility, nay, the necessity of religious change may be seen to be ingrained in its very self-understanding as a historical revelation. Even though this revelation is believed to contain timeless truth, the very fact that this truth has come to expression in a series of historical events grounds the tradition in the reality of change. This defines what can fairly be understood as the perspective and the task of the theologian at the frontier of the tradition: one must continuously engage with elements of truth as they present themselves in the course of history, and "entertain whatever can be assimilated" as Henri de Lubac puts it.[57] Engagement with other religions may be regarded as a privileged occasion for religious change and growth through the encounter with new ideas, images, practices, and principles that may prove amenable to assimilation to the Christian tradition.

Dialogue conducted from religious commitment thus generally involves openness to change, while preserving the integrity and truth of one's own fundamental religious convictions. In some cases, however, openness to the truth of the other religion may lead all the way to also embracing the fundamental worldview and beliefs of the other. It is worth asking how this may occur. One way would be through the very exercise of empathy that is essential for dialogue as such. All genuine dialogue involves an attempt to understand the internal coherence and the plausibility of the position of the other, or its "substantive rightness" as Gadamer put it.[58] Expanding upon Gadamer's hermeneutics and applying it concretely to the context of interreligious dialogue, David Tracy argues that "to recognize the other as other, the different as different is also to acknowledge that other world of meaning as, in some manner, a possible option for oneself."[59] This option need not be immanent and live, but it may present itself as what Tracy calls a "suggestive possibility."[60] In some cases, and through a configuration of any number of factors, this possibility may turn into a reality. The shift from one primary frame of religious reference to another may occur suddenly or gradually, as the result of a momentous experience or a conscious process of deliberation. Engagement with the truth of the other religion may lead to a profoundly transformative experience and insight that changes one's whole perception of reality. Or it may result in a gradual realization of the superior truth of the other religion, of its greater capacity to integrate various dimensions and facts of life within a coherent system of meaning and purpose. Conversion may be prompted by a positive appeal of the other religion, but also by a critical confrontation with one's own tradition. The questions raised by the other in the dialogue may at times cause a rupture in one's relationship to one's own tradition and a greater receptivity to the truth of the other. While conversion thus certainly belongs among the possible results of interreligious dialogue, it can scarcely be factored into the religious conviction by which one adheres to and lives from one's own tradition.

◆ ◆ ◆

Emphasis on the need for religious conviction and commitment in dialogue may be seen to place an unnecessary limitation on interreligious dialogue. It limits one's freedom of thought and practice to the contours of a particular faith tradition, and it ties one's own fate to that of the predetermined religious imagination and to the more conservative tendencies of religious authorities or of the tradition as a whole. The practice of dialogue with other religious traditions often elicits profoundly enriching experiences and elevated insights that one's own religious tradition may not (yet) be able to integrate or accept. And the checkered history of relations between religious traditions often weighs upon attempts to engage in constructive dialogue. It is thus not surprising that individuals engaged in dialogue are often tempted to break from their respective tradition and to practice dialogue unencumbered by a sense of answerability to any higher truth or authority. Yet a firm foundation within a particular religious tradition may just as well, and indeed — I have contended — better be regarded as an asset in dialogue. The tradition represents a necessary point of departure and place of return in all genuine interreligious dialogue. It offers a storehouse of religious experiences and insight to bring to the dialogue and to reconsider as a result of the dialogue. Commitment to a particular religious tradition, moreover, delivers one from the burden or temptation of individual judgment and represents the only promise of moving the tradition itself forward. While traditions may be slow to change, this reluctance may also save the tradition from easy syncretism or from the integration of ideas and practices that may come to confuse believers or disrupt the integrity of the faith and the coherence of the tradition. On the other hand, it is only through openness to other traditions and to the possibility of change and growth that traditions may themselves hope to gain from the dialogue and secure the continued commitment of those engaged in the adventure of interreligious dialogue.

CHAPTER THREE

INTERCONNECTION

One of the basic conditions for interreligious dialogue is a sense of commonality or solidarity among religions, and of the relevance of the other religion for one's own religious tradition. Any notion of the radical singularity or the fundamental incomparability of religions would render dialogue superfluous, if not impossible. Interreligious dialogue thus presupposes a conviction that, in spite of important and ineradicable differences in belief and practices, religions may find one another in a common ground. This meeting point between religions may be located in the past or in the future, in a common origin or goal outside or within religious traditions. It may be the starting point or the very goal of dialogue. But some belief in the interconnection or interrelatedness between religions is necessary in order to render dialogue both possible and meaningful.

This idea of interconnection between religions is far from evident. It runs first of all against religious self-understanding. Every religion tends to regard itself as unique, self-contained, and in no way comparable to the other religions of the world. But the notion of interconnection also flows against the current intellectual climate, with its emphasis on particularity and difference. All truth, religious or otherwise, is regarded as radically singular, fragmented, and perspectival, and any attempt to compare or relate different personal, cultural, or religious features is regarded as suspect, the likely expression of moral and epistemological violence. On this line of thinking, each religion derives from a different source, pursues different goals, and develops its own culturally specific set of values and beliefs. Indeed, even the term "religion" no longer serves as a ready basis for presuming a set of common characteristics. Not only do scholars fundamentally disagree on the definition of the term, but the very validity of the term "religion" has been questioned, associated as it has been with Western and monotheistic connotations.[1]

Even though the existence of a common essence, ground, or goal among religions cannot be presumed, we shall here focus on certain areas that have or may become a meeting point between religions and a starting point for dialogue. One of the areas in which members of different religions have indeed found one another is in the confrontation with common social, political, and economic challenges: secularization, world peace, human suffering, or the damages visited upon the environment. These external challenges facing all religious traditions alike may be seen to point to shared fundamental values and concerns uniting religions and to offer a basis for genuine collaboration and joint commitment. In the first part of this chapter, we will focus on some examples of dialogue and collaboration that have emerged from such confrontation with common social and political challenges.

Rather than in external challenges, some have found the meeting point between religious traditions within the religious traditions themselves, in particular in the domain of mysticism or spiritual experiences. Mysticism has long been regarded as the area of convergence between religious traditions, and the dialogue between monastic traditions and between spiritual masters of different religions has often been presented as the model and epitome of interreligious dialogue. In the second part of the chapter, we will reflect on the implications of the notion of a mystical unity of religions for interreligious dialogue.

A third area in which religions may be thought to meet is in their common reference to a transcendent ultimate reality. The idea that all religions derive from or to point to the same ultimate reality may indeed offer a basis and foundation for dialogue. The question, however, is how that ultimate reality is to be understood or where it is to be located. In an attempt to establish a neutral common ground for dialogue, some have developed a conception of a transcendent ultimate reality beyond that of any particular religion. However, religions may also find in their own particular conceptions of ultimate reality a sufficient basis for affirming the interconnection with other religions. In the end, each religion must find its own reason and motive for dialogue, according to the possibilities afforded by its own set of beliefs and teachings. While the existence of external challenges may offer an immediate occasion for dialogue, it is only insofar as the teachings of other religions are considered to be related to one's own that dialogue will become not only possible but also necessary.

COMMON EXTERNAL CHALLENGES

One of the avenues by which religions frequently discover a sense of solidarity is in the confrontation with a common threat or challenge. Concern with issues like secularization or ecological devastation may stimulate religions to forge an alliance, or perhaps simply exchange ideas dedicated to achieving a positive religious response. Even though the occasion for dialogue here lies outside of any particular religion, the very fact that more than one religion identifies the same points of concern suggests a set of basic commitments recognizably similar in each of them without which dialogue would be at best unlikely. In the case of secularization, it is the shared commitment to a reality beyond the purely immanent world that may be seen to bind religions together in a common cause. Likewise, the need to confront global threats to peace, or to work for the preservation of the environment, also calls for a religious collaboration beyond the solutions offered by any one religious tradition. Globalization and its social and political challenges thus seems to offer an immediate and urgent occasion for dialogue.

Secularization

Limiting ourselves to only the most frequently cited features of modern secularism, we may concentrate on the manner in which technology and capitalism have touched all but the most remote parts of our world, carrying with them a this-worldly attitude and a logic of material gain and progress that puts tremendous pressure on religious thinking and values. Even though the full-blown secularization thesis — according to which mechanical reason and a certain pragmatism would lead to the end of religion — has lost much of its plausibility, it is impossible to deny the powerful effect of that worldview on religious consciousness. Life in the modern world not only shifts religious conviction and practice out of the public and into the private domain, but also opens itself increasingly to a scientific rationality that at the very least calls upon religious reflection to redefine its tenets in a new, contemporary light. It seems evident that some religions possess a greater metaphysical facility with these developments than do others.

Yet few, if any, could claim that scientific rationality has not challenged their basic commitments and articles of faith in a significant way.

This virtually tells us how and why the religions may collaborate in the face of secular materialism: each represents by its very nature a resistance to the onslaught of mechanistic rationality and a defense of a life that aims beyond the visible and tangible world. The ways in which other religions have found themselves able to engage secularization may prove highly instructive in this regard. For the Muslim philosopher Seyyed Hussain Nasr, it is the very fact that Christianity and Judaism have long been engaged with the challenges of modernity that makes them particularly interesting dialogue partners. This is also the sentiment of the Buddhist philosopher Masao Abe, who regards the problems of secularization as the main, if not the only reason for engaging in dialogue with Christianity:

> Apart from the context of the issue between religion and irreligion there wouldn't be much sense in taking up the problem of Buddhism and Christianity. If a discussion of the theme should not throw any light on our search for the being of religion itself which can overpower all negation, then it would be indeed futile to engage in it. It is precisely on the meeting point of the two problems, namely the interreligious problem of Buddhism and Christianity on the one hand, and the problem of religion and irreligion on the other, that the most serious question for modern man, the question of his self-estrangement should be asked; and it is precisely there that we should expect to find an answer to it.[2]

This is an early statement, and it is true that Abe's views on the use of interreligious dialogue expanded as he became one of the main representatives of Kyoto School philosophy and Zen practice in the dialogue with Christianity. But the threat of a purely secular or irreligious worldview never ceased to inform much of his dialogical agenda. He was firmly convinced that only collaboration between the religions could bring out the *sui generis* nature and the distinctive function of religions in the face of nihilism and the challenges of secularist critiques. This is unmistakable in his more recent work, such as the widely read essay "Kenotic God and the Dynamic Sunyata," which directs mutually critical and constructive dialogue between the Christian and the Buddhist understanding of ultimate reality toward a better response to modernity from both religions.[3]

While other religions have come to probe Christian attempts to come to terms with modernity, Christians in turn have at times sought inspiration in Eastern religious traditions. This would be how to understand the great popularity of Fritjof Capra's book *The Tao of Physics*,[4] which claims to see significant parallels between modern physics and Eastern forms of mysticism. Thus, without doubting that secularism remains a challenge for all religious traditions, Capra argues that Eastern religions may be better equipped to deal with that challenge and indeed with the materialistic malaise of modern Western society in general. This of course concedes a great deal to contemporary physics which must be accepted, but it also comes close to making the phenomenon of secularization a fortuitous development, since it at last turns Christianity toward dialogue with Eastern religions, with their exceptionally versatile mystical current.

The negative counterpart of this attitude of openness toward other religions can be found in another child of modern secularization: the reactionary, innovative, and aggressive form of traditionalism we call "fundamentalism." Understood as a radical rejection of modernity, fundamentalism has manifested itself in various forms within many of the major religious traditions. It is characterized by a return to some form of religious authority (scriptural, personal, or ethical principles) that is elevated beyond any critical reflection and that forms the rallying point for radicalism. Fundamentalism has been the cause of tension and dissonance not only among but also within religious traditions. Acts of violence have been perpetuated as much against co-religionists who do not agree with the radical views of fundamentalists as against members of other religious traditions. The volumes of the Fundamentalism Project provide a thorough analysis of the various social, political, economic, and religious dimensions apparent in the many forms of fundamentalism that have emerged throughout the world.[5] One recognizes similarities alongside important differences among the many instances of fundamentalism. Each such instance is, of course, best addressed from within the particular religious tradition in which it emerges. It is only through exposure to the religious exaggerations and distortions of fundamentalist ideologies that believers may eventually acquire a more critical understanding of the ideologies that have captured the imagination of many a believer, especially those in need of security and religious clarity. However, the very fact that fundamentalism is an almost universal problem for religious traditions, and moreover one with significant structural similarities, suggests that attempts to come to terms with it within a particular religion can serve and be served by a dialogue with other religions that face the same problem. Like the secularization against which it reacts, fundamentalism is based on social and psychological causes that are uncontained by any one religious situation or identity. At the very best, this invites

101

interreligious collaboration in pursuit of adequate diagnosis and an effective, humane response to both fundamentalism itself and the various factors that give rise to it.

World Peace

Unsurprisingly, a concern with world peace has been one of the most powerful catalysts for unifying different religious traditions in dialogue. Since the middle of the twentieth century, numerous interreligious organizations and initiatives have arisen dedicated to the promotion of peace and justice in the world. One of the most established of these is the World Conference on Religion and Peace (WCRP), founded in 1970 through the collaborative efforts of prominent leaders from various religious traditions. Once every five years, it organizes World Assemblies, where representatives of all the major world religions meet to discuss various topics related to peace and disarmament. The WCRP focuses not only on religious leaders and scholars but also on grassroots education and training in conflict resolution in areas affected by religious and ethnic violence. It prides itself on being "active on every continent and in some of the most troubled areas on earth, creating multi-religious partnerships that mobilize the moral and social resources of religious people to address their shared problems."

Another permanent structure of interreligious dialogue for peace is the "United Religious Initiative," founded in 1995 by the Anglican bishop William Swing. According to its mission statement, "the purpose of the United Religions Initiative is to promote enduring daily interfaith cooperation, to end religiously motivated violence and to create cultures of peace, justice and healing for the Earth and all living beings." This has also been the mission of the "International Committee for the Peace Council" founded in 1995 and with a concerted interest in training peace counselors who support local initiatives through advice and example.

In addition to these and other overarching or interreligious peace organizations, there are events staged by single religious movements. These are almost too numerous to catalogue, but suffice it to observe that religious groups ranging from many new Japanese religions to the Pontifical Council for Interreligious Dialogue have been actively engaged in the promotion of peace through small or large gatherings of representatives of different religions. A particularly memorable instance of this was the 1986 gathering of the leaders of the major world religions in Assisi, at the invitation of John Paul II, to pray together for world peace. An equally inspiring if smaller instance was the first meeting of the World Congress of Imams and Rabbis for Peace, in Brussels in 2005.

The proliferation of different religious organizations and initiatives dedicated to world peace responds to the equivocal or even duplicitous role that the religions themselves have often played in generating war or qualifying peace. While all religions preach the importance of peace and harmony, there is no denying the fact that they have been and continue to be profoundly implicated in the logic of war and violence. All interreligious dialogue for peace requires a willingness to recognize and apologize for the sins of one's own tradition as well as forgive those of the other.[6] That said, it has to be recognized that most religions do possess plentiful ethical and social resources for cultivating peace between peoples and nations. The very existence of the aforementioned initiatives plainly testifies to this. A proper interpretation and mobilization of such resources may thus become a powerful tool not only for breaking through the cycle of religious violence and retaliation, but also for keeping feelings of hatred and antagonism from arising. Since religions offer not only a higher legitimation for ethical commitment to peace, but also a vision of hope and energy to transform the world, dialogue is not only an interesting possibility but a moral obligation.

Hence, Hans Küng's famous dictum: "There can be no peace among the nations without peace among the religions" and "there can be no peace among the religions without dialogue between the religions."[7] For Küng, this dialogue has taken the form of the development of a global ethic, the formulation of a set of four fundamental ethical principles or "irrevocable directives" upon which all religions agree: commitment to a culture of nonviolence and respect for life, commitment to a culture of solidarity and a just economic order, commitment to a culture of tolerance and a life of truthfulness, and commitment to a culture of equal rights and partnership between men and women. These principles for a global ethic were ratified at the 1993 World Parliament of Religions in Chicago and signed by representatives of all the major religions present. They are meant to serve as the basis for mutual understanding and collaboration toward the creation of a just and peaceful world.

Alleviation of Suffering

A third phenomenon stimulating collaboration and dialogue among religions is the suffering caused by economic and ecological exploitation. Without digressing into the classical and current status of theodicy, it may safely be asserted that suffering, especially in its physical forms, elicits an appeal that transcends ideological and religious differences. The widespread and apparently endless experience of human suffering renders dialogue between religions particularly imperative. In recent times, we have come to recognize that this is no less true of the suffering of the planet itself. Both of these forms of suffering have been made the focus of religious reflection and interreligious dialogue in the work of Paul Knitter. Pointing out that all religions are confronted with "the same context of human and ecological suffering that now menaces the world," Knitter calls for a concerted effort of all religious traditions to jointly address their causes.[8] For him, this is a matter above all of the lethal combination of globalization and capitalism, as they infect virtually every region and culture of the world. Insatiable material greed and the seemingly unstoppable laws of macro-economics lead to the rampant exploitation of both human and natural resources with a force and range that call for a global response and for collaboration among religions.

While religions may not be equipped to address the macro-economic issues involved in the phenomenon of globalization and economic and ecological exploitation, they do possess the tools to critique its source and to promote alternative attitudes and behavior. It is probably true that each religion has its own focus or perspective on those causes and factors, which is to say its own relative competence with some of them. After all, some religions see no positive meaning in suffering of any kind, whereas others attribute a degree of salvific or liberatory power to it. Yet all religions tend to oppose and condemn the materialism, selfishness, and greed that often drive capitalist economies and that inflict, directly or indirectly, so much suffering on others. Religions may thus join voices to offer a united and powerful critique of the system and behavior that result in social injustice and human exploitation.

With regard to ecological exploitation, there can be no doubt that religious beliefs and attitudes have a direct effect on how human beings relate to nature, either positively or negatively.[9] One of the most concerted efforts to bring about dialogue between religions on this issue is the Harvard project on "Religion and Ecology" spearheaded by Evelyn Tucker and John Grim. The goal of this project is "to describe and analyze the commonalities that exist within and among religious traditions with respect to ecology"; "to identify the minimum common ground on which to base constructive understanding, motivating discussion, and concerted action in diverse locations around the globe; and to highlight the specific religious resources that comprise such fertile ecological ground: within scripture, ritual, myth, symbol, cosmology, sacrament, and so on."[10]

One particular form of human suffering that is common to most religions and that has become a focus for dialogue is that of gender inequality and the subordination of women. While the position of women certainly differs from one religion to the next, some of the same dynamics of domination and exclusion are present among many of the world religions: male monopoly on the knowledge and interpretation of scripture, preoccupation with and control of women's sexuality, and exclusion of women from positions of authority and power (except insofar as these positions are based on purely spiritual gifts or charismatic qualities). These conditions may be brought to light by direct, internal feminist analysis of a particular tradition. But the fact that similar patterns of patriarchal domination and control are in evidence across religious traditions may shed new light on the origins and dynamics of the religious subordination of women. Dialogue may thus lead to a deeper understanding of the structures of religious patriarchy and to shared inspiration and an exchange of resources for developing new liberative strategies.

Naturally, dialogue between women from different religions has also generated a sense of solidarity and a commitment to collaboration not only in the pursuit of feminist causes, but also in addressing many of the challenges mentioned above: world peace, ecological concerns, and social justice. The very fact that women share common experiences of exclusion within and beyond their religious traditions may render them particularly open and receptive to one another and to the potential of other religious traditions to bring about change and growth within their own. It is tempting to suppose that the scope of this potential is due to the depth of the critique that accompanies it. Few forms of critique are as penetrating as feminism, and if one accepts its basic claims few propose a concept and an experience of liberation nearly as expansive. The authority of the tradition itself, in each case if not in general, is put to the test of experiences that it is said to generate.

External Challenges and Dialogue

There is little doubt that common external challenges may bring members of different religions to a new sense of interconnection and an enhanced sense of solidarity in commitment to a common cause. Insofar as the occasion for dialogue lies outside of any particular tradition, it also contributes to a sense of equality or equivalence among all partners. In this case, it is no longer the distinctive beliefs of any particular religion, but rather the challenge to all of them that becomes the rallying point and the standard for efficacy and truth in dialogue. Each religion is evaluated and judged not on the basis of any particular religion's convictions, but according to the degree to which and the way in which it addresses a particular social or political issue. Dialogue on secularization will naturally focus on the manner in which the religions have come to terms with this particular problem, just as dialogue on poverty and forms of economic exploitation will lead to an assessment of religions in terms of their effectiveness in overcoming these particular forms of suffering. And dialogue between women from different religions will likewise focus on the liberative force of any particular religion, or of particular teachings within any religion.

This is why Paul Knitter, for example, regards the various forms of human and ecological suffering caused by globalization as a "new hermeneutical kairos for interreligious dialogue":

> It is a "kairos" because it is a unique constellation of events that constitutes both new opportunities and responsibilities; it is "hermeneutical" because it enables followers of different religious paths not just to feel the need for each other but to understand *and* to judge each other. It is a global situation consisting of concerns and questions that transcend differences of culture and religion and so touch all peoples.[11]

For Knitter, the voices of the victims of globalization represent the ultimate point of entrance into the hermeneutical circle of dialogue as well as the ultimate norm of truth. Here, the truth of any particular religion is thus measured, not by any internally religious criteria, but by the degree to which the teachings of such religion empower and motivate people to bring about liberation from social, economic, and political exploitation. This "soteriocentric" approach is thus believed to offer a criterion for dialogue that all religions are able to embrace. Attending more closely to this criterion, Knitter states that the norms operative in this form of dialogue "will be multiple, correctable, expandable — and always established in the dialogue." [12] Here, the result is on one hand something like a principle of equality among all religions that submit to a common criterion, and on the other hand an appeal to dialogue as source and site of the creative process that may further our sense of commonality, or at least solidarity among religions.

It is difficult to imagine disagreeing with much of this. However, it is one thing to conceive of a criterion as neutral or common, but quite another to relate oneself to it from one's own perspective. And that means: according to one's own convictions, and for reasons that are, in the final account, one's own. It is clear that for any believer, the compelling force of a particular criterion will ultimately lie not in its neutrality or commonality, but in the fact that it arises from or coincides with one's own deepest religious beliefs and principles. Any attempt to elevate neutral criteria beyond the truth claims of particular traditions thus runs against the grain of religious self-understanding.

All this also begs another, perhaps more penetrating, question: Where do religions derive their sense of commonality or solidarity once the external challenge or threat subsides? Or better: Where do they derive it apart from any such challenge or threat? Dialogues focused on common external challenges often remain limited, both in content and time, to that particular challenge or issue. One may certainly hope and expect that the friendship and solidarity forged by this kind of dialogue will also generate a broader interest in the religious beliefs of the other and lead to a genuine openness to learning from one another. But this does not necessarily or naturally evolve from the experience of solidarity in facing common challenges. A dialogue instigated by common external challenges may, of course, lead to the discovery of interconnections that do not depend on and are not limited by relative capacities to respond to the same challenges. But it may also remain confined to collaborative response to common challenges and contingent upon the existence of such challenges. In order for dialogue to be more than episodic, it may thus need to be grounded in a sense of interconnection that is more inherently religious, or internal to religious self-understanding.

COMMON EXPERIENCE

The search for a common religious origin or meeting point between religious traditions has often led to a focus on ultimate religious experiences. In particular, mystical experiences have appeared to offer a promising focal point for the idea of the interconnection between religions. After all, while religious discord generally responds to and insists on conflicting claims to truth, mystics speak of experiences that are, in the most positive sense, ineffable. It is impossible to deny the many similarities between spiritual paths or disciplines of various religions, or between the personal and spiritual qualities of mystics of different religions. This is why some have come to regard all religions as different historical and cultural expressions of the same fundamental experience. This conception of a common ground among religions may be regarded as both the result of and the motivation for dialogue.

The Mystical Unity of Religions

The notion of a mystical unity of religions or the idea that all religions meet in their greatest spiritual depth became especially prominent during the twentieth century. It has been proposed in one or another form by psychologists, philosophers, historians, and theologians, and within religious traditions that otherwise appear quite diverse. One of the earliest systematic elaborations of the idea is found in the work of William James. In *The Varieties of Religious Experience,* James explores the phenomenon of religion from the perspective of the subject, drawing on examples from many different religious traditions.[13] Comparing accounts of mystical experience in various religions, he points to the existence of "a certain composite photograph of universal saintliness, the same in all religions, of which the features can easily be traced."[14] These universal features include, he says, a sense of being in a life that transcends this world's selfish little interests, a commitment to self-surrender, freedom, and loving and harmonious affections. All of these are manifested in a basic tendency to asceticism and self-sacrifice, the achievement of detachment, equanimity and humility, and in a high degree of purity, moral perfection, and charity.[15] With these features universally in view, James thus considered mysticism a generic phenomenon, transcending the particularities of all religious traditions:

> In mystical states we become one with the Absolute and we become aware of our oneness. This is the everlasting and triumphant mystical tradition, hardly altered by the differences of time or creed. In Hinduism, in Neoplatonism, in Sufism, in Christian mysticism, in Whitmanianism, we find the same recurring note, so that there is about mystical utterances an eternal unanimity which ought to make critics stop and think, and which brings it about that the mystical classics have, as has been said, neither birthday nor native land.[16]

This account of mysticism came to resonate deeply with philosophers grounded in the Hindu and Buddhist traditions, and with proponents of perennial philosophy. One hears echoes of James in Nishida Kitaro's *An Inquiry into the Good,* where — in what becomes a founding moment of Kyoto School philosophy — he develops the notion of "pure experience": a direct and unmediated experience of reality in a state of consciousness that is undivided and universal, as exemplified by mystics of all religious traditions. "The true meaning of religion," states Nishida, is found "in breaking beyond one's own consciousness and experiencing the lofty universal spirit that functions at the base of consciousness."[17] Such would be the true aim of all religions, and the true achievement of their mystics.

A similar notion is advanced by the Hindu philosopher and statesman Sarvepalli Radhakrishnan, when he invokes a universal experience and mode of consciousness "which is distinct from the perceptual, imaginative or intellectual, and carries with it self-evidence and completeness."[18] Though Radhakrishnan describes this experience in terms of *Advaita Vedānta* as the overcoming of all dualities between the self and the Ultimate Reality, he argues that this in fact represents the experience of mystics of all religious traditions.[19]

This is also the thrust of Frithjof Schuon's *The Transcendent Unity of Religions,* which locates the ultimate unity of religions in their esoteric experiences.[20] According to Schuon, a Sufi philosopher, exoteric religious life is characterized by dualistic forms of thought and attachment to the particular teachings and practices of their own tradition, whereas esoteric experiences involve an overcoming of all duality and a realization of the relative and partial nature of all religious language and expression.

The notion of the mystical unity of all religions became one of the central tenets of the school of perennial philosophy.

Aldous Huxley, one of the protagonists of this school, describes the basic principles of perennialism as follows:

> The metaphysic that recognizes a divine Reality substantial to the world of things and lives and minds; the psychology that finds in the soul something similar to, or even identical with, divine Reality; the ethic that places man's final end in the knowledge of the immanent and transcendent Ground of all being — the thing is immemorial and universal.[21]

Drawing on accounts of mystics from a wide variety of religious traditions, perennial philosophy aims to demonstrate the common experiential core at the heart of all religious traditions by emphasizing the difference between the experience itself and its expression in the doctrines and cultic practices of each one of them. Similar notions of the unity of all mystical experiences may also be found in the Theosophical tradition and in its later expressions in the New Age movement.

Though scholars of mysticism rarely go so far as to affirm the unity of all mystical experiences, the similarities between the thought and experiences of mystics of different religions have led to important comparative work. While some have come to develop typologies of mystical experiences within and across religious traditions,[22] others have focused on the comparison of particular mystics or mystical traditions.[23]

Though many implicitly or explicitly recognize a certain unity or analogy of mystical experience, the idea of a mystical or spiritual unity among religions has also met with strong criticism. In general, scholarship on mysticism has become polarized between so-called "essentialists," who tend to regard mysticism as a unified and undifferentiated phenomenon transcending the particularities of culture and religions,

113

and "constructivists" who argue that every mystical experience is thoroughly shaped by the religious and cultural context in which it occurred, concluding therefore that the mystical experiences of different religions are in fact fundamentally divergent. The latter position has been argued vigorously in a series of edited works by the Jewish philosopher Steven Katz, who attempts to demonstrate that mystics remain profoundly rooted in their own respective traditions, continue to identify with the religious and philosophical categories particular to their tradition, and engage the religious language of their scriptures in creative, but nevertheless determined ways.[24] In terms of what people like James or Nishida have argued, the position of Katz and of other constructivists comes down to rejecting above all the very possibility of pure experience, or of experience unmediated by scriptural, doctrinal, or ritual categories and contexts. Since all experience is thought to remain embedded in and conditioned by its particular religious context, the experience of a Jewish Kabbalist is believed to be fundamentally different from that of a Taoist sage, and that of a Christian mystic different from that of a Zen Buddhist one, their many evident congruencies and unmistakable resonances notwithstanding. While the debate between essentialists and constructivists has reached an impasse, with arguments for both sides becoming more or less exhausted, it seems evident that the constructivist position has succeeded in removing the self-evidence with which some have come to assume the idea of the unity of all mystical experiences.

Lessons from the Inter-Monastic Dialogue

While the idea of the unity or diversity of mystical experiences is often debated on purely rational or theoretical grounds, the actual experience of dialogue between spiritual masters and monks from different religious traditions may also shed some light on the question of the universality of mysticism and its role in the dialogue between religions. It must first of all be noted that much of the original impetus for Christians to enter into dialogue with other religions was spurred by interest in the spiritual or mystical traditions of those religions. Several of the Christian pioneers of interreligious dialogue were themselves monks (Thomas Merton, Henri Le Saux, Bede Griffiths), and the shift from a purely missionary relationship to other religions to one defined more by reciprocal interest and respect was largely inspired by a respect for the mystical depth of those traditions.

A remarkable feature of the spiritual dialogue is the ease and spontaneity with which spiritual masters and monks from different religious traditions seem to acknowledge one another and move in and out of each other's religious traditions. A prominent and enduring instance of this is the interreligious dialogue that takes place between monks from different religious traditions — the so-called "inter-monastic dialogue." Here monks belonging to one tradition spend extended periods of time immersed in the monastic life and religious discipline of the other tradition, and what they discover, across the expected language and cultural barriers, is a meeting place in deep mutual understanding. Thomas Merton, one of the pioneers of this dialogue, expresses this as follows:

> The deepest level of communication is not communication, but communion. It is wordless. It is beyond words, and it is beyond speech, and it is beyond concept. Not that we discover a new unity. We discover an older unity. My dear brothers, we are already one. But we imagine that

we are not. And what we have to recover is our original unity. What we have to be is what we are.[25]

In 1978, the Catholic Church established a formal structure for inter-monastic dialogue. Cardinal Pignedoli, then prefect of the Vatican Secretariat for dialogue with non-Christian religions, made it the occasion for extraordinary words: "the monk," he said, "represents a point of contact and of mutual comprehension between Christians and non-Christians. The presence of monastics in the Catholic Church is therefore, in itself, a bridge that joins us to all other religions."[26] Of course, this stops well short of claiming actual unity at the heart of mystical practices or experiences, and any official statements by those involved in inter-monastic dialogue have stayed clear of argumentation for or against mystical unity. This may be seen to reflect a monastic reticence to engage in highly speculative disputation. But it may also be understood to respect the ultimate ineffability of the mystical experience itself, which arguably rules out the possibility of defending either the unity or the diversity of different mystical experiences. Pierre de Béthune, one of the pillars of the inter-monastic dialogue, puts this beautifully:

> We will never be able to formulate in an adequate way the mystery, the silence, the luminosity and the joy into which we journey. But communion in this spiritual journey defines dialogue's ultimate task. [27]

Dialogue between spiritual and monastic traditions has led to considerable mutual fecundation. The immersion of Christian monks in the spiritual traditions of Hinduism and Buddhism has led them to integrate spiritual practices originating in these traditions within Christian monastic life. As such,

116

practices such as yoga and Zen meditation have become part of monastic life and discipline in more than a few Christian monasteries. And Zen gardens may be found in the courtyard of some. In all of this, there is a striking lack of worry about possible incongruencies, and thus an interesting suggestion of, if not communality, then at least congeniality between spiritual traditions.[28]

Another form of spiritual dialogue between religions that may offer some food for reflection on the possibility of grounding the interconnection between religions in mystical experiences is the phenomenon of interreligious master-disciple relationships. As spiritual masters and disciples from different religious traditions have become increasingly more mobile, individuals belonging to one religious tradition have sometimes become disciples of spiritual masters of different religious traditions, but without changing their original religious affiliation. An early example of this is Henri Le Saux, who became the disciple of the famous Hindu sage Ramana Maharshi. Le Saux describes his experience of spiritual resonance with the guru in the following terms:

Before my mind could even grasp or express it, the intimate aura of this Sage had been perceived by something in me, in the depth of my Self. Unknown harmonies awakened in my heart.... In this Sage of Arunachala and of this time, it was the unique Sage of eternal India which appeared to me; it was the unbroken lineage of sages, of renouncers, of seers; it was the very soul of India which penetrated into the depth of my own soul and entered into a mysterious communion with her. It was a call which shattered everything, which dissolved everything, which opened wide an abyss.[29]

117

Though Le Saux continued to struggle throughout his life to reconcile the Hindu and the Christian spiritual traditions, the difference in religious affiliation of the guru did not seem to represent a barrier for spiritual exchange and awakening. This experience has become more common as Hindu gurus, Tibetan lamas and Zen masters have come to attract numerous Western disciples. And conversely, Christian gurus such as Bede Griffiths have counted among their disciples Hindus who were neither inclined nor encouraged to convert to Christianity. It is tempting, of course, to attribute the evident and growing appeal of spiritual masters of different religions and the ease with which spiritual masters and disciples relate across traditions to a common mystical experience or spiritual goal. The very idea that one may remain faithful to one's own tradition while surrendering to a spiritual master of a different religious tradition requires some belief — on the part of both masters and disciples — in the spiritual interconnection between religious traditions.

While the spiritual dialogue between religions often shows signs of an implicit or explicit assumption of a unity or continuity of spiritual experiences, it must also be pointed out that a number of individuals immersed in this dialogue continue to emphasize the difference between mystical experiences. Even while using Zen Buddhist practices within his own teaching and practice of meditation, the Jesuit William Johnston, for example, argues that the Zen Buddhist experience lacks the Christian dimension of a gratuitous "love rising out of faith."[30] And after decades immersed in the study of Zen Buddhism, Heinrich Dumoulin insisted that "Zen meditation 'without thoughts or images' does not usurp the place of Christian meditation, which is dialogal and leads to the higher states at which the confrontation of subject and object issues in *unio mystica*."[31] Needless to say, this somewhat more pronounced interest in differences hardly prevents one from recognizing the similarities that accompany them whereupon mutual understanding becomes substantially a matter of exploring the complex fiber of interconnection.[32]

Mystical Unity and Dialogue

Though the experience of inter-monastic dialogue does not offer unequivocal support for the idea of the *unity* of all mystical experiences, the ease with which monks and spiritual masters from different religious traditions engage and adapt to the spiritual practices of another tradition does suggest that it may be possible to ground interreligious dialogue at least partly in a sense of deep spiritual connection between religions. At minimum, the inter-monastic experience can encourage and inspire: there, at the spiritual heart of the tradition, in the lives of those given over to it and it alone, it is possible to respect those of other traditions and to recognize the importance of what they live by. This, in turn, gives reason to hope that the religious life and experiences of the other religion are in some way related to one's own and that dialogue is thus both possible and relevant. Emphasis on the radical discontinuity and distinction between religious experiences would indeed render dialogue futile. If every religious path terminates in a different experience, then the symbols and practices of that other path might be seen to have little relevance for one's own. Such a view may still have some reason and some room for dialogue, but precious little positive interest: one would learn in the greatest possible depth and detail precisely what one is not, which is to say the experiences and expressions of the other would have virtually no significance for one's own religious understanding. If, on the other hand, religious traditions are seen to be based on or oriented to similar or corresponding religious experiences, dialogue may not only lead to a deeper and broader understanding of one's own ultimate spiritual goals, but may also enrich the path by which one seeks them, with whatever help one may gain from the resources of another tradition.

That said, it is also the case that too much emphasis on the spiritual unity between religions may diminish the impulse to dialogue. It is well known that the emphasis on a transcendent unity of religions often coincides with a devaluation or relativization of the concrete content of religious beliefs and practices. If, for instance, the ultimate experience itself is considered to be radically ineffable and beyond any religious expression, every such expression is inevitably regarded as a mere sign, as a "finger pointing to the moon" that must be somehow abandoned in order to attain the ultimate experience. Religious symbols, categories, and rituals are then treated as instruments that are themselves devoid of ultimate meaning and importance. The negative implications for dialogue are evident enough: if the distinct religious teachings and practices of a religion are not constitutive of the experience itself, or if they are thought to lead, each in their own way, to the same experience that is already expressed within one's own tradition, it is no longer clear that engagement with any other religious teaching is necessary except for the general acquisition of facts. Genuine interest in dialogue thus presupposes some commitment to the constitutive role and truth of religious expressions and to the possibility of enhancing one's own religious understanding through a creative engagement with the teachings and practices of the other. Dialogue between religions thus seems to require a proper balance between faith in the interconnection between spiritual experiences, and belief in the distinctiveness of religions as revealing different modes of the ultimate experience, or different aspects or stages of the experience.[33]

UNIFYING TRANSCENDENT REALITY

While the religious conception of the interconnection between religious traditions may be located in the immanent realm of religious experience or the personal experience of the ultimate reality, it may also be located in that ultimate reality itself. All religious traditions refer to a reality transcending the immanent world. This reality may be personal or nonpersonal, male or female, characterized by a dualistic or nondualistic relationship to the world, and unified, internally diversified, or plural. The conception of the transcendent reality operative in any particular religion is often complex, combining even opposite characteristics into one. As such, Hinduism may be regarded as both polytheistic and monotheistic, and Buddhism has expressed itself in both nonpersonal and personal representations of ultimate reality. But in the end, all religions affirm the unity and ineffability of this ultimate reality.

This ultimate reality presents the natural focal point for the idea of the unity or interconnection between religions. If the ultimate reality is one, then all truth must derive from or be oriented to it. Monika Hellwig thus states that "interreligious dialogue is based on an act of faith that reality is not absurd, and that therefore what is truly ultimate is unified so that all quests for communion with the ultimate are in process of converging."[34] Any belief in the unity of ultimate reality may thus itself provide the necessary common ground and goal for dialogue.

121

However, the very fact that this unifying transcendent reality may be understood in different ways may itself result in inter-religious tension and aggression, rather than dialogue, as the history of the relationship between the monotheistic religions sadly illustrates.[35] In reaction to this, pluralist theologians tend to focus on a meeting of all religions in an ultimate reality transcending all religious conceptions of it. The most notable example of this view may be found in John Hick's notion of "the Real" as the unifying transcendent ground and goal of all religions. Let us now attend to it, and to its possible implications for dialogue.

Neutral Ultimate Reality

Theological attempts to develop a notion of the transcendent reality beyond that of any particular religion are generally based on a strong awareness of the historical atrocities committed in the name of particular religious conceptions of absolute truth, and on a desire to overcome the reality of conflicting claims to truth. In the work of John Hick, this is accomplished through recourse to the Kantian distinction between the ultimate reality *an sich* and the phenomenal instances in which it appears. He calls this ultimate reality transcending all religions "the Real" or "Reality"[36] and regards the religions themselves as "different ways of experiencing, conceiving, and living in relation to an ultimate divine Reality which transcends all our varied versions of it."[37] Here, the word "different" seems to entail a notion of distinctiveness without supremacy or privilege: "Different forms of religious awareness are not necessarily competitive in the sense that the validity of one entails the spuriousness of the others, but...are better understood as different phenomenal experiences of the same divine noumenon, or, in another language, as different experiential transformations of the same transcendent informational input."[38]

Now as the expression "informational input" indicates, Hick does not advocate the sort of relativism that reduces all religious traditions to their respective historical and cultural contexts. Rather, each tradition in its own way and perhaps to varying degrees contains within itself, and elaborates through time, a deposit of the one ultimate reality. Each may thus be seen to express a certain facet or aspect of that ultimate reality. This also affects Hick's views on the unity or diversity of mystical experiences. Over against the idea of the mystical unity of religions, he states that "it seems more probable that they undergo characteristically different unitive experiences (even though with important common features), the differences being due to the conceptual frameworks and meditational disciplines supplied by the religious traditions in which they participate."[39] The various religious traditions are thus seen to contain genuinely distinctive experiences and conceptions of the ultimate reality, which, one might expect, would render dialogue indispensable. If every religion is considered to contain a partial reflection of the truth, engagement with other religions may be regarded as essential in order to gain a fuller or more comprehensive understanding of that transcendent ultimate reality.

While Hick's conception of the unity and interconnection of all religious traditions in a radically transcendent ultimate reality may thus be seen to offer a solid theological basis for dialogue, it also raises critical questions. The first of these concerns the criteria or criterion to be employed when discerning religious truth and growth. As Hick himself indicates, not all religions or religious expressions may be regarded as authentic manifestations of the ultimate reality. Rather than applying religion-specific criteria (which would involve an undue imposition of the criteria of truth of one religion upon the others), Hick proposes a criterion that he finds common to all religions, namely, the relative capacity of a practice or belief to bring about a "transformation of human experience from self-centeredness to Reality-centeredness."[40] This is not unproblematic for religious self-understanding and for dialogue. It may well be the case that Hick's criterion represents the highest common denominator among religions. Yet whatever plausibility and truth it may have for any believer or group of believers can be derived only from within the normative teachings of their particular religion. If, for instance, Muslims regard the transformation from self-centeredness to Reality-centeredness a valid criterion in dialogue, this would only be insofar as they can root it in Koranic revelation or in the tradition of the Prophet. And so if Hick's criterion of truth does play a role in the process of interreligious discernment, this will have to be due not to its neutrality or commonality, but rather to its presence, explicit or implicit, in the teaching of one's own tradition. To this it should be added that believers are not on the whole inclined to subordinate their own religious criteria to any common religious denominator. Not only would this contradict religious self-understanding, but it would almost certainly impoverish dialogue, which ideally includes the creative and constructive engagement of one's own highest criteria of truth with those of the other.

This comes close to a second question for Hick's position, which applies to its tendency to diminish the importance of distinctive teachings and ritual practices, and thus the very occasion for dialogue. Mark Heim has been particularly forceful in voicing this critique. Heim argues that if all religious beliefs and practices are believed to express the same ineffable reality, they lose their referential value, or relevance in reflecting and pursuing particular religious ends. He states that "since for Hick differences over factual matters (such as whether Jesus was crucified or Mohammed traveled from Mecca to Medina) or commitments to differing mythic truths do not deflect people from realization of the same salvation/liberation, it is worth inquiring whether any differences at all are relevant."[41] For Heim, it is only in acknowledging the distinctiveness of religious ends that the particularities of different teachings and practices maintain their proper cognitive or referential value. While it must be recalled — against Heim's critique — that Hick does recognize the informational input of the different religious conceptions of ultimate reality, it is nevertheless true that his emphasis on the unity of all religious traditions in the Real does tend to minimize the existence and importance of particular claims to truth, and indeed the fact that religious teachings claim ultimacy.

A final question for Hick pertains to the supposed neutrality of his concept of the "Real." What for Hick signals an ultimate reality beyond any concrete religious conception appears to some critics as subtly theistic in definition. Gavin D'Costa, one of Hick's staunchest critics, argues that the position as a whole "masks the advocation of liberal modernity's "god," in this case a form of ethical agnosticism."[42] According to D'Costa, it is characteristic of liberal modernity to withdraw from any claim that one may gain insight into the ontological nature of ultimate reality, whereupon the religious shows up only, or properly, in ethical concerns and in their guiding principles. Emphasizing the particularity of this understanding, D'Costa even designates Hick's position as a form of "Enlightenment exclusivism."[43] This may be an overstatement, but it does point to the fact that claims to neutrality or universality sometimes conceal a highly particular outlook, indeed epistemics. The thought also lies behind Masao Abe's objection to Hick. Responding from a Buddhist perspective, Abe finds his approach "too narrow and provincial" and containing clearly theistic overtones.[44] Rather than rejecting all attempts at arriving at a common ground, which he believes would lead to a "vicious relativism,"[45] Abe proposes an alternative to Hick's category of the Real: a "positionless position" or a standpoint of "no-common-denominator":

> I am suggesting the importance and necessity of the clear realization of the "no-common-denominator" in both the affirmative and the negative sense. If we realize "no-common-denominator" in all religious traditions thoroughly, by overcoming both the affirmative view of the presence of a common denominator and the negative view of its absence, then a complete emptiness is opened up. This is a *positionless position,* a standpoint that is free from any standpoint.[46]

At first sight, this "positionless position" may appear to promise a genuinely neutral or nonconfessional common ground for dialogue. But on closer inspection it may also appear as a distinctively Mahāyāna Buddhist conception of reality, which focuses on *emptiness* as the middle way between affirmation and rejection of ultimate reality. This cannot be the occasion for a thorough reckoning with this position as either no position at all or in fact a standpoint in its own right. But the difficulty alone tells us that it is far from clear that a neutral conception of ultimate reality is possible under any condition.

Similarly, John Cobb also questions the neutrality of John Hick's notion of a transcendent common ground, which he regards as "an abstract expression of the biblical understanding of creation and hence not a neutral ground for dialogue among the great traditions."[47] However, unlike Abe, Cobb does not propose an alternative transcendent common ground, which he believes "offends all equally"[48] and introduces "a new form of imperialism."[49] All conceptions of the ultimate, he insists, remain conditioned by a particular worldview or point of departure — even those that well might appear to transcend it. This, moreover, has lived experience on its side. After all, believers worship not the Real, but a particular conception of ultimate reality that thus retains all the meaning and the power proper to the religions. From this perspective, a genuinely neutral conception of ultimate reality would be not only unobtainable but also undesirable. Perhaps the unifying ground for interreligious dialogue is therefore to be sought in confessional conceptions of the ultimate.

Confessional Ultimate Reality

The natural tendency of any religious tradition is to situate the origin or basis for interconnection between religions in their own particular conception of ultimate reality. Religions indeed presuppose that the fullness of truth is concentrated in their own conception of ultimate reality and that whatever form or degree of truth is found elsewhere will be derived from or oriented toward this truth. Hence do Christians and members of the other Abrahamic faiths believe that, as Cobb puts it, "in God all things cohere, [and] there cannot be another truth that is alien to God's truth."[50] So, likewise, might Buddhists relate all truth of other religions to the *Dharmakāya*. It is the unquestioned merit of a confessional approach to the interconnection of religions that it coincides with the self-understanding of most religious traditions. From the point of view of the believer — and this is the point of view that matters in dialogue — there is no ultimate reality higher than the one addressed within one's own religious tradition, and if there is truth to be found in other religious traditions, it will have to be related to one's own conception of ultimate truth.

One of the more systematic attempts to develop a Christian understanding of ultimate reality capable of recognizing the truth of other religious traditions within itself may be found in the work of Mark Heim. Heim's theological project is based on an attempt to "save the greatest referential value for the largest number of religious experiences"[51] or to grant "the maximum truth value in the specifics of the traditions."[52] Like most other Christian theologians engaged in dialogue with other religions from such an inclusivist position, Heim turns specifically to a Trinitarian conception of absolute reality as the basis for recognizing the truth of other religions. However, while those others (D'Costa, Dupuis), focus mainly on the Holy Spirit as the basis for openness, Heim embraces the complex reality of the Trinity as a whole. In reaction to John Hick's approach, which tends to abolish all distinctions between religious ends and the referential value of particular religious teachings, Heim argues that a robustly Trinitarian approach to religious ends may give credence to the distinctive goals of the different religions while acknowledging their ultimate unity and interconnection. On that account, he contends that each of the goals of other religions represents one or another facet of the Christian Trinitarian relationship to God. Whereas Buddhist and Hindu traditions may shed light on the nondualistic and impersonal dimensions of the absolute, Islam may be seen to have cultivated a personal conception of God. It is thus only through dialogue with other religions that Christianity comes to a full realization of the meaning of its own central teachings. There is no doubt that Heim believes that the Christian conception of the ultimate goal as a participation in the Triune life of God offers the most integrative and thus the highest of conceptions of the ultimate end.[53] Yet he also recognizes the religious particularity from which all of this unfolds and moreover calls for other religions to develop their own theological understanding of the unity and interconnection of religions within their own particular conceptions of ultimate truth.

Interestingly, the Buddhist theologian John Makransky uses Heim's model precisely in this manner. Whereas Heim's Christian approach draws crucially on Trinitarian thought, Makransky's Buddhist approach makes a corresponding turn to *Dharmakāya*.[54] The notion is rich and suggestive. While the Mahāyāna Buddhist understanding of *Dharmakāya* refers to the empty ground of being, it is believed to be manifest in perfect forms (*rupakāya*), which may become the focus of meditation and devotion. This permits Makransky to suggest, from a Buddhist perspective, that Christ may be regarded "as a remarkable Rupakāya manifestation of Buddhahood itself, a powerful means through which followers of Christ have indeed communed with and learned to embody liberating qualities of Dharmakāya."[55] Similarly to Heim, Makransky does not merely reduce Christ to an expression of Rupakāya already fully grasped and realized within the Buddhist tradition. On the contrary, he insists that Christian beliefs and practices "engage Dharmakāya so intensively in communion through Christ as Rupakāya that much light can shine back on Buddhist thought and practice from Christian reflection upon Christology, communion, and ecclesiology."[56]

A critique that may be leveled against this confessional approach to the unity and interconnection of all religions is that it tends to a domestication of the truth of the other religion and to a distortion of its self-understanding. Heim's considerable efforts notwithstanding, he is still able to integrate the distinctive ends of other religions only insofar as they resonate with the Christian understanding of ultimate reality. Thus subsumed within the Christian perspective, they acquire a "penultimate" status that no longer squares with their status within their own tradition.[57] And though Makransky's approach is highly sympathetic to Christianity, it similarly redefines the Christian teachings from a Buddhist perspective, conceiving of them as "skillful means to be harmonized to the empty ground of being and its liberating qualities in cultures where the Buddha's teaching of emptiness is little known or too challenging yet for many to accept."[58] Every confessional understanding of the relationship between religions thus seems to inevitably entail a certain degree of domestication of the truth of the other.

However, this does not necessarily imply a simple reduction of the distinctive truth of the other to one's own established teachings. Both Heim and Makransky affirm the validity and truth of teachings that are not fully ingrained or developed within one's own tradition, and that thus allow for the possibility of genuine dialogue and growth. Heim insists that this theology of religious ends allows for the recognition of "unique, religiously determinative and final truths of the sort that the religions themselves claim" and that this "widens the dialogue by allowing that it may reveal not only variations on one theme and one result but sharper challenges and crucial options."[59] In the same vein, Makransky's focus on the Christian practices of love and communion as a dimension or component of Buddhist practice seeks not so much to confirm existing beliefs and practices as to send "Buddhists back to the resources in their own traditions with fresh eyes."[60] It is thus clear that a confessional understanding of the interconnection of all religions does not preclude genuine dialogue.

A powerful testimony to this is found in the work of Raimon Panikkar. From his early, pioneering book *The Unknown Christ of Hinduism* to his latest work *Christophany: The Fullness of Man*,[61] Panikkar continues to insist that Christians cannot but refer to the ultimate reality as Christ.[62] And yet his entire theological endeavor is in fact directed to arguing that the reality of Christ is manifest in every authentic religious tradition:

> Christ is the only mediator, but he is not the monopoly of Christians and, in fact, he is present and effective in any authentic religion, whatever the form or the name. Christ is the symbol, which christians call by this name, of the ever-transcending but equally ever-humanly immanent Mystery.[63]

In order to maintain this position, and above all to uphold the universality of Christ, Panikkar emphasizes the distinction between the historical Jesus and the Cosmic Christ. While Jesus is the human face through which Christians have come to know the Christ, the reality of Christ transcends any particular religious tradition. And Christ then may be — indeed must be — understood according to the religious beliefs and practices of the different traditions. Though this conception of the absolute is formed and grounded in Christian scripture and tradition, it is also reminiscent of a worldview likely to be associated with the Hindu and Buddhist traditions. This becomes evident in Panikkar's notion of "christophany," which is evidently a synthesis of Hindu, Buddhist, and Christian worldviews, none of which assumes a dominant hermeneutical position.[64] While believers may thus engage in dialogue from a conception of the coherence of all truth in their own representation of ultimate reality, this representation may itself become enriched, even transformed, as a result of the dialogue.

What dialogue puts at stake is thus not commitment to a particular conception of ultimate reality, but the degree to which that reality is able to embrace the truth of other religions. "The issue," as John Cobb puts it, "is not whether one holds some truth as absolute, but whether one considers oneself to be in possession of all truth worth having."[65] The integration of teachings and practices of other religions into the perspective opened up by one's own conception of ultimate reality calls for an exercise in theological imagination that itself presupposes a deliberate attempt to expand one's own traditional self-understanding in order to make room for distinctive conceptions of the other. While a certain openness to the truth of the other religion is a necessary condition for dialogue, it is dialogue itself that often leads to theological creativity and an attempt to enrich one's conception of ultimate reality by welcoming as much as possible what is expressed in other religious traditions. If, moreover, we attend to the lessons of our mystical and apophatic texts, which remind us that the nature of the ultimate always exceeds all human and religious conceptions, then dialogue must appear as a deeply, even essentially theological enterprise. It would therefore be one-sided and unfortunate to reduce the confessional conception of the interconnection of religions to an interest only in what is relevant for members of that particular religion, since that same conception is far from devoid of its own motivation for dialogue. And though it is true that such an understanding of other religions from within one's own conception of ultimate reality entails a certain degree of domestication of the other, it may fairly be said that this is an

inevitable condition of the irreducible particularity of all religious perspectives. It is the recognition that all participants
engage in dialogue from their own conceptions of the interconnection of religions, and that each engages the other from
within their own hermeneutical framework, which forms the
basis for the balanced and sincere exchange that occurs in
genuine dialogue. Moreover, the fact that all religions enter
dialogue from a distinct understanding of how the truths of
all religions cohere within their own perspective does not rule
out considerable overlap between them even on the matter of
ultimate reality itself, thus offering a fertile ground for further dialogue both from and on the particularities of each
religion.

◆ ◆ ◆

All dialogue takes place in the field of tension between similarity and difference, between a sense of religious interconnection
and recognition of the distinctiveness of the other tradition.
In spite of the contemporary emphasis on difference and resistance to any notion of a common essence or universal
characteristic such as would warrant the generic term "religion," individuals belonging to different religious traditions
continue to find common ground and goals both within and
outside their respective traditions. Though the differences between religions are most often identified as the proper food
of dialogue, it is from the realization of a connection with
other religious traditions that dialogue is felt to be in fact
possible. What I prefer to designate with the cautious word
"interconnection" may be found in a common confrontation
with external challenges or in a shared commitment to any
number of social, political, or economic causes. Often, this external meeting ground creates a strong sense of interreligious

solidarity and collaboration. And it may become the basis for dialogue on the contribution of distinctive religions to such external causes. Yet it does not as such form the basis for sustained dialogue on distinctly religious questions. This requires belief in the inherently religious connection between different religious traditions: it is only insofar as the other religion is thought to be related to one's own experience or conception of ultimate reality that dialogue becomes not only possible, but also necessary. Against every claim that the differences between religious experiences are irresolvable, the religious resonance and communion among spiritual masters and monks of different religions provide an important spiritual foundation for dialogue. Perhaps with that foundation in view, ongoing practical dialogue requires genuine interest in the distinctive teachings and practices of the other religion and in their relevance and importance for one's own religious tradition. Without rejecting the sheer possibility of securing the interconnection of all religious traditions in a transcendent reality beyond all religions, it must be recognized that for believers, and thus for the communities represented in dialogue, there is no ultimate reality beyond that conceived within their own religious tradition. In that case, one can hardly turn elsewhere than to a confessional understanding of ultimate reality for a vital sense of interconnection with other religions. This does not provide a "neutral" meeting place for dialogue or a sense of interconnection shared by all participants in the dialogue, but it does establish the religious foundation from which dialogue becomes possible. The very belief that the teachings or practices of the other religion are somehow related to one's own conception of ultimate reality is evidently a sufficient ground and reason for dialogue. For believers, and for those who speak for them, dialogue is a process through which one both discovers and reconfirms the interconnection with the teachings of other religious traditions and continues to deepen one's own self-understanding through a progressive, though not unlimited, integration of the truth of other religions.

CHAPTER FOUR

EMPATHY

One has not really heard the message of one of the real religions that have moved millions of people over centuries if one has not been really moved by it, if one has not felt in one's soul the power of it. — LESSLIE NEWBIGIN[1]

The possibility of genuine dialogue between religions requires not only a series of internally religious conditions, but also epistemological ones. One of the most basic requirements for dialogue is proper understanding of the other. While interreligious dialogue is decidedly about more than an exchange of data, the question of whether or to what extent one can understand the other tradition does have a certain priority over the question of whether what has been discovered or understood can also be regarded as true. This epistemological question has been at the heart of the disciplines of comparative religion and history of religions. In the course of the twentieth century, the study of religion has gone through a series of dramatic swings as it has tried to find its place and status among the human sciences. From a cataloguing of data, it has moved through the development of grand narratives or theories about the essence of religion and religious phenomena, to more specialized studies of texts and traditions, and more limited and controlled comparisons. From an emphasis on differences, it has shifted to a focus on similarities and universal structures to a renewed interest in difference and particularity. In the process, an enormous wealth of data about other religions has been accumulated. The major religious scriptures have been (repeatedly) translated, doctrinal and philosophical teachings studied, ethical systems analyzed, and ritual practices recorded. There is thus no shortage of factual data to generate a considerable degree of historical and theoretical understanding across religious traditions.

However, real understanding of the religious other involves more than an intellectual grasp of the teachings and practices of the other religion. It also presupposes a willingness and ability to penetrate into the religious mind-set of the other and understand him or her from within. Even though religion is certainly more than a feeling, the affective dimension does play a crucial role in the religious life of any person, and a proper understanding of another religion would thus be seriously impoverished without access to the meaning of a particular belief or practice for the person involved. As Simone Weil, an ardent student of religions, puts it:

> The comparison of religions is only possible, in some measure through the miraculous virtue of sympathy. We can know men to a certain extent if at the same time we observe them from outside we manage by sympathy to transport our own soul into theirs for a time. In the same way the study of different religions does not lead to a real knowledge of them unless we transport ourselves for a time by faith to the very center of whichever one we are studying.[2]

This process of transposing oneself into the feelings, the thoughts, and the experiences of another has generally been called "empathy." Though the term came into general use only in the latter part of the nineteenth century, it has been the object of considerable debate with regard to its heuristic utility in the human sciences in general and in religious studies in particular. Wilhelm Dilthey, one of the founders of modern hermeneutics, regarded empathy as the distinctive methodological tool for the humanities, providing access to the original intentions and the deeper meaning of texts and other cultural products. The notion of empathy became the focus of considerable philosophical reflection in the work of early phenomenologists such as Edmund Husserl and his student Edith Stein. And early phenomenologists of religion such as Gerardus van der Leeuw and Joachim Wach similarly assigned a constitutive role to empathy in the process of understanding other religions. To understand a particular phenomenon, van der Leeuw states, we must ourselves "experience the appearance, and this, indeed, not involuntarily and semi-consciously, but intentionally and methodically."[3] Wach uses the Greek term *methexis* to point to the essential dimension of participation and engagement of feeling in the understanding of religious others, while the idea of "reliving" the existential situation of the other religion and understanding their "mode of being in the world" constituted the heart of Mircea Eliade's methodology.

With the shift from an epistemological to a more dialogical approach to hermeneutics, and from a phenomenological to a strictly historical and philological approach to the study of religions, the term "empathy" was all but banned from methodological discussions. Emphasis on the difference between the insider (*emic*) and the outsider (*etic*) perspectives[4] led to an association of empathy with the bygone days of romantic or "subjectivist" hermeneutics[5] and with the naïve belief in the possibility of understanding others better than they understand themselves. Gavin Flood, for example, refers to the notion of empathy as "deeply problematic" since it "does not take account of communication and active understanding...does not take into account the historicity of the understanding encounter, and...cannot deal with conflict, or the other's being closed to empathic penetration."[6]

While the term "empathy" has thus largely disappeared as a heuristic tool within the study of religions, one cannot deny that it continues to profoundly shape much of what transpires in interpersonal, intercultural, and interreligious communication. From the choice of objects or subjects to be studied to the filling in of innumerable small and larger gaps in the interpretation of data, empathy may be seen to function as the unacknowledged methodological God of the gaps. In the dialogue between individuals belonging to different religious traditions, empathy also continues to play an indispensable role. It not only allows one to gain a deeper understanding of the other, but it also functions as a measure of what may possibly come to enrich one's own tradition. The ethos of a true dialogue presupposes a certain reciprocity in which, just as I would like the other to understand me in the depth of my religious experience, the other also appeals to my willingness to enter into his or her self-understanding. Empathy thus represents the means to gain understanding of the affective dimension of the other religion, of the religious desires and needs that lie at the origins of particular beliefs and practices and of the experiences generated by them. It is precisely because this dimension of affectivity, desire, and attunement can never be fully expressed in words that, as Jacques Dupuis puts it, each partner in dialogue "must rise above the level of the concepts in which this experience is imperfectly expressed, to attain, insofar as possible, through and beyond the concepts, to the experience itself."[7] Empathy not only offers a more comprehensive understanding of the other religion, but also plays an important role in negotiating the truth and relevance of the other tradition — or at least of particular teachings and practices — for one's own religious life. It is only insofar as one is capable of resonating with the spiritual meaning of a particular belief or practice that it may come into contact with one's own tradition and possibly lead to change or growth. While empathy is certainly not the only heuristic tool in understanding other religions, its role in the process of interreligious dialogue can thus not be overestimated. This is why a proper understanding of the dynamics of empathy, its nature, procedure, and epistemic status forms a key to the epistemological questions raised in dialogue.

Much of the general approach to the issue of empathy in the context of dialogue has been framed in terms of John Dunne's popular notion of "passing over":

> What seems to be occurring is a phenomenon we might call "passing over," passing over from one culture to another, from one way of life to another, from one religion to another. Passing over is a shifting of standpoints, a going over to the standpoint of another culture, another way of life, another religion.[8]

Taken at face value, this seems to express an unquestioned belief in the possibility of entering into the standpoint of the other, whereupon one may understand the world from his or her particular perspective. Such a naïve epistemological position is no longer tenable. The critique of empathy by scholars of the comparative method has made it impossible to use the term or claim the capacity without constant critical awareness of its epistemological status and indeed its limits. Is it truly possible to "pass over" into the religious tradition of the other and understand it from within? Or is the understanding and experience of the other always colored and conditioned by one's own religious and historical context? And what are the implications of this for the dialogue between religions? We shall here address these questions by focusing on the philosophical discussion in which the concept has been properly defined, and by using examples that might be relevant for the dialogue between religions.

THE NATURE OF EMPATHY

Even though the experience of imagining oneself into the life and feelings of another person belongs to the very nature of human solidarity,[9] much of the theoretical reflection on empathy dates from the turn of the twentieth century. The term "empathy" was introduced in the late nineteenth century to describe what takes place in the process of esthetic enjoyment and came to be applied to the psychological understanding of others by Theodore Lipps.[10] It soon played an important role in the early hermeneutical tradition as well as in phenomenology. Building on both of these traditions, empathy also became an integral part of the phenomenology of religion of Gerardus van der Leeuw. Since then, empathy has largely disappeared, though it has continued to inform certain branches of psychology and even returned in the discipline of folk psychology, where it represents the epistemic ground for understanding other minds.[11] Leaving aside the various nuances debated for the meaning and goal of empathy, it may be argued that its general purpose is the understanding of the mental life and experiences of others. Edith Stein defines empathy succinctly as "the experience of foreign consciousness"[12] or the "comprehension of mental persons."[13] Needless to say, and herein lies the particular importance of the phenomenon for interreligious dialogue, this will include the affective and volitional dimensions of life that are the source of thoughts and actions, but that do not usually feature in historical accounts or in factual data. Let us examine this more closely.

Empathy as Transposition

In most of the early discussions, empathy is generally described as a form of "transposition" (Dilthey's *Hineinversetzen, Transposition*) into the mental lives of others in order to recognize the original intentions of the author of a text. Exploring intersubjectivity as such, Husserl similarly regards empathy as a process of entering into the mental life of another and understanding the motives and desires that lie at the origin of his or her actions:

> I put myself in the place of another subject, and by empathy I grasp what motivates him and how strongly it does so, with what power. And I learn to understand inwardly how he behaves, and how he would behave, under the influence of such and such motives, determining him with such and such force, i.e., I grasp what he is capable of and what is beyond him. I can understand many inner correlations, having fathomed him so. In this way I grasp his Ego, for it is precisely the identical Ego of these motivations, ones that have this direction and power. I secure these motivations by placing myself in his situation, his level of education, his development as a youth, etc., and to do so I must needs share in that situation; I not only

empathize with his thinking, his feeling and his action, but I must also follow him in them, his motives becoming my quasi-motives, ones which, however, motivate with insight.[14]

For both Dilthey and Husserl, empathy thus involves putting oneself into the mind-set and intentions of the other. It contains both affective and cognitive dimensions. The affective dimension of empathy is expressed in the original German term *einfuhlung* and reflected in Titchener's original English translation of the term: "Not only do I see gravity and modesty and pride and courtesy and stateliness, but I feel them in the mind's muscle. That is, I suppose a simple case of empathy, if we may coin that term as a rendering of *Einfuhlung*."[15] The term empathy, however, also came to be invested with clear cognitive associations. Max Scheler, for example, clearly distinguishes sympathy as "fellow-feeling" from empathy, which he describes as "all such attitudes as merely contribute to our apprehending, understanding, and in general, reproducing (emotionally) the experiences of others, including their states of feeling."[16] This pronouncedly cognitive definition comes clearly to the fore in later accounts of empathy, such as that of Lauren Wispé, who defines it as "the attempt by one self-aware self to comprehend non-judgmentally the positive and negative experiences of another self."[17]

In the context of interreligious dialogue and understanding, this conception of empathy as a transposition involves much more than a simple identification with familiar thoughts and feelings. While all empathy requires knowledge of the context and causes of the experience of the other, interreligious empathy entails a process of immersion in a completely different set of fundamental beliefs and practices. This reminds us of the indispensable role played by communication and language in a manner that rejoins the more hermeneutical conception of the role of transposition in the process of understanding the other. Reacting against the purely phenomenological account of empathy, Gadamer states that:

> it belongs to every true conversation that each person opens himself to the other, truly accepts his point of view as valid and transposes himself into the other to such an extent that he understands not the particular individual but *what he says*.[18]

The appearance of language between oneself and the other informs us that the understanding of the meaning of the beliefs and practices of another tradition takes the form of a transposition into the worldview of the other. Empathic understanding of the meaning of Krishna, for example, would require from a Christian some form of identification with Vaishnava mythology, and with the particular set of religious associations informing the life and thought of a particular Hindu sect or school. This, then, may lead to a more affective resonance with the teachings of the other, or to some grasp of the religious intentions and motivations underlying particular teachings.

In the dialogue between religions, such empathy may come about through the reading of texts, through prolonged participation in the religious life of the other, or through profound engagement with members of the other religion. It may involve a sudden or a gradual passage from a purely rational or intellectual understanding of the other to a direct experience of the religious or spiritual import of a particular teaching or practice. But it arises from a mind-set in which the worldview and

teachings of the other religion are held to be (at least hypothetically) true. Even though interreligious empathy is often
mediated or facilitated through close relationships with individuals belonging to the other religion, it is not the experience
of any particular individual that is the goal of empathy. It is obvious that any one text, teaching, or ritual practice may have
a variety of meanings within different schools or among individuals belonging to a particular school. No single religious
experience may thus be regarded as normative for the tradition
as a whole. However, the experiences of individuals belonging to a particular tradition do remain the negative measure
or criterion for the integrity or authenticity of my empathic
understanding of the other. An empathic account that does
not at all resonate with members of a particular religion must
probably be regarded as suspect.

Foundations of Empathy

Most theories of empathy are based on some implicit or explicit belief in universal mental structures and patterns of
experience. Already in the eighteenth century, David Hume
suggested that the possibility of empathic understanding of the
feelings of others was based on inborn and universal emotional
and mental structures:

> Nature has preserved a great resemblance among all
> human creatures, and that we never remark any passion
> or principle in others, of which, in some degree or other,
> we may not find a parallel in ourselves. The case is the
> same with the fabric of the mind, as with that of the body.
> However the parts may differ in shape or size, their struc-
> ture and composition are in general the same...and this

146

resemblance must very much contribute to make us enter into the sentiments of others.[19]

Among twentieth-century historians and phenomenologists of religion, it is Gerardus van der Leeuw who grounds the possibility of empathy most explicitly in theories of a universal or common human nature. Appealing to Terentius Afer's ancient maxim "homo sum, humani nil a me alienum puto" (I am human and nothing human can be alien to me) as well as to Goethe's statement that "in every man there dwell all the forms of humanity," he proposes that while "this is no key to the deepest comprehension of the remotest experience, [it contains] nevertheless the triumphant assertion that the essentially human always remains essentially human, and is, as such, comprehensible."[20] Apart from these more poetic sources, van der Leeuw was also deeply influenced by the work of the German psychologist Eduard Spranger. In his *Lebensformen,* Spranger develops the idea of "eternal mental laws" or "general structural laws of the mind" (*Ubergreifende Geistesstructuren*) according to which reality is structured and understood. Understanding, he claims, presumes "that we take the total structure of the individual mind as the standard, that is, presuppose in him the entire differentiated act and experience complex from which the mental individual is made up, just as it is given in us as the basic mental structure."[21] For Spranger, the thesis of general and formal structures of the mind does not imply a complete transparency or intelligibility of the other. On the contrary, he takes great pains to emphasize that understanding is always partial and provisional. But it did provide him, and after him, van der Leeuw, with a basic confidence in the possibility of understanding the minds and

feelings of others, even across religious, cultural, and historical boundaries. In *Religion in Essence and Manifestation,* van
der Leeuw suggests that, given the proper knowledge and disposition, it would be no more difficult for him to enter into
the mind-set of an Egyptian scribe "who wrote his notes on
papyrus four thousand years ago" than it would be to understand the lines he himself wrote as a child in a school essay.
"That he [the Egyptian scribe] was 'another' than myself," he
states, "makes no difference whatever, since the boy who pre-
pared the school work thirty years ago is also, to my own
contemplation, 'another,' and I must objectify myself in my
experience of those bygone days."[22] While few would sub-
scribe to this extraordinary optimism about the intelligibility
of human experience across history, cultures, and religions,
van der Leeuw was hardly the last theorist of interpersonal or
intercultural understanding to defend some notion of universal mental structures. One thinks immediately of the work of
the anthropologist Claude Lévi-Strauss, who argues that "it
is through the properties common to all thought that we can
most easily understand forms of thought which seem alien to
us."[23] More recently, there are also contemporary versions of
folk psychology, where the capacity for understanding other
people's minds is based on neurobiologically fixed mechanisms
of perception. Since all humans react in the same way to external stimuli, it is believed that "nature simply provides us
with the capacity for projective changes of perspectives and
empathetic, imitative duplication of the (emotional) situation
of others."[24]

Eschewing the quasi-Kantian belief in the existence of universal mental structures, Dilthey grounds the possibility of
interpersonal understanding and empathy in a common sphere

of expression and understanding, which he calls the "objective mind":

> Every single expression represents a common feature in the realm of this objective mind. Every word, every sentence, every gesture or polite formula, every work of art and every political deed is intelligible because the people who expressed themselves through it and those who understood them have something in common. The individual always expresses, thinks and acts in a common sphere and only there does he understand.[25]

Not only thoughts, but also experiences and feelings are thus made possible through a preexisting field of communication that both shapes the internal life of a person and makes that life of experiences and emotions intelligible to others. Scheler appears to adopt a similar line when he argues that empathy is not so much a matter of projecting one's own prior experiences into the other (as Theodore Lipps had proposed) as of recognizing feelings and experiences that are shaped in the process of interaction with others. This comes down to suggesting that empathy is based on the fact that the experience of the self and the experience of others are not differentiated: "the child feels the feelings and thinks the thoughts of those who form his social environment, and there is one broad roaring stream of living in which he is totally immersed."[26]

This notion of community and interrelatedness prior to any isolated individuality dominates the later hermeneutical tradition. It in fact renders empathy a secondary, derivative category of experience. Hence does Heidegger, for whom "being" (*Dasein*) is essentially "being-with" (*Mitdasein*), state that "only those who cut the I off from the other must latch onto 'empathy' as that act that is supposed to instate the initially absent bond between the I and the other."[27] And Paul Ricoeur points out that "otherness is not added on to selfhood from the outside, as though to prevent its solipsistic drift, but it belongs instead to the tenor of meaning and to the ontological constitution of selfhood."[28] From here, and with this understanding of our situation, the notion of empathy quickly fades from hermeneutical discourse. If self and other are always already interconnected, there is no radical "other" to be understood, and all understanding must be conditioned by one's own subjectivity. Just as there is no objective and final understanding of a text, there is thus no possibility of pure empathy, so that all understanding of the other occurs in a continuous and open-ended process. From the perspective of philosophical hermeneutics, empathy is less a reality grounded in human nature than an aim and an ideal that the encounter with others compels us to seek.

There is therefore no reason to think that any of this rules out the possibility of empathy so much as it highlights certain essential limits for it. To put a fine point on it, it now requires us to ask whether and how, against those limits, it might be possible to resonate — even imperfectly — with the religious life of another religious tradition. This is evidently the proper point of entry for a closer review of the epistemological status of empathy. Borrowing Husserl's succinct terminology, empathy is here understood as a form of "analogical apperception"[29] in which one's own experiences and orientations form the basis for understanding the other. The idea of analogy points to the impossibility of ever fully duplicating the primordial experience of the other. But it also suggests the presence of at least structural or formal similarities or points of rapport that allow for some level of mutual comprehension. In the relationship between members of different religions, these points of rapport may be found in basic and universal religious needs as well as in recurrent patterns of religious experience and expression. All religious beliefs and practices respond ultimately to a basic human need for meaning and purpose. In itself, this may be seen to offer only scant ground for the possibility of interreligious empathy. Yet it directs one to the desires and motivations that lie at the very heart of the actions and experiences that qualify as religious in this or that particular tradition. As such, in attempting to understand the experience of a Hindu offering *pūjā* to the god Krishna, I attempt to grasp the deeper religious desires and impulses that gave rise to this act of devotion. I may be able to empathize with a person offering *pūjā* insofar as I am able to locate and resonate with the motivation of that act as being a pure act of loving devotion — or else, quite differently as the case may warrant, an experience of a wish for a healthy pregnancy, or again a good harvest, marital harmony, and so on. Of course, this effort is immediately complicated by the fact that desire and impulse are themselves informed by teaching and practice, which is also to say, belief. The relationships between all of these facets of the religious life are complex. While religious beliefs and actions may be regarded as responding to particular desires, they may themselves evoke particular desires and motivations or else broaden and refine existing ones. Still, there evidently are recurrent religious motives that come to expression in various ways in different contexts. For example, most religious traditions — each no doubt in its own way — address the broadly religious desire for wholeness and harmony and respond to a wish for freedom from suffering and death, as well as a wide range of particular desires for happiness, health, wealth, fertility, success, control, longevity, justice, wisdom, knowledge, peace, or courage. It is in this broad pool of common human and religious desires that one may find some basis for interreligious empathy.

A second set of elements providing some basis for the possibility of interreligious empathy is found in the constancy or recurrence of certain experiences that may or may not correspond to basic religious desires. While all religious experiences are of course colored by the religious context from which they arise, one nonetheless finds expressions of religious ecstasy, deep absorption, detachment, equanimity, solidarity, hope, possession, and even more specific, well-defined but rare experiences such as religious weeping or levitation across different religious traditions. Thus, while the practices of a whirling dervish may seem alien to Christians, the sense of religious ecstasy or absorption it produces may strike some chords of resonance with a Christian observer. Similarly, the Hindu experience of *darshan* or the feeling of joy and excitement at seeing and being seen by God may awaken a Christian to past or latent layers of religious emotion. The necessary condition for interreligious empathy is thus relative familiarity. This also explains why it is at times easier to empathize with individuals belonging to a different religious tradition than with those in one's own tradition whose religious life is shaped by a different set of experiences. A Christian of more contemplative bent, for example, may in some respects be more capable of empathizing with a Hindu belonging to the Vedanta society than with, say, the experience of a born-again Christian. Another way of putting this would be to say that empathy in general is at least partly a matter of the kind or quality of an experience and not only of its particular content.

CONDITIONS FOR EMPATHY

This brings us to a discussion of the more personal conditions for the possibility of empathy. The first of these conditions lies on the side of general affective predisposition, where empathy requires *sympathy,* or what Gabriel Marcel has termed "availability" (*disponibilité*).[30] Since empathy generally entails some degree of inference by analogy, it secondly presupposes a reservoir of personal religious *experiences* that may form the basis for resonance with those of others. And if empathy entails more than a repetition or recognition of one's own past experiences, it thirdly requires a rich *imagination*. This much calls for an immediate caveat: as crucial as they are, each of these conditions may also lead to a distorted understanding of the other, to a projection of one's own experience, imagination, and desire for meaning onto the other. But this only serves to remind us that the conditions for empathy, like empathy itself, function properly only if they remain focused on the religious life of the other as their aim and endpoint.

Sympathy

The terms "empathy" and "sympathy" were long used interchangeably and remain intimately related, sympathy requiring some degree of empathic understanding of the other, and empathy an attitude of positive disposition toward the other. Sympathy is here understood not only as an attitude of personal warmth and affection toward the other person, but also of openness to the meaningfulness and worth of his or her religious life. It thus includes respect for and interest in the beliefs and practices of the other. Such an attitude of sympathy "strengthens the energy of re-living," as Dilthey already noted,[31] and provides the basic motivation and impulse for

153

engaging the other in the process of understanding. Using religious language, van der Leeuw states that a true understanding of the other "can only follow after a spontaneously warm, self-denying devotion (*Hingabe*),"[32] and that a phenomenologist is entitled to interpret religious data only after "the persistent and strenuous application of this intense sympathy."[33] Against the positivist emphasis on detachment and neutrality, Joachim Wach argues with Nietzsche that "grey cold eyes do not know the value of things" and that a proper understanding of the religious other requires "engagement of feeling, interest, metexis, or participation."[34]

The importance of sympathy toward the other individual and/or religion becomes obvious when considering the impact of the reverse on the process of empathic understanding. One needs only observe the history of Christian attitudes toward other religious traditions in order to realize how negative prejudices against the other can distort one's understanding. This may take place through imparting a sense of religious fear of other religions, thus preventing any possibility of religious identification, or through the cultivation of pronounced negative feelings and emotions toward the religious other. As long as the worship of Hindu gods was regarded as rote idolatry, Christians were forbidden to even glance at the images of Hindu deities, thereby severely limiting any possibility for empathic understanding of the meaning of worship of these images.[35] Empathy thus requires personal sympathy toward the religious other, which itself is to be grounded in a doctrinal openness toward other religions. The greater sense of freedom and license to enter into the sacred spaces of other religions and to participate in their ritual life indeed goes hand in hand with a greater theological recognition of other religions in the course of the twentieth century. And all this cannot but enhance the possibility of genuine empathic understanding of the other. Given this general openness, however, individuals may still feel a spontaneous sympathy or antipathy toward particular religions or religious practices, which in turn may be expected to affect their capacity for empathy.

Greater sympathy for other religions and a sense of freedom to participate in their ritual life does not, however, erase all obstacles to interreligious empathy. First, ritual participation in other religions may raise certain deontological questions. Such participation may be regarded as a form of betrayal by members of one's own religious tradition and hypocrisy by those of the other. Performance of ritual gestures without corresponding conviction may be experienced as disrespectful, or as a trespassing of proper religious boundaries, and as lacking an essential ingredient for proper understanding: personal belief. Secondly, religions often contain restrictions and regulations with regard to participation of nonbelievers. One thinks, for instance, of the manner in which Roman Catholicism welcomes anyone and everyone to the liturgy of the Word, but restricts participation in the Eucharist to baptized members in good standing. As the example suggests, there are inevitable limits for the empathic understanding to be gained in participating in the rituals of another tradition. Still, one cannot a priori preclude the possibility of empathic understanding of the meaning of rituals to which one has no personal access.

While sympathy toward the religious other may enhance the possibility of empathic understanding, it may also at times be a source of subtle distortion. Eagerness to render the beliefs and practices of the other meaningful to everyone of good will may lead one to attribute or impose meaning, as it were, from the outside, rather than welcoming the meaning that is inherent. This can occur by projecting one's own past experiences on the other, or by ascribing to the other a meaning and coherence that in fact derives from one's own religious preconceptions. As such, while Western scholars and feminists have developed various highly sophisticated and seemingly coherent conceptions of the meaning of the goddess Kali within the Hindu religious system, one cannot but wonder at times to what extent the meaning of this goddess for Westerners corresponds to the experience of Hindus themselves. Sympathy for the other religion indeed often carries the risk of over-interpretation and well-willing projection.

Experience

Insofar as empathy is understood as "analogical apperception," personal experience plays a crucial role in the process of empathy. The experiences of others are indeed initially grasped by way of recognition or by way of similarity to one's own past experiences. Non-Muslims will thus start to gauge the meaning and experience of Ramadan by reference to their own experience of religious fasting, while empathic understanding of the devotion to Krishna will probably proceed by way of analogy with one's own personal experience of devotion. Attending to the role of previous experience, Dilthey in fact seems to believe that empathy is possible only "if the context which exists in one's own experience and has been encountered in innumerable cases is always — and with all the potentialities contained in it — present and ready."[36] In reading a text, he states, "the soul follows the accustomed paths in which it enjoyed and suffered, desired and acted in similar situations. Innumerable paths are open, leading to the past and dreams of the future, innumerable lines of thought emerge from reading."[37] This is how we might understand Husserl's reference to one's own experience as the "originary norm" for understanding others.[38]

One immediate implication of this would be that the richer and more diverse one's own religious life is, the more chance one may have of understanding that of others. Joachim Wach expresses this in terms of the relationship between a spiritual master and disciple, according to which "it is possible for the higher to comprehend the lower and the older (master) to perceive what is going on in the younger (disciple), but not vice versa."[39] Leaving aside the hierarchy implied, there seems to be little point in denying that the capacity for empathy is based on and to a significant degree restricted by the range of one's own religious experiences and sensitivity. Individuals with little or no experience of or tendency toward religious enthusiasm may find it difficult to empathize with the religious life of Hare Krishna members, just as persons inclined toward a devotional relation to the divine may find a nontheistic experience of ultimate reality unimaginable and inaccessible.

Another implication one might derive from the emphasis on personal experience is the fact that empathy cannot provide access to new or different experiences. The implications for the dialogue between religions are evident. If all empathic understanding of the other is limited to experiences that are already part of one's own religious history — if there is no escaping a territory mapped in advance by past experience — dialogue has little chance of learning anything new about the other, let alone expanding one's religious and experiential horizon or leading to genuine religious growth. In spite of the emphasis on experience, it is interesting to note that most theories of empathy do not limit empathic understanding to those experiences which are already part of one's own lived reality.[40] This is already manifest in Dilthey's account of his experience in reading the letters of Luther:

157

The possibilities of experiencing religious states in one's own life is narrowly limited for me as for most contemporaries. But when I read through the letters and writings of Luther . . . I experience a religious process, in which life and death are at issue, of such eruptive power and energy as is *beyond the possibility of direct experience for a man of our time.*[41] (my italics)

Dilthey here clearly attests to empathic resonance with an experience or a religious process that appears completely alien or unfamiliar to him. Max Scheler similarly suggests that "we can have a lively and immediate participation in joy or sorrow, can share with others their appreciation of value, and can even enter into another commiseration for a third party, without ever having sampled that particular quality of experience before. A person who has never felt mortal danger can still understand and envisage it, just as he can also share in it."[42] While empathy with physical experiences of pleasure and pain may require previous experience of the same, Scheler believes that with regard to mental or spiritual experiences, every human is equipped with an "innate capacity" for comprehending the feelings of others and for imaginatively drawing on the great range of emotional qualities capable of emerging at any time in any person. The more purely internal or, as he puts it, the more "vital" the experience, the higher the capacity for empathy without prior experience. As an example of this, Scheler points to the experience of despair of Jesus in Gethsemane, and argues that:

[it] can be understood and shared regardless of our historical, racial, and even human limitations. And for every candid heart which steeps itself in that desolation it operates, not as a reminder or revival of personal sufferings,

great or small, but as the revelation of a new and greater suffering hitherto undreamed of.[43]

This proposal receives a more thorough discussion in the phenomenology of Edith Stein. Rather than immediate personal experience, Stein refers to one's mental and emotional disposition or "structure" as the basis for empathy, stating that "all foreign experience permitting itself to be derived from my own structure can be fulfilled, even if this structure has not yet actually unfolded."[44] It is thus not so much direct experience, but a propensity toward the experience that is seen to be the basis for empathic understanding of the other. Her account of this capacity for entering into new experiential territory appeals to what the phenomenologists call "fulfilling intuition": it is by filling out the elements not yet present within one's own life experience that one gains an empathic understanding of the other. In the case of interreligious empathy, this involves situating oneself in the broader religious context of the other and taking stock of the essential variables shaping the experience of the other. This may then lead to an expansion of one's own experiential horizon and to an intuition of distinctive forms of religious life and experience. Stein emphasizes that not all types of experience are universally accessible. Experiences and attitudes that are radically discontinuous with or opposed to one's own present themselves "in the manner of empty presentation" or unfulfilled intuition. The example she gives is one of a skeptic trying to empathize with a religious person who sacrifices all for the sake of his faith:

> I see him behave in this way and I empathize a value experiencing as a motive for his conduct. The correlate of this is not accessible to me, causing me to ascribe to him a personal level I do not myself possess. In this way I

159

empathically gain the type of *homo religiosus* by nature foreign to me, and I understand it even though what newly confronts me here will always remain unfulfilled.[45]

This, of course, also applies the other way around, unless the person was once a skeptic or experienced strong religious doubt. Individuals with no propensity to ecstasy, religious or otherwise, are indeed likely to remain completely unmoved by Hare Krishna *kirtans,* while conversely individuals with a high inclination to religious joy and ecstasy may feel completely puzzled by the lack of such emotions in others.

With regard to interreligious empathy, this opens wide the possibility of empathic understanding of experiences that are not directly part of one's own religious repertoire. Though the capacity for empathy is highly personal and unpredictable, one might surmise that one's own religious tradition and the range of experiences it generates does play a certain role in one's empathic understanding of others. As such, it might be easier for individuals belonging to theistic traditions to understand the experience of devotion, even if this experience differs in kind and intensity. The more continuous those experiences are with one's own religious beliefs and practices, the more uninhibited the process of empathy. And yet the religious or spiritual potential of individuals is not necessarily limited to the range of experiences available within their own tradition. In the attempt to understand others, individuals may come to resonate with experiences that do not have an immediate, perfect connection, or are not wholly continuous with their own religious tradition. This is made possible through the power of imagination.

Imagination

The study and discussion of empathy has always been sensitive to the fact that the experience itself is always at risk of collapsing into simple projection of oneself onto the other, and to be sure few scholars have doubted that some degree of projection is always entailed in any empathic understanding. After all, if my own experiences orient my understanding of the other, as the condition for its possibility, or if there must be some minimal continuity between myself and even the most alien or novel features of my experience of the other, then I am in an important sense apt to rediscover myself, or some variation of myself, in any possible interlocutor. The question faced by scholars has not been whether projection is an original feature of empathy, but instead what one may do to recognize and perhaps overcome it. Standard phenomenology from Husserl to van der Leeuw has invoked the possibility of stepping back away from one's own experiences so as to catch sight of and to set aside the particularities that the subject brings into its sense of the other. Husserl in fact goes further or becomes subtler than van der Leeuw, who, though later, seems to have learned from only some of the philosopher's efforts. Applied to empathy, what the phenomenological *epoche* uncovers is precisely that this requires us to abandon, or at least destabilize, the ego-centered stance from which we ordinarily constitute meaning. Empathy is explicitly dynamic, and its relationship is one of personification: insofar as I put on the persona of the other without in fact becoming the other, it occurs in the mode of "as if." But I am also not fully myself in empathy, or at least not the self who constitutes things as objects. Husserl speaks here of a "disempowering decentering": I become a "quasi-I" — though also, again, "a quasi-other," that is to say, the closest approximation to the other, that I can, in all sincerity, manage. In adopting this perspective out of which to understand the other "I make of myself not only a means to the understanding of the other, but also its object, an object that admittedly only represents what really has to be understood."[46] From here, as the result of this process, I not only recognize what my own experience delivers into the meaning of the other who I now perceive — whereupon I might already begin to look beyond, into new vistas of the genuinely alien — but I may also become more critically aware of what is my own and what is not.[47] A constant effort to free up and seize upon every opportunity for genuine illumination defines the role of imagination.

The imagination plays an essential role in all religious life. To begin with the obvious, it is a crucial factor in our human capacity to conceive of a reality beyond the purely immanent and of a state of being free from suffering and temporality. Imagination allows the human mind to enter into the world of symbolic and mythical representation and to assimilate the highly complex and often contradictory meanings embedded in one's own religious symbols. But it also allows one to conceive of forms of symbolic expression different from one's own. While religious imagination tends to be shaped by a particular symbolic universe, this very particularity may help in imagining alternate forms of religious expression. After all, every religious belief or expression points beyond itself to any number of alternative possibilities, belief in a male God at least suggesting the possibility of female expressions of the divine, or belief in a personal God the possibility of nonpersonal conceptions of ultimate reality. And these different alternatives may become live options through the power of the imagination. Encounter with other religions may thus stretch the imagination to conceive of radically new forms of religious representation. Imagination also forms the means by which one may be transported into the ritual life and religious practices of others. Through contemplation of the ecstatic dance of Hare Krishna members or the masterful execution of the Japanese tea ceremony, the imagination may awaken one to forms of religious joy or control scarcely developed within one's own religious tradition. It may also help one expand upon the set of meanings traditionally associated with particular religious symbols or images. It is through the imagination that traditional associations of religious symbols may be left behind and the possibility of new meanings and affective connotations released. While the heart plays an important role in many religious traditions, each religion informs it with particular meaning and feeling, accessible only through the imagination. In empathy, the imagination thus represents the faculty of movement, helping one to cross from one religious constellation into the other. It frees us from imprisonment in our own determined experiences and helps us to tap into forms of religious experience hitherto unimagined.

The question of how far beyond our lived experience the faculty of imagination may reach is open to debate. Most theories of empathy continue to ground the imagination within one's own actual or potential life experience. Eduard Spranger believes that "in imagination we have ready a manifoldness of situations on which we model our future behavior" and "this stock of individual life situations helps us to enter into the other person with our interpretive imaginary powers."[48] According to Dilthey the imagination works to "strengthen or diminish the emphasis on attitudes, powers, feelings and ideas contained in our own lives and this enables us to reproduce the mental life of another person."[49] All this points to

163

the fact that the imagination remains a highly subjective faculty, difficult to predict or to control. While certain individuals within one religion may be able to enter imaginatively a particular belief or practice of another religion, others may be left cold by it.

Though the capacity for expanded religious sensitivity depends on the power of imagination of any particular individual, certain exercises may stimulate the process. The interreligious imagination may be awakened through the simple reading of texts or through attentive listening to the testimony of believers. But a particularly effective way of stimulating the imagination is through participation in the religious life of the other.

Most ritual theories point to the fact that rituals do not merely reflect but produce particular religious attitudes and experiences. This is due to total sensory immersion in the religious context of the other, which awakens one to dimensions of religious life and experience that remain hidden when contact is only via written or verbal communication. This gives new life to Theodore Lipps's early description of empathy as a process in which "we understand the feelings of others by a process of analogical inferences based on imitating the expressive movements of those others in our imagination."[50] While the meaning and importance of surrender in Islam may be obvious from the study of the tradition or the reading of texts, the actual visual perception of, or participation in, Muslim prayer may point to dimensions of the experience closed to purely theoretical study. Similarly, visits to Hindu temples and submersion in the sounds and smells of Hindu devotion may sharpen one's senses to the particularity of this experience. And while Jews and Christians profess to share belief in the same God, participation in the ritual life of the other tradition nonetheless offers an immediate sense of the differences in the experience of God that distinguish the two traditions. This is why participant observation has come to play such an essential role in the study and understanding of other religions.

Related to this is the importance of time or prolonged immersion in the religious context of the other. While chance or distant encounter with the religious images of another religion may give rise to a sense of alienness, aversion, or projection, it is only through long and patient attention to the religious life of the other that one may overcome habitual conceptions and enter slowly into the experiential life of another tradition. The phenomenon of religious globalization and the coexistence of members of different religions has removed some of the barriers to such interreligious imagination. Not only does it enhance the possibility of enduring encounter with the religious other, but it has also come to remove some of the cultural obstacles for the imagination. The understanding of Zen Buddhism in the West no longer requires quite so stringently an imaginative transposition into the particularities of Japanese culture, just as the adaptation of Christianity in India allows Hindus to focus on specifically religious, rather than cultural, differences.[51] The process of adaptation or inculturation of religious traditions may thus enhance the possibility of empathy.

EMPATHY AND DIALOGUE

Enough has been said about empathy itself to now conduct an informed inquiry about its possible role in the dialogue between religions. The goal of empathy in dialogue involves a deeper understanding of the meaning of particular beliefs and practices through an attempt to identify with the experiential life of the other. This exercise, we shall see, is never complete.

With the exception of some early phenomenologists, few theorists of empathy have seriously considered it to lead directly to some form of "objective" understanding of the other, or to perfect duplication of the pristine experience of the other. Not only does the object of faith generally remain beyond the empathic grasp of anyone not belonging to the tradition, but our experience of the other always remains conditioned by our own past experience and categories of understanding. I wish to suggest, however, that while this may be regarded as a fundamental epistemic problem in the study of religions, it does not necessarily preclude the possibility of a constructive dialogue between religions.

Empathy and Alterity

Interreligious empathy involves an understanding of the experiences of other people insofar as they are representative of a particular tradition. Though this distinction cannot be drawn too sharply — since access to the experiential dimension of another religion is generally through the experiences of its members — it does have some bearing on our reflection on the epistemic status of interreligious empathy. If empathy is conceived in terms of access to the personal experience of a particular individual belonging to another religious tradition, it is evident that no amount of knowledge, sympathy, experience, or imagination will ever provide access to the fullness of the experience in question. This much is generally acknowledged in most theoretical discussion of empathy. Spranger observed that "the subjective experiential context of another person is never wholly revealed to us"[52] and Husserl pointed out that "the other is never in the sphere of my ownness"[53] and that "the other cannot be actualized originally in my primordial sphere."[54] Every experience entails an inscrutable whole of prior experiences and events, conscious and unconscious desires and motivations, which are never fully transparent, either to the observer or to the person undergoing the experience. To this may be added the temporality of all experience, or the fact that, as van der Leeuw puts it, "the immediate is never and nowhere given" and that "pure experience, upon which our experiences are grounded, has always passed away irrevocably by the time our attention is directed to it."[55] As reflective agents, in other words, we start out after the fact of our encounter with the other, which in its immediate form is thus always beyond our empathic grasp. We sense this already when probing the religious experiences of individuals belonging to our own religious tradition, where testimony often limps and words sometimes simply fail in the attempt to achieve a feeling of community. But of course this sense is much more powerful when we turn toward individuals belonging to other religions, whose experiences are shaped in relation to a different object of faith. Initial attempts at empathy, and perhaps an entire sequence of them, fall evidently short of any perfect understanding, let alone a verifiable one.

Another obstacle to gaining genuine empathic understanding of another religion is the absence of actual faith on the part of the one who attempts to enter into the life of the religious other. Even though one may be deeply familiar with all of the elements comprising the experience of devotion within another religion, the feeling of love for the *particular object of devotion* — that which is arguably the most important dimension of the experience for believers — remains inaccessible for anyone not belonging to the tradition. Though one's own experience of faith may provide some sense of analogical imagination, each experience of devotion is itself always shaped by its object, whether Krishna or Allah or Christ, and is as such attained only through the experience of surrender to it. This was brought home to me very directly during a visit to a Ganesha temple in South India. I had studied Hinduism for many years, and so the temple, the images, and the ritual gestures I observed seemed quite familiar. I was accustomed to the ritual etiquette of the temple, to the main themes of Hindu mythology, and to the details of Hindu iconography. Comfortably strolling around in the temple, my attention was suddenly drawn to an old Hindu woman who was performing *pūjā*, offering flowers, incense, and water in front of the god with the elephant head. In an instant, this image shattered all sense of familiarity, and brought me back to a realization of the difference between my own Christian religious experiences and those of the Hindu other, and to the limits of my empathic understanding of the other. Short of personally developing a love of Ganesha, I would never be able to fully access the experience of the other.[56] To some degree, of course, this applies to all forms of empathy. The feelings of empathic joy for someone who has fallen in love do not usually include empathic love for her beloved, and the empathic sorrow for someone's loss is generally based on one's own experiences of bereavement at a loss of one's own. However, it should not be forgotten that religious experiences also include a conviction of the ultimate truth of the beliefs and practices, or at least of the principles that command them. This dimension of the experience, moreover, is not incidental or secondary, but defines it as such. The Christian who cannot enter into the faith of the Hindu thus misses empathy with what is essential, even while empathizing with the general feeling of devotion she seems to undergo.[57]

All empathic understanding of the other thus proceeds by way of analogy in which one's own experience, and thus also to a considerable extent one's own tradition, remains the basis and norm for understanding the other. Husserl expresses this sharply when he states:

> What I can re-understand (*nachverstehen*), to what ex-
> tent I can empathize is determined by the ideal variations
> of the archetypal human being: I, who am this human
> being, achieve normal empathy as the perception of the
> other; in so doing the other body that resembles mine
> is supplemented with the same supplementary meaning
> content that belongs to my body under corresponding cir-
> cumstance and with the possible variations which belong
> to mine. My body given to inwardly directed or solipsistic
> experience is thus the archetypal apperception and pro-
> vides the necessary norm. Everything else is a variation of
> this norm.

Husserl's understanding of the ego as the ultimate norm for understanding the other may be regarded as too static and solipsistic. The ego is itself always shaped in interaction with others and is itself constantly in a process of dynamic change. This fluidity accounts for the fact that the norm can be put under pressure or, in dramatic cases, overturned by the data of empathy. However, it does rightly emphasize the epistemic limitations of our understanding of the other. Not only is our empathic understanding of the other always colored by our own experiences, but those experiences also determine the ex-tent to which I can grasp any particular experiences. Some forms of religious life may indeed remain beyond my em-pathic understanding. As Joachim Wach pointed out, "There will never be a lack of those differences (difference in tem-perament is one example) which make it difficult even for the student of broad concerns and deep sympathies to comprehend various kinds of religiosity, types of religious thought, or devotional practices which differ sharply from his own."[58] This kind of inaccessibility of the experience of the other may be due to one's own limited powers of imagination, or else to the nature of the belief, attitude, or experience itself (or a combination of the two). Certain religious experiences may indeed be so particular as to require past experience in order to be understood. The experience of spirit possession, for example, is quite probably beyond the imagination of most people who have not actually undergone something like it.

Insofar as my experiential life is largely shaped by my own religious tradition, its beliefs and practices and the range of experiences generated by them also function as an epistemic norm in the process of interreligious empathy. This means that all empathic understanding of the other religion is always colored, to some extent, by the experiences generated within one's own tradition. Rather than implying flat projection, this may point to the vital necessity of one religion in order to understand another. It is indeed only through analogy with one's own religious life that the other is understood. But it is also in the process of resonating with similarities as well as subtle differences between one's own religion and that of the other that differences in shades of experience may come to light.

On the other hand, limitations of one's empathic understanding of the other may point to the incompatibility between that particular religious teaching or practice and one's own religion, and may thus become one parameter in discerning the possibility of fruitful exchange between religions. This is not to deny the possibility of empathizing with experiences that are not immediately reconcilable with one's own religious tradition, but to observe that the more continuous an experience is with one's own religious tradition, the more easily the process of empathy unfolds. As such, and again with all proper caution in mind, one is entitled to suppose that the relative difficulty one might have in achieving an empathic understanding of the experience of the other is in fact a preliminary indication of the degree to which that experience may be irreconcilable with one's own religious tradition. It is of course a risky thought, but one cannot easily dismiss the notion that experiences that are inaccessible to a majority of believers might be truly incompatible with the basic features of one's own tradition. But this need not function only negatively. Perhaps the widespread empathic resonance to and appeal of a particular teaching or practice points to its relevance for one's own religious life. Here, one cannot help thinking of how a widespread Christian resonance to Hindu and Buddhist forms of meditation has called attention to an area of religious experience that may well be compatible with Christian faith and that seems well on its way to stimulating religious growth.

Dialogue on Empathy

If empathy always involves a certain degree of projection or superimposition of one's own experiential framework upon the other, then empathy requires dialogue as much as dialogue presupposes empathy. It is only through a continuous process of engagement with the religious other that one's exercise in empathy may be corrected and one's insights confirmed, enhanced, or changed. In this sense, empathy as a process requires a specific attitude we have already encountered as humility. Even though the experiential life of another religion remains beyond the purview of someone not belonging to the tradition, it is still this life of experience that remains the goal of interreligious empathy. While dialogue without empathy may involve a lifeless and maybe even meaningless exchange of data, empathy without dialogue may lead to simple projection and a distortion of the experiential dimension of the other.

While the religious life and experience of the other thus constitutes the ultimate aim and horizon of interreligious empathy, the impossibility of perfect empathy does not itself impede constructive dialogue. In his book *The Dialogical Principle,* the Russian philosopher Mikhail Bhaktin relativizes the importance of complete identification with the other as a necessary or relevant element in the dialogue (between cultures). He argues that it is the very fact of standing outside and perceiving the other from a different perspective (*exotopy*) that constitutes the basis for a constructive dialogue:

> There is an enduring image that is partial, and therefore false, according to which to better understand a foreign culture one should live in it and, forgetting one's own, look at the world through the eyes of its culture. As I have said, such an image is partial. To be sure, to enter in some measure into an alien culture and look at the world through its eyes is a necessary moment in the process of understanding; but if understanding were exhausted in this moment, it would have been no more than a simple duplication and would have brought nothing new or enriching. Creative understanding does not renounce its self, its place in time, its culture; it does not forget anything. The chief matter of understanding is the exotopy of the one who does the understanding — in time, space, and culture — in relation to what he wants to understand creatively. Even his own external aspect is not really accessible to man; he cannot interpret it as a whole; mirrors and photographs prove of no help; a man's real external aspect can be seen and understood only by other persons,

thanks to their spatial exotopy, and thanks to the fact that they are other. In the realm of culture, exotopy is the most powerful level of understanding. It is only through the eyes of another culture that the alien culture reveals itself more completely and more deeply, but never exhaustively, because there will come other cultures, that will see and understand even more.[59]

His comments about intercultural understanding are directly applicable to the interreligious context: it is by seeing one's own tradition through the eyes of the other that one may become aware of new dimensions of one's own tradition. Rather than empathy, Bhaktin uses the term "live-entering," understood as "a creative understanding in which something new is produced through the dialogical interaction of self and other."[60] From this perspective, the question of accuracy in empathy may thus be regarded as a misnomer. The meaning of any religious phenomenon is always complex and fluid and can never be fully grasped, either from within or from outside a tradition. The impossibility of fully entering into the experience of the other is here thus regarded as a potential source of creative growth for both partners engaged in dialogue. For the one being understood, it may become an occasion for deepening one's self-understanding.

But it may also lead to growth for the one who has come to attain imperfect empathy. It is indeed not necessary that a new experience or insight be fully understood or wholly taken over in order for real change to result. While Hindus may not be able to integrate the robust Chalcedonian conception of Christ within their own self-understanding, their empathic understanding of the person and teaching of Jesus Christ may still lead, and has led, to an enrichment of the Hindu tradition.

And even though Christians may not be able to completely recognize the experience of emptiness as the ultimate goal of their religious life, Zen meditation has nonetheless come to constitute an important enrichment of Christian spiritual practice. The very attempt at understanding the other from within itself leads to an expansion of one's religious horizon and experiential life. The Christian attempt to empathize with the Hindu teaching and practice of yoga may generate a genuinely new experience of mental calm and control while the Buddhist experience of Christian love may reveal dimensions of love less in evidence in Buddhist teachings and practices. And even though my own experience of Christian devotion remains the basis for understanding Krishna *bhakti,* the attempt to understand that experience from within awakens the religious imagination to a more playful and joyful relationship to God. In cases such as these, growth undoubtedly occurs in part as a process of maturation, as one acquires a better understanding of one's own identity, including its hidden or unsuspected potential. But in some instances, this maturation is accompanied by a process of expansion, of augmentation through the acceptance of something genuinely new.

All the same, it would be shortsighted to suppose that all forms of empathic understanding of the experiences of other religious traditions lead necessarily to growth and change within one's own religious tradition. What one finds in some instances of empathy undoubtedly contradicts what one already holds as a matter of profound conviction, or more simply as a matter of unshakable value. Buddhists, for example, might well gain a solid empathic understanding of some features of Christian forms of devotion, while judging them inferior to their own spiritual practices, whereas Christians may make considerable progress toward grasping the experience of Krishna as the embodiment of divine bliss and play, yet continue to regard that experience as incompatible with the Christian devotional relationship to Christ. Rather than an opportunity for mutual learning, the empathic understanding of the other may also at times illumine the particularity or the singularity of different religious paths and the futility of any attempt to reconcile them. Interreligious empathy may indeed at times offer a glimpse or a taste of a different way of being religious that simply opens one's religious horizon, without necessarily changing one's religious tradition.

◆ ◆ ◆

Scholars have referred to empathy as "a mysterious capacity" (Spranger),[61] "an art" (van der Leeuw),[62] or a "miraculous virtue" (Weil), which, though essential to the process of understanding the religious other, escapes complete comprehension and control. We have attempted to grasp some of the salient features of empathy. It consists of a transposition into the religious life of the other by identifying with the worldview, the belief system, and the ritual practices of the other in order to resonate with the spiritual impact of particular teachings on the life of a believer. The possibility of such empathy is to some extent grounded in the universality of certain basic religious desires and emotions and in the existence, across religious traditions, of certain recurrent religious attitudes and orientations. However, the experience of interreligious empathy is never guaranteed. It may be stimulated by a positive disposition toward the other, by a broad reservoir of personal experiences, and by a rich religious imagination. But whether one will be moved by a particular religious teaching or practice remains ultimately unpredictable. In the dialogue between

175

religions, empathy may, however, function as a basic principle of orientation. Teachings and practices of the other religion that elicit absolutely no empathic resonance or else negative empathy will probably not lead to a constructive dialogue or religious growth. On the other hand, the experience of profound empathic resonance with the religious other may point to similarities or compatibilities between religions and may open the way to religious growth and change. Even though one's own religious life and experience always remains the basis for empathic understanding of the religious other, empathy may still lead to an expansion of one's religious horizon and to a discovery of religious feelings and experiences hitherto unimagined. These experiences may then become the basis for an enrichment of one's own religious tradition.

Even though empathy may offer some indication of the compatibility of the teaching or practice of the other religion with one's own religious tradition, the possibility of religious growth will ultimately be determined not on epistemological but on theological or religious grounds. At the end of the day, whatever one gains by way of empathic resonance with the religious teachings and practices of the other religion, unless those teachings and practices are thought to contain a certain degree of truth, there can be little or no motivation to respond to them, let alone impulse toward change in oneself. The very possibility of dialogue itself, as an activity oriented to exchange and enrichment, depends finally on an attitude of theological openness by which one welcomes the presence of the other as a potential source of goodness and truth.

CHAPTER FIVE

HOSPITALITY

When all of the necessary conditions are fulfilled, the possibility of interreligious dialogue still ultimately depends on the ability of one religion to recognize truth in the other. This attitude of generous openness to the (possible) presence of truth in the other religion may be called hospitality.[1] This term designates a recognition of the other as other and openness to learning from the other. Such hospitality constitutes the sole sufficient condition for dialogue. The very possibility of discovering authentic truth in the other should automatically awaken the desire for dialogue. And conversely, the denial of any truth beyond the boundaries of one's own tradition would eliminate all desire for dialogue, even when all of the other conditions are met.

In the context of the dialogue between religions, the term "hospitality" is often used to designate the need to welcome the religious other in spite of religious differences.[2] Here, however, we use it to imply an attitude of openness and receptivity to those very differences as a possible source of truth. The possibility of growth and change in dialogue indeed depends on the recognition of truth in difference.

In the practice of dialogue, hospitality may be seen to have a special relation to humility: hospitality toward the truth of the other requires recognition of the limitation or the partiality of one's own understanding of truth, while humility in turn is reinforced or enhanced by the discovery of new elements of truth in other religions. Though openness toward the possibility of discovering truth in teachings and practices different from one's own thus constitutes an essential condition for a constructive dialogue, religions are not on the whole inclined to such hospitality. Most religious faith is based on a belief in the fullness and sufficiency of one's own religious teachings and practices. The very idea that other religions might harbor truth that has not yet been captured within one's own tradition may thus be experienced as a threat to one's epistemic and religious confidence. This is why religions tend to deny the presence of truth in other religions, or else extend hospitality only to those beliefs and practices that are the same as or similar to their own. Against this, true hospitality — hospitality in its most robust form — involves the recognition of the other as other and openness to the possibility of being transformed by that difference. This recognition of distinctive truth beyond the boundaries of one's own religious perspective, however, often presupposes considerable hermeneutical creativity and effort.

Within the Christian tradition, it is primarily in the area of theology of religions that this effort has been attempted, with an appeal to any number of theological resources. It is to be noted that beliefs that at one time have been used as a basis for denying truth in other religions may at other times be used to open the tradition to the presence of truth in difference. For example, while the symbol of the Cross has often been understood as an expression of Christian uniqueness and exclusivism, it may also be seen to point beyond itself to the other, as reflected in the words of Stanislas Breton:

The weight of the Cross is identified with the weight of the other as other, with the mysterious weight that draws us to the region of our dissemblance.[3]

In marking the specificity of Christianity, the Cross may thus be seen to open the tradition to that which is different and which must be engaged in pursuit of the fullness of truth. Given the fact that religious symbols and teachings may be used to deny as well as facilitate hospitality to the truth of other religions, we will need to review the different degrees and kinds of hospitality that may be found within any one religious tradition, and their effect upon the dialogue with other religions.

NO HOSPITALITY

It is probably no exaggeration to state that few religions are spontaneously inclined toward much generosity or hospitality toward the truth of other religious traditions. As an a priori attitude, this lack of hospitality may at times apply to all religions equally or to certain religions in particular. Religions often tend to develop negative prejudices toward so-called new religions, or religions that have emerged at a later date than their own.[4] And the attitude of hospitality is often paradoxically more difficult with regard to family religions than with regard to religions with no historical or religious connection. Some of the reasons for this are obvious: new religions by their very existence challenge the truth of existing ones, and in the case of religions bearing substantial similarities, any difference comes to be experienced as a direct threat to one's own claims to truth. At times, religions also come to develop negative attitudes toward the truth of other religions in response to external pressures or threats. The Christian expression *extra ecclesiam nulla salus* (outside the church, no salvation), for example, was only used with explicit reference to non-Christians at the Council of Florence (in 1442), at a time when the tensions between Christians, Jews, and Muslims ran high. And many of the pronouncedly exclusivist truth claims found in fundamentalist ideologies must probably be regarded as a direct reaction to the pressures of the modern world, including its religious diversity.

Though instances of explicit and blanket denial of truth in other religions are in fact relatively rare, most religions develop strategies of exclusion meant to juxtapose their own beliefs and practices with those of the other. In some cases, these strategies focus on the content of the other religion, singling out its conception of ultimate reality for attack. Thus, for instance, Justin Martyr's denunciation of pagan religion refers to their gods as fallen angels (*angeli fornicatores*) or as "evil demons" who "both defiled women and corrupted boys, and showed such fearful sights to men, that those who did not use their reason in judging of the actions that were done, were struck with terror; and being carried far away by fear and not knowing that these were demons, they called them gods, and gave to each the name which each of the demons chose for himself."[5] In other cases, however, a subtler strategy of exclusion may focus not on the content of the other religion but on its *nature*, which is then accorded a different, i.e., lesser status. Within Christianity, this has been accomplished by introducing oppositional categories such as "religion" versus "revelation," and "faith" versus "belief."

Faith versus Belief

A well-known Christian instance of exclusion by way of differentiation is found in the work of the famous Swiss theologian

Karl Barth, and in particular in his manner of distinguishing between religion and revelation. For Barth, religion contains the whole of human forms of groping toward the divine, while revelation is defined as "the act by which in grace God reconciles man to Himself by grace."[6] While Christianity also contains certain characteristics of a religion, it is for him the only one that may be regarded as revelation. For Barth, this unique status is based not so much on the content of its teachings as on the reality of its divine election:

> For the Christian religion is true, because it has pleased God, who alone can be the judge in this matter, to affirm it to be the true religion. What is truth, if it is not this divine affirmation? And what is certainty of truth, if not the certainty which is based solely upon this judgment, a judgment which is free, but wise and righteous in its freedom, because it is the freedom of God?[7]

It is thus the unmerited grace of God that renders the Christian religion both true and fundamentally distinct from all other religious traditions. One element that confirms or expresses the status of Christianity as a true religion is its emphasis on faith and grace as the means to salvation. Clearly aware of the fact that religions such as Hinduism and Buddhism also contain such devotional strands, Barth moves on to argue that it is not faith itself, but faith in the person of Jesus Christ that renders the Christian religion true:

> Beyond all dialectic and to the exclusion of all discussion the divine fact of the name of Jesus Christ confirms what no other fact does or can confirm: the creation and election of this religion to be the one and only true religion.[8]

Barth's theology offers a clear example of the fact that the denial of truth in other religions is generally based on a priori religious grounds and can be maintained only through isolation from other religions. Recognizing that a commitment to Christianity is rooted specifically in faith, Barth discourages comparison with other religions, believing that it would "always and very quickly mean uncertainty regarding the truth of the Christian religion," and that Christians would maintain confidence in the unique truth of its own revelation only insofar as they "can look away from themselves to the fact of God which alone can justify them."[9] In light of the revelation in Christ, all other forms of religion cannot but be regarded as "unbelief." While extreme, this theological position is internally consistent, according to a logic that is particularly suited to religions based on divine revelation. If all truth is ultimately seen to derive from a single transcendental source, all forms of religion that do not acknowledge this source cannot but be regarded as deficient or false, or of an altogether different nature.

A second and somewhat related form of exclusivism by way of differentiation is found in Christian texts that emphasize the difference between faith, which is the proper Christian response to divine revelation, and "belief," which may be found in other religious traditions. This distinction comes to the fore in the Vatican document *Dominus Iesus,* which, without denying that there may be elements of truth in other religions, nonetheless insists that "the distinction between *theological faith* and *belief* in the other religions must be *firmly held.*"[10] Here faith means "the acceptance in grace of revealed truth which makes it possible to penetrate the mystery in a way that allows us to understand it coherently," while belief is "that sum of experience and thought that constitutes the human treasury of wisdom and religious aspiration, which man in his search for truth has conceived and acted upon in his relationship to God and the Absolute." As a result, the document emphasizes that only the canonical scriptures of Christianity may be referred to as "inspired texts"[11] and that while there may be some elements of truth in other religions, "it is also certain that *objectively speaking* they are in a gravely deficient situation in comparison with those who, in the Church, have the fullness of the means of salvation."[12]

There can be little doubt that such an attitude of limited hospitality in Barth and in *Dominus Iesus* may be understood in part as a reaction to the threat of religious relativism emerging from liberal and pluralistic theologies. Barth underlines the form in which that threat appeared in his day when he acknowledges that a purely historical comparison between Christianity and other religions could never in itself support the superiority or uniqueness of Christianity. And in the introductory paragraphs of *Dominus Iesus,* we find a pointed and insightful discussion of the various challenges to traditional Christian self-understanding posed by "relativistic theories which seek to justify religious pluralism, not only *de facto* but also *de jure (or in principle)*."[13] Even though it is under duress that religions often come to emphasize their own uniqueness and turn away from the truth of other religions, there is no denying that such absence of hospitality resonates with much religious self-understanding.

Dialogue as Apologetics

Strategies of exclusion render the teachings and practices of the other radically alien, so that the attitude of religious hospitality and the practice of dialogue appear either futile or pointless. While belief in the election of Christianity to be the true religion should not give Christians a sense of superiority or arrogance with regard to other religious traditions, Barth also discourages all forms of engagement with other religions. Instead, he advocates an attitude of "tolerance," understood not in terms of acceptance of the validity or legitimacy of the teachings of other religions, but in terms of "forbearance" and recognition of one's own unmerited election. In the end, Barth believes that it is the responsibility of Christians to bring members of other religions to the true religion, for "it alone has the commission and authority to be a missionary religion, i.e., to confront the world of religions as the one true religion, with absolute self-confidence to invite and to challenge it to abandon its ways and to start on the Christian way."[14]

While this absence of hospitality toward the truth of other religions is unlikely to lead to dialogue, it may generate a form of mutual apologetics. We have already seen that apologetics forms an integral part of all serious interreligious dialogue.[15] As such, the rejection of truth in other religions may shed some light on at least one dimension of dialogue. Religious apologetics first of all requires a profound understanding of the other religion. As such, Barth's arguments for the superiority of Christian revelation are all the more impressive for also demonstrating an awareness of the Buddhist and Hindu traditions of grace, which he nonetheless rejects. Likewise, Henri de Lubac's confession of the uniqueness of Christ is particularly striking, or perhaps unsettling, when cast in a book-length study of the figure of Amida, the heavenly Buddha of the Pure Land. Having evoked the image of Amida in the most laudatory terms, de Lubac concludes:

> All of this, however, remains far from the Christian supernatural. Disengaged from the puerility of its fable,

Amidism remains profoundly driven in the crepuscular thought and spirituality belonging to all "natural" religion as to all "natural" mysticism.[16]

While Barth and de Lubac may have acquired a — for their times — impressive understanding of the other tradition, one's knowledge of the other religion can always be deepened and enhanced and arguments against the truth of the other will be all the more convincing if based on genuine expertise. Francis Clooney thus points out that "if a disciple of Barth today dismisses the Srivaisnava understanding of grace, Hindu theologians who know that theology well can dispute the point and argue against it persuasively if they also know Barth's theology."[17]

Though the exercise of apologetics may lead to a deeper understanding of the other tradition, and occasionally to a rectification of misconceptions of the other, there is little chance that it will lead to any form of religious change or growth. Barth's position is a powerful case in point. Whatever his knowledge of Hindu and Buddhist forms of devotion, it did little more than strengthen an argument for the superiority and uniqueness of Christian revelation that was for him never in doubt. Insofar as his attitude toward other religions was based on a faith commitment rather than on historical evidence, it is difficult to see how any amount of counter-argumentation could ever change his point of view. At best, it would seem capable only of stimulating a sharper awareness of the confessional source of one's own rejection of the presence of truth in other religions.

This does not mean, however, that interreligious dialogue has nothing to learn from theological apologetics. Apart from

the fact that the latter has long been, and remains, a useful feature of reflection within most traditions, and without denying
the fact that apologetic approaches have often been highly bi-
ased and poorly informed about their interlocutors, it remains
the case that some arguments appearing here are theologically
sound, and in some cases still quite pertinent. After decades of
religious deference, itself hardly unwarranted, the unscripted
and unabashed judgments on the teachings or practices of the
other religion sometimes reawaken us to areas of religious incompatibility or conflict that had been neglected or suppressed.
Likewise, though the vocabulary used in some forms of traditional apologetics is no longer adequate or constructive in the
contemporary context, a raw religious reaction to the teachings and practices of other religions, or an adamant defense
against some of the critiques and accusations of other religions,
may also remind us of some of the most genuinely challenging
dimensions of the dialogue with any particular religion. And
this holds both for the view looking out at the other and for
the one looking within oneself: attention to the nature and intensity of some apologetics may point directly to elements in
the other religion that are difficult to reconcile with one's own,
but also to elements within one's own tradition that stand in
the way of genuine dialogue.

Dialogue as Mutual Affirmation/Suspicion

While resistance or limited inclination to dialogue with other
religions may be based on confessional beliefs in the exclusive truth of one's own tradition, it may also derive from more
philosophical conceptions of the nature of religious truth as
such. Confrontation with the reality of religious plurality has
indeed led to various new approaches to the truth of religions,
some with the unintended consequence of inhibiting genuine

dialogue. Such is the case, for example, with George Lindbeck's cultural-linguistic approach to religious truth. In an attempt to overcome the problem of competing religious claims to truth, Lindbeck situates the truth of religious claims not in their correspondence to external states of affairs, but in terms of their internal coherence.[18] This, however, may lead to the conclusion that the teachings of one religion are unintelligible, or at least irrelevant, to individuals of a different religion. Needless to say, this is not a concession Lindbeck is willing to make: discussing the implications of his account of religious truth for the dialogue between Christianity and other religions, he states that these religions may contain "highly important truths and realities, of which Christianity as yet knows nothing and by which it could be greatly enriched."[19] Yet one searches in vain for an explanation of how such enrichment might actually take place. Moreover, everything else here seems to urge against that possibility. If different religions and doctrinal systems are truly incommensurable, as he certainly seems to think, then dialogue could never go beyond mutual affirmation (or denial). Lindbeck also admits this much when he states that the goal of dialogue is for "Jews and Muslims to become better Jews and Muslims, and Buddhists to become better Buddhists."[20] Now, the meaning of such a notion, often encountered in the dialogue between religions, remains notoriously ambiguous. Its intention is clear enough: the goal of dialogue is not to convince other religions of one's own superior truth or still less to convert individuals from one religion to the other, but to allow each participant to realize more fully the truth of their own religious tradition, and integrate that truth into their own lives. There is, of course, nothing objectionable about this. Even so, the term "better" can be somewhat equivocal. Whether one realizes it or not, suggesting that the other might become a better member of their religion often implies a greater conformity to the ideals and goals of one's own tradition, or at least realizing what is best about that tradition *as viewed from the perspective of one's own*. It would indeed seem disingenuous to wish for the realization of ideals that diverge from or oppose one's own. A simple example makes this plain. If, hypothetically, my own religion emphasizes the fundamental personal and spiritual equality of all human beings while another openly supports the subjugation of one gender to the other, it would be incongruous for me to wish that members of that other religion realize more fully ideals that I myself oppose. What we may take from this, then, is that in actual interreligious dialogue, the idea of becoming a "better" Muslim, Christian, Jew, or Buddhist is most often informed by a certain judgment of what that would entail, based on one's own beliefs, or else by a belief in the unity of all religious goals.

Rather than to mutual affirmation, John Milbank's emphasis on the internal coherence and mutual incompatibility of different conceptions of truth leads to a suggestion to replace dialogue with "mutual suspicion."[21] Reacting against various pluralist proposals for a possible meeting point between religions in ethical concerns, and to religious conceptions of unity beyond religious differences, Milbank emphasizes the irreducibility of each religion to the other. In the encounter between religions, each religion can at most aspire to resist any hegemonic movement or universalizing pretense on the part of other religions. Whether or not this position is philosophically cogent, the theological position it stakes out does bring into view another important feature of interreligious dialogue, this time contained within the notion of mutual suspicion — that of a mutual challenge in which the possible discrepancies and limitations of each religion are exposed in the confrontation with the beliefs and ideals of another. One of the fruits of interreligious dialogue is undoubtedly a more critical self-understanding.

HOSPITALITY TOWARD SIMILARITY

While the wholesale rejection of truth in other religions is rare in the history of religions, hospitality generally begins — and often ends — with the recognition of truth in teachings and practices which mirror or resemble one's own. If such hospitality is rather common in the encounter between religions, this may well be due in no small part to the fact that it poses little or no threat to traditional religious self-understanding. It also places less pressure on the data of empirical reality. As Paul Griffiths points out, rejection of all truth in other religions "commits anyone who holds it to the claim that no alien religious teaching is identical with any teaching of the home community. For if there were any such instance of identity, it would immediately follow that if the relevant teaching of the home tradition is true, that of the alien religion must also be."[22]

Under a qualified form of hospitality to the other, one may still adhere to the absolute or ultimate truth of one's own religious teachings while avoiding the logical inconsistency of denying the truth of teachings of other religions that might be identical to one's own. Accordingly, one's own tradition remains the basis from which similarities in the other are discerned, and all truth may be seen to ultimately derive from one's own tradition. In short, the epistemic advantages of this position are considerable.

Similarities may take the form of direct or structural correspondences, external resemblance, or semantic equivalence.

It is of course true that surface similarities often reveal profound semantic differences, while seemingly different religious teachings or practices may at times point to remarkably similar religious contents. The discernment of similarities in another religious tradition thus requires an extensive knowledge and profound understanding of that religion. Since all similarities between religions are qualified by the distinctive religious context in which they are embedded, the recognition of truth in similarity also always entails a certain negotiation of difference. Either those differences are disregarded and considered inferior to one's own religious truth, or they are seen to contain certain elements from which one may learn something new. Either way, the other religion is regarded as a mirror in which one recognizes truth only insofar as it corresponds to one's own beliefs.

Insofar as each religion believes itself to be in possession of the truth, that truth functions as the natural point of orientation and departure for building bridges and generating hospitality toward other religious traditions. In meeting the religious other, the discovery of similarities often signals a moment of recognition and assurance. These similarities may derive from common historical origins, from mutual or unilateral influences, or from historical contingency and the finite nature of religious imagination. They may involve similar worldviews, the same ethical teachings, analogous conceptions of the divine, similar ways of theological reasoning, or analogous sets of religious virtues. In any case, the appearance of similar elements logically calls for a recognition of at least some truth in the other religion.

Of course, the many beliefs shared by religions with common parentage (e.g., the Abrahamic religions) cannot but be some of what provides for religious hospitality. But religions with no direct historical relationship also often display important similarities in segments of beliefs as well as modes of theological reflection.[23] Here, it is of course less the object of devotion than the religious attitude or insight itself that may be regarded as an expression of truth. But it is predominantly in the domains of ethics and spirituality that religions have moved most easily to recognition of similarities and to an affirmation of truth in the others. As Hans Küng has shown, all of the great religious traditions of the world call upon their adherents to abstain from killing, from stealing, from lying, and from adultery or sexual immorality.[24] Numerous other correspondences may be found between the ethical teachings of any two or more religions, from the Golden Rule that appears in positive or negative formulation in the sacred texts of most religions to the call to love of neighbor that is also expressed in various ways in many of them. And remarkable similarities exist between the monastic disciplines of the various religions, as well as among the qualities of individuals practicing such disciplines. Perhaps the consonance in their basic intentions is enough for those principles to become the ground and starting point for religious hospitality, even if the difference in context and orientation might complicate the task significantly.

The Other as "Preparatio"

It is clear that in the recognition of truth in similarity, one's own religious beliefs always remain the basis and norm for recognizing such truth. This perspective defines an inclusivism that is operative in all religions, even as their theologians labor variously to refine, reject, or redefine it. In its natural attitude, each religious tradition tends to evaluate and affirm the truth of the others according to its own religious principles.[25]

A corollary of the possibility of recognizing truth in similarity is the idea that truth found in another religious tradition is partial and provisional in comparison with the truth of one's own religious tradition. The most common or familiar version of this idea may be found in the Christian church father Eusebius of Caesaria's conception of the truth of Greek philosophy as *preparatio evangelica*. The general Christian inflection is captured in the image of the elements of truth in other religions as "seed of the word" (*logos spermatikos*) awaiting fulfillment in the truth of Christian revelation. Other religions, Buddhism for example, or at least particular schools within that tradition, developed hierarchies of truth, predicated on the proximity of the teachings of the other to one's own. Here, all truth in other religions is seen to be derived from or oriented toward one's own conception of ultimate reality, thus safeguarding the ultimate truth of one's own tradition.

One of the main proponents of this attitude within the Christian tradition is Karl Rahner. Against the traditional Christian belief that there is no salvation outside of the church, Rahner argued that other religions may be "a positive means of gaining the right relationship with God and thus for the attaining of salvation, a means which is therefore positively included in God's plan of salvation."[26] However, remaining fast to the Christian notion that all truth is derived from the grace of God in Christ, he still insisted that whatever truth was to be found in other religions could only be understood as derived from Christ:

If there can be a faith which is creative of salvation among non-Christians, and if in fact it may be hoped that it in fact is found on a large scale, then it is to be taken for granted that this faith is made possible and is based upon the supernatural grace of the Spirit. And this is the Spirit who proceeds from the Father and the Son, so that as the Spirit of the eternal Logos, he can and must be called at least in this sense the Spirit of Christ, the divine Word who has become man.[27]

In focusing on the presence of truth in similarity, teachings and practices that differ from one's own tend to be regarded as false or as deficient when compared to one's own, or as valid until the moment when the fullness of truth of one's own religion encounters the other. Other religions are thus looked upon as a mixture of truth and error. Whereas the Vatican Document *Dominus Iesus* recognizes elements of truth in other religions, regarding them as "preparation for the Gospel,"[28] it also states that "it cannot be overlooked that the other rituals, insofar as they depend on superstitions and other errors constitute an obstacle to salvation."[29] Other religions are thus regarded as merely partially and provisionally true. For Rahner, other religions are valid or lawful only "until the moment when the gospel really enters into the historical situation of the individual."[30] This conception of the truth of other religions as fulfilled or completed within one's own is far from unique to Christianity, even if the specific language of *preparatio* almost certainly is. Whether in the form of crude religious supersessionism or alloyed to a vision of personal spiritual progression from one religion to the next through one or many lifetimes, any number of religions have addressed the riddle of plurality in the context of a positive vision of fulfillment in time: whatever truth is present in other religions is grasped in its fuller context and is opened to its deeper meaning when it is defined from within one's own religious tradition.

193

Dialogue as Monologue

Recognition of elements of truth in teachings and practices of other religions similar to one's own certainly represents a first step toward a fruitful dialogue between religions. It may lead to a more open and respectful attitude toward the other religion and to a rediscovery of neglected or forgotten dimensions of one's own religious tradition. It is indeed through the appeal of beliefs or practices of another religion that one may recover teachings or practices buried in history or left in the margins of the tradition. This is the case, for example, with some features of the resurgence of interest in the Christian Hesychast tradition in the West, which has been awakened largely through encounter with Hinduism and Buddhist forms of meditation. And much of the attention to the apophatic mystical tradition has likewise been inspired by contact with similar strands of thought in Hindu and Buddhist philosophy. As such, focus on similarities in the dialogue with other religions may certainly bring about some degree of growth insofar as it leads to a reawakening to the richness of one's own tradition.

Moreover, insofar as all similarities between religions are couched within different religious contexts, the meaning of particular teachings and practices is never seamlessly the same, and these differences also come into play in the dialogue between religions. Even when understood from within a different religious context, the teachings and practices of a religion tend to preserve at least some of their original meaning and flavor. This comes into view in the practice of verbal translation the moment one detects a semantic slippage from the word by which a tradition expresses the meaning of an experience or insight, and to the word by which another tradition tries to take that original meaning into itself. The result is almost inevitably a hybrid term in which some of the original meaning makes its way into a new language while that new language is changed to the degree that it admits a certain newness. In the inculturation of Christianity in non-Western cultures, indigenous religious terms have often been used to express the Christian message, thereby also often enhancing and at times even challenging it.[31]

Even though the attitude of hospitality toward truth in similarity may thus lead to a certain degree of religious growth, it still falls short of an open and reciprocal exchange between religions. Insofar as the other religion is viewed as a mirror of one's own, dialogue remains narrow, devoid of much challenge or surprise. One of the main critiques of this type of hospitality, and of the attitude of inclusivism in which it appears, is that it tends toward a domestication of the truth of the other religion. This is clearly expressed in Gavin D'Costa's account of what transpires in inclusivist approaches to other religions:

> If religious traditions are properly to be considered in their unity of practice and theory, and in their organic interrelatedness, then such "totalities" cannot simply be dismembered into parts (be they doctrines, practices, images, or music) which are then taken up and "affirmed" by inclusivists, for the parts will always relate to the whole and will take their meaning only in this organic context. Hence, what is included from a religion being engaged with is not really that religion per se, but a reinterpretation of that tradition in so much as that which is included is now included within a different paradigm such that its meaning and utilization within that new paradigm can only perhaps bear some analogical resemblance to its meaning and utilization within its original paradigm.[32]

This process of domestication of the religious other may thus be seen to erase religious differences, thereby minimizing the opportunities for learning from the other.

In judging the truth of another religion solely on the basis of one's own religious framework and norms, dialogue also tends to become a monologue, and part of a larger missionary agenda. Insofar as one's own religious tradition is regarded as the ultimate truth and the norm against which the truth of the other may be discerned, dialogue becomes primarily a means of rendering the other aware of the actual truth of its own tradition. Proposed as a matter of constructive criticism, this approach to dialogue involves presenting oneself and one's own tradition as the occasion by which the other religion can recognize and overcome its own errors and obscurities. As a matter of solidarity and compassion, it involves the promise to lift the truth of the other, itself imperfectly or incompletely understood, and bring it to its rightful place and full meaning. In short, one's own religion becomes the norm, not only for the meaning and truth of one's own religion, but also for that of the other. Thus, a dialogue between Christians and Hindus might take the form of Christians pointing out to Hindus that it was Gandhi's life of self-giving love (rather than, e.g., his worship of Ram or his vegetarianism) that reflected the highest truth, while Hindus might in turn attempt to convince Christians of the superiority of a figure such as Meister Eckhart over less congenial Christian figures. In such a dialogue, each tradition in fact speaks across the other, engaging the truth of the other only insofar as it fits one's own religious aspirations and system of beliefs. Here, the goal of dialogue would appear to be the edification of the other, rather than one's own enrichment and growth.

HOSPITALITY TOWARD DIFFERENCE

While hospitality or receptivity toward the truth of the other religion may be relatively effortless when limited to those teachings that are similar to one's own, hospitality in difference forms an important challenge to most religious traditions. It involves a recognition that there might be elements of truth in the other religion of which one's own tradition has no previous knowledge or understanding. This may lead to a questioning of the attitude of self-sufficiency and epistemic security that characterizes most religious traditions. It also challenges religions to account for the presence of distinctive truth in another religion and to determine its status relative to one's own. Is this truth to be regarded as autonomous or as somehow dependent on one's own religion? And how is one to discern the presence of truth in difference?

These two sets of questions are related, and answers to them line up in a manner that defines the basic positions on the matter. The affirmation of the autonomous nature of the truth of the other is generally consistent with a call to recognize the truth of the other on its own terms, while on the other hand the proposal that the truth of the other can be countenanced only according to the conditions of one's own tradition is consistent with a call to apply one's own criteria to such alien truth. The former position has generally come to be identified with pluralism and the latter with "open" inclusivism. We shall here attempt to ignore these labels and focus instead on the way in which religions — in this case Christianity — may come to open themselves to the possibility of finding truth in religious teachings and practices different from their own. Such openness often requires a great deal of theological creativity and hermeneutical effort. But it is only in discovering such

197

resources for affirming truth in difference that dialogue may lead to genuine change and growth.

Accounting for Truth in Difference

There is no denying that Christian teachings are not essentially predisposed to recognizing truth in teachings and practices that differ from its own. Christian faith in the fullness of truth and salvation in the person of Jesus Christ would indeed seem to leave little room for elements of distinctive truth beyond Christian revelation. While the understanding of the meaning of Christian revelation may grow and develop through time, all of the basic elements for such development are believed to be contained within the tradition. On some rare occasions, however, one may find texts — even official documents — suggesting the presence of distinctive truth in other religions. While Catholic theologians have debated the question of whether or not the Vatican II document *Nostra Aetate* recognizes the possibility of salvation in other religious traditions, few have paid much attention to the remarkable fact that the document expresses "high regard for the manner of life and conduct, the precepts and doctrines which, *although differing in many ways from her own teaching,* nevertheless often reflect a ray of that truth which enlightens all men."[33] This short clause thus appears to recognize the possible presence of truth in difference, thereby opening the way for constructive dialogue.

In coming to terms with the reality of religious pluralism and with the exigencies of genuine dialogue, Christian theologians have generally turned to the Trinity as the basis for recognizing truth in difference. While some (Jacques Dupuis and Gavin D'Costa) have focused primarily on the Holy Spirit, others (Mark Heim) take their bearings from the dynamic relationship among all three persons of the Trinity. Without denying the inseparability of the Spirit from the Son, Dupuis emphasizes the distinctive role of the Holy Spirit in an economy of salvation capable of admitting the presence of distinctive truth in other religions. "It is," he states, "from this permanent integrity and continued 'distinction' of the divine action of the Word that the possibility of a continuing action of the Word as such is derived, distinct from that which takes place through the humanity of Jesus Christ."[34] On this basis, Dupuis describes the relationship between Christianity and other religions as one of "mutual complementarity" by which "an exchange and a sharing of saving values may take place between Christianity and the other traditions and from which a mutual enrichment and transformation may ensue between the traditions themselves."[35]

Unlike Dupuis — and partly in reaction to him — D'Costa insists that the divine revelation in the Spirit is inseparable specifically from the historical incarnation in the person of Jesus Christ. Still, he too regards the Holy Spirit as the basis for recognizing the presence of genuine truth and goodness in other religions. Though the working of the Holy Spirit in other religions cannot, according to D'Costa, denote the presence of any new revelation in them, it can express itself distinctively according to the different forms in which the grace of God works in other religions. And this may lead to a "non-identical repetition of the revelation which is given"[36] and to a "mutual fulfillment" between religions:

> If one were to retain and utilize the category of fulfillment in a very careful sense, then it is not only the other religions that are fulfilled (and in one sense, radically transformed) in their preparation being completed through Christianity, but also Christianity itself that is

fulfilled in receiving the gift of God that the Other might bear, self-consciously or not.[37]

As distinct from the positions of Dupuis and D'Costa, Heim's focus on the inner complexity of the triune God grounds an approach that sets out first to avoid reducing the religious ends of all traditions to one and the same goal. It is an interesting achievement of Heim's work that it emphasizes the distinctiveness not only of the ultimate religious ends of every religion but also of the teachings and practices leading to such ends, and yet grounds the capacity — even the desire — to do so in something as quintessentially Christian as Trinitarian theology. For Heim, the very dynamism of the Trinity models and endorses an affirmation of the integrity and truth of these diverse religious ends, each of which must be regarded as "an intensified realization of one dimension of God's offered relation with us."[38] Each of the distinctive religious ends may thus contain elements of truth that have not yet been integrated or explored within the Christian tradition. As such "Christians need humble apprenticeship to other religions in regard to dimensions of the triune life that those faiths grasp with profound depth."[39]

Now as far as each of these Trinitarian models goes toward opening the Christian tradition to the distinctive truth of other religions, it must be clear that none actually affirms the equality or equivalence of the truth of other religions. It should also be pointed out that openness toward the truth of other religion entails a certain qualification. In the end, Dupuis, for example, comes to speak of an *"asymmetrical"* complementarity,[40] while D'Costa's notion of "mutual fulfillment" does not indicate anything like complete reciprocity between religions, but rather the possibility for Christianity *too* to be fulfilled by learning from what it finds in the other.

The force of a Christian center of gravity can be felt elsewhere in D'Costa's account of dialogue. While seeking to attend to the "auto-interpretation" of religious traditions, he nonetheless eventually concedes that on his analysis all that can be hoped for is that the Christian "hetero-interpretation" (interpretation of the truth of a tradition from a perspective outside of it) might sometimes coincide with their auto-interpretation. A similar force is noticeable in Heim's position. While he plainly does attempt to grant the maximum amount of distinctive truth to the different religious goals of each tradition, in the end his model must set a recognizably Christian theological limit on that effort. Whereas every religious tradition of course regards its own goal as "ultimate," from within a Christian perspective, as Heim himself observes, those ends can be regarded only as "penultimate."[41] Moreover, given the fact that one thus always views penultimates from a perspective that must be considered ultimate, it is probably not by chance that there is in his work little discussion of the problem of conflicts or irreconcilability among the differing religious ends, as well as among their attendant teachings and practices.

None of this serves to discredit the Trinitarian models for dialogue, but only to draw attention to a point where the theological impetus for openness, hospitality, and finally growth becomes precisely that: theological. Their important differences aside, each of these models outlines and exemplifies the creative possibilities to be found within the tradition itself for recognizing the presence of distinctive truth beyond its own boundaries. And though the recognition of the truth of the other may not fully coincide with the self-understanding of the other, still the appreciable movement that can be made in that direction is already enough to stimulate a positive attitude toward newness or difference, and thus a real chance for growth.

Normativity and Difference

If religions are able to recognize some degree of truth in difference, the question remains how that truth is to be discerned. The issue of normativity is contested in the dialogue between religions. Out of concern for the equality and integrity of all religions, some have come to reject the legitimacy of all religion-specific criteria of truth, or the process of subjecting the teachings of one religion to the criteria of another. Instead, they propose criteria that are neutral or common to all. John Hick, for example, proposes as such a criterion the degree to which a particular teaching or practice "makes possible the transformation of human experience from self-centeredness to Reality-centeredness,"[42] while Paul Knitter centers his judgment of the truth of religion on the extent to which it promotes "eco-human well-being."[43] Perhaps sensing that these notions are too abstract to be joined to specific religious criteria, Roger Haight has developed the notion of "mutual normativity," arguing that "Christians may regard Jesus as the normative revelation of God, while at the same time being convinced that God is also revealed normatively elsewhere."[44] While this may be true from within a generally descriptive account of religious normativity, it is difficult to see how the religious criteria of another religion may become normative for one's own. Moreover, it cannot be denied that in a dialogue between religious traditions, religious criteria will always take precedence over neutral ones, and neutral criteria will be normative only insofar as they correspond with religious ones. For believers, religious norms are, after all, derived from divine revelation or sacred teachings and not from human discretion or from a lowest or even highest common religious denominator.

Resistance to the idea of confessional criteria of truth or religious normativity often lies in the fact that it tends to religious arrogance, subjecting the truth of one religion completely to the criteria of another, thereby precluding any genuine dialogue or growth. However, the notion of normativity may be understood in a more dynamic and open way. Rather than representing the fixed and final truth against which the teachings of other religions may be judged, religious norms may themselves be open to change and growth and represent a minimum, rather than a maximum, criterion of truth. Roger Haight, for example, proposes distinguishing a "positive" norm that "positively rules out what does not agree with it" and thus "implicitly denies alternatives" from negative norms that rule out "only those alternatives which contradict it."[45] The latter leaves considerable room for hospitality to truth in difference, insofar as any teaching or practice that is not directly opposed to, or not discontinuous with, one's own basic religious norms may be considered as possibly true. While from a Christian perspective the person of Jesus Christ is thus the *norma normans* (Dupuis),[46] this normativity may well permit Christian hospitality to a wide variety of religious practices and beliefs, from the Muslim names for God to the Confucian cardinal virtues, from the Hindu practice of yoga to the Buddhist notion of the *bodhisattva,* all of which do not in and of themselves contradict the basic teaching and conception of the person of Jesus Christ.

The distinction between positive and negative norms may be complemented with a distinction between static and dynamic approaches to the normativity of one's own tradition. Religious norms are often regarded as fixed and final. Etched in stone — fixed in timeless doctrines and unchangeable ritual gestures — one's norms are then regarded as the immutable criteria against which the world and other religions are judged. Against this, a more dynamic understanding of normativity favors the notion that one's own basic set of normative principles may evolve and indeed improve over time. As such, while representing the basic criterion against which the truth of the other religion is discerned, dialogue may itself also lead to a deepened understanding of the criterion itself. Insofar as dialogue may allow for the recognition of teachings that are not in contradiction with one's own, these teachings may in turn come to affect the understanding of one's own criteria. If, for example, the Buddhist Madhyamika philosophy is judged compatible or not incompatible with Christianity, dialogue with this philosophical tradition might significantly affect the Christian understanding of the meaning of Jesus and of his teachings.[47]

Considered together, the distinction between positive and negative normativity and the distinction between static and dynamic normativity — or rather the possibility of focusing on negative, dynamic normativity as a central component of dialogue — defines a hospitality that does extend beyond one's own established beliefs to truth in difference, but not without limit. The Christian engaged in genuine and vital dialogue does have at her disposal resources for at least considering the possibility of truth in principles and practices that remain beyond her Christian reach, but only insofar as they are not evidently discontinuous with, let alone opposed to, what can be reasonably extrapolated from her basic beliefs. This leaves aside numerous teachings and practices that are either incompatible with or irrelevant for her own Christian tradition as she understands it. Such teachings and practices may commonly relate to the particular symbolic and ritual expressions that distinguish one tradition from the other (names and images of gods, dietary rules, commemorative religious festivals and feasts). But they may also involve teachings that are directly mutually exclusive (such as the eternity or temporality of the soul, etc.). There may be relatively few religious beliefs that must be considered as radically incompatible. And religious texts and teachings tend to be hermeneutically flexible, as well as open to forms of interpretation far beyond those which have been explored within any particular religion. Yet every true dialogue must also come to terms with the reality of fundamental religious differences and the existence of teachings and practices that are unlikely ever to become the occasion for change. Part of the art of dialogue must surely consist in a capacity to recognize and set aside the latter, so as to devote oneself more fully to what remains.

Dialogue and Growth

If hospitality toward truth in difference may lead to growth, it remains to be seen what types of religious change and growth one may reasonably envision through the process of dialogue. It is of course impossible and against the very grain of dialogue to determine a priori the possible outcomes of any particular dialogue. The parameters of growth will always depend on the particular context and focus of any dialogue. But allowing for the necessary vigilance against what is irrelevant or opposed to one's own basic convictions, there are a number of avenues along which growth may exceed both the dull abstraction and mutual ethical edification so often envisioned in interreligious dialogue.

First, hospitality to truth in difference may lead to a more profound self-understanding. That is to say, it may carry one beyond an enhanced awareness of the specificity or the particularity of one's own religion to a genuinely new understanding of what one is, now informed by the teachings of the other. This may have a humbling effect on those who undergo it and come to recognize with new and greater lucidity that at least some of what was previously thought to be unique turns out to have any number of correlatives elsewhere. But more than this, it may also yield an enhanced capacity for engagement of one's authentic identity and, indeed, responsibility. "In the recognition of its limits," writes Stanislas Breton, "Christianity [or any other religion] regains a precision of its outline, and by that very fact the possibility of an effective presence in the world."[48] However, the new self-understanding gained through dialogue may involve not only a sharper view of what was always there to see (though occluded through the power of habit or arrogance). It may also involve radically new elements, provided by the teachings of other religions. For example, whereas the Christian belief in the uniqueness of Jesus has traditionally been understood purely from within the Christian conception of salvation history, the dialogue with Judaism, Islam, Hinduism, and Buddhism may provide Christian theology with new accents, connotations, and even full-fledged conceptions of what remains the central category of Christian faith. The dialogue with Judaism, for instance, has called for new reflection on the distinctiveness of the person and teachings of Jesus in comparison with other charismatic prophets of his time, whereas the dialogue with Hinduism has shed new light on the relationship between his humanity and his divinity.

A second, and related area of possible growth is that of an increased capacity for healthy self-criticism. Of course, religions have long mustered critical self-reflection in response to a confrontation with various social and historical realities, but it is through the encounter with religious others that specifically religious lacunae or distortions may come most easily to light. This may include a sudden realization or direct awareness of the ways in which one's religious teachings have contributed, consciously or not, to the suffering and denigration of other religions. Much of the dialogue between religions to date has indeed focused on the healing of historical memories. But it may also entail critical awareness of certain areas of under-developed insight and expression within one's own religion. Here the lesson can be made almost automatically, since it will arise from a contrast between areas where the other tradition appears vital and sophisticated while one's own is plainly wanting. Thus, for instance, a widespread commitment to social action in the teaching or practices of one religion may, when placed alongside a comparative lack of that commitment in the other, spur members of the latter to probe their tradition for untapped resources. Likewise, the advanced spiritual practices of one may shed light on the other's lack of attention to particular forms of spiritual life, long since forgotten and submerged beneath other practices, or maybe simply never developed. The powerful self-critique of one religion may also serve the other in this way. This may be seen in the ways in which forms of feminist critique developed within one tradition have inspired feminists in other religions. Or in the ways in which the critique of certain forms of mysticism within one religion may inspire critical self-reflection within another.[49]

In addition to enhanced self-understanding and critical self-reflection, the growth resulting from interreligious dialogue may on some occasions involve the integration of genuinely new religious insights and practices. The fact of interreligious borrowing of symbols, teachings, and ritual practices is of course nothing new. But while in the course of history, such religious appropriation has typically occurred unconsciously and without recognition of the other religion, dialogue between religions offers a chance for more deliberate and reflective integration of religious teachings and practices originating in other traditions. This may involve the adoption of new forms of prayer and practice or the integration of new categories of interpretation. And, at least occasionally, a borrowed category or practice may transform the tradition in which it arrives. A vivid and well known example of this is the Christian relation to the Buddhist notion of "emptiness" (*śūnyatā*). For various Christian thinkers, this term has become the basis for a purification of traditional Christian conceptions of God (O'Leary, Cobb), the foundation for a new Christology (Keenan), or the name of an insight that sheds new light on the Christian notion of kenosis (Abe). As Cobb points out, it is through the integration of such categories that "our own heritage may be illumined in new ways" and that we may come to a "richer and purer grasp of the meaning of the God we have come to know through Jesus Christ."[50] While the Christian concept of God may be purified and chastened by encounter with a notion as profound as the Buddhist notion of emptiness, one can scarcely expect Christian theology to go all the way to abandoning its belief in a personal Creator God. Whether or not the effort to learn from what is expressed in the Buddhist category meets its limit precisely there, it is incontestable that religious growth of that sort certainly will meet some such limit eventually. On the other hand, those limits are probably far less predetermined than we are often inclined to think, and the hermeneutical possibilities of religions always exceed their present self-understanding.

◆ ◆ ◆

In the second half of the twentieth century, at the height of the burgeoning excitement about interreligious dialogue, some of the pioneers of this dialogue nurtured high hopes that such dialogue might eventually lead to a convergence of religions. Inspired by Teilhard de Chardin's notion that "everything that rises must converge," Frank de Graeve proposed that "convergence" did not mean annihilation of differences, but separate and distinct inner conversion of religions, along lines that draw ever closer without actually meeting.[51] Perhaps Bede Griffiths had something similar in mind when he suggested that "in each religion, as you go deeper into it, you converge on the original source."[52] Griffiths did not anticipate or hope for the dissolution of all religious differences any more than de Graeve. But both of them did see the differences between religions as "a sign of the creative abundance that is supposed to enhance unity, and not necessarily a sign of particularism that precludes it."[53]

Few would still share the optimism of these pioneers of the dialogue. After some decades of significant effort at interreligious dialogue, there is little noticeable growth within religious traditions. In fact, one too often notes a contrary tendency to sharpen and reassert the boundaries of one's own distinctive identity in the face of religious diversity. Interpersonal hospitality between individuals belonging to different religions does not often translate into doctrinal hospitality. The meeting between leaders or representatives of different religions often has only a ceremonial function, and initiatives toward more serious and searching dialogue are often met with passivity, indifference, or even active resistance.

Yet as good people of faith know well, not every fruit is immediately visible. It need not be otherwise with dialogue. In the meantime, individuals from a large and growing number of traditions engage in theology of religions and comparative theology with a view to pursuing avenues for hospitality toward the distinctive truth of other religions and to exploring both the vital possibilities and the basic limits of dialogue for their respective traditions. Their efforts may seem daunting no less than promising. Beyond the immediate task of simply understanding one another (and there is not always anything simple about it), they meet each religious text and tradition as an occasion to stretch the imagination and to consider the possibility of forms of religious experience hitherto unexplored within their own traditions. And where they succeed, however briefly and however minimally, they exhibit an interreligious hospitality that can inspire others. With the inspiration comes the challenge: the actual discovery of truth in the distinctive teachings of other religions may itself put pressure on traditional religious concepts of hospitality or the refusal thereof. Successful dialogue, after all, is an incitement to bolder efforts. To make progress — to grow — is to immediately push the limits of religious hospitality toward still greater openness to truth in difference, which is also to say, to a truth that makes a difference.

CONCLUSION

Each of the five conditions I have identified for dialogue challenges traditional religious self-understanding, or — for various reasons — falls short of perfect realization. In the Christian case, some conditions appear to be directly at odds with traditional teachings, while others create institutional tensions or else test the very limits of understanding itself. With regard specifically to doctrinal or epistemic humility, there is no mistaking a serious challenge to the traditional belief in the ultimate and final truth of Christian teachings. Such belief does not typically include a sense of the limited and finite nature of one's own teachings and practices or openness to change or growth. Humility, as commonly understood, characterizes an attitude to be adopted toward, rather than about, the truth of one's own tradition. Rather than doctrinal humility, it thus tends to generate doctrinal pride and attachment to the truth of one's religious teachings and practices. Insofar as such attachment defines religious commitment, commitment to a particular religious tradition also seems to be at odds with the attitude of openness necessary for dialogue. Exceptions notwithstanding, strong identification with a particular religious tradition seems to bring about an attitude of indifference or hostility toward other religions, while profound interest in other religions often derives from or leads to greater religious autonomy. The need for a proper balance between openness and commitment thus places considerable pressure upon individuals engaged in dialogue as well as on religious traditions themselves.

If dialogue presupposes some degree of interconnection or commonality, it has become far from evident that such common ground exists, or that religions agree on a common ground or goal for dialogue. Some have come to focus on social and political challenges facing all religions alike, while others locate the unity of religions in an ineffable mystical experience or in an ultimate reality transcending all religions. Neither, however, seems to provide a basis for sustained dialogue. While in the former case, dialogue tends to last only as long as those external challenges are in place, the latter approach severely limits the impulse for dialogue since all religious teachings are regarded as but finite expressions of an incommunicable experience or reality.

The need for mutual understanding in interreligious dialogue entails both factual knowledge and some degree of empathic resonance with the other. Whereas the former may be acquired through extensive study, it has become clear that the latter is rarely if ever perfectly realized. Some of the meaning and experience of particular teachings and practices always escapes those lacking the dimension of faith. All empathic resonance with the religious other is thus at best approximate or analogical, and one's understanding of the religious other never complete. But the greatest obstacle to genuine dialogue lies in the recognition of truth in distinctive teachings or practices of the other. Such hospitality to truth in difference is necessary if dialogue is to include the possibility of growth and change. However, it may also threaten the epistemic confidence of any religion or suggest the incompleteness of one's own teachings or practices. As a result, hospitality is generally confined to those teachings and practices that are similar to or the same as one's own, thereby limiting the chances for genuine growth.

All of this may lead to the pessimistic conclusion that a constructive dialogue between religions is, at the end of the day, impossible. At the very least, it may shed some light on the reasons why interreligious dialogue remains the provenance of a relatively small group of individuals, why those individuals are often viewed with a certain degree of suspicion by mainstream traditions, and why the fruits of interreligious dialogue do not often come back to nourish the religions themselves. There is still a widespread perception within most religious traditions that dialogue is an extraneous activity that does not derive from or touch upon their own self-understanding. In that understanding, it may be practiced as a form of mutual edification or as an expression of sympathy and solidarity, but without any essential effect on the inner reality of religions.

These concerns notwithstanding, I hope to have shown that religions may contain various resources that may move them closer to the fulfillment of the conditions for genuine dialogue. In focusing mainly on Christianity, it has become clear that those resources are to be found both in religious teachings and in the hermeneutical principles that are brought to bear on them. The Christian virtue of humility may not necessarily imply doctrinal humility, but it does offer a basis for the development of a humbler attitude toward doctrinal formulations. To be sure, humility is in the first place a spiritual attitude, an orientation toward the realization of union with God. Yet thought through to the end, it is the very realization of the ineffability of the ultimate reality that brings into perspective the contingency of all finite expressions of that reality, whereupon dialogue finds a basis that is both spiritual and theological.

As for the tension between openness and commitment, its resolution lies primarily in the realization of the other conditions for dialogue. Genuine commitment to a particular religious tradition becomes less of a challenge if that tradition is itself oriented toward dialogue with other religions. And this in turn may come about through the efforts of individuals who, while engaged in serious dialogue with other religions, remain firmly committed to their own religious traditions and to the realization of the conditions for dialogue.

While the interconnection with other religions is often sought outside and beyond the self-understanding of any particular religion, I have tried to demonstrate that any religious conception of connection with other religions in fact forms a proper ground for dialogue. If, indeed, one comes to an awareness that the teachings of the other religion are somehow related to one's own, the engagement of such teachings becomes a matter of internal necessity. The Christian belief that the grace of God is operative throughout creation and in particular in a religious search for truth renders the search for traces of such grace a theological imperative. Different religions thus operate on the basis of very different, and at times mutually incompatible, conceptions of interconnection. But the particularity of various grounds and motives need not as such impede genuine dialogue.

Even though one may never presume to attain perfect understanding of the religious other, the very attempt to enter into the religious worldview and experience of the other may widen one's religious horizon and lead to the discovery of new and at times profoundly enriching forms of religious life. Profound resonance with certain teachings or practices of the other religion may in fact point not only to similarities with one's own religion, but also at times to areas in which one's own religion may be found wanting and in need of growth. The possibility of such growth, however, will always remain predicated upon the degree to which a religion is able to recognize truth in difference. While such radical religious hospitality remains a challenge for most religious traditions, I have demonstrated the possibility of realizing such hospitality, even within Christianity.

Since my focus has been largely and by personal necessity on the situation of dialogue in Christianity, I should not fail to recognize that each religion faces different obstacles for dialogue, and that each will have to find within its own teachings and practices the resources for overcoming them. Some conditions may in fact be more congenial to some religions than to others. While Buddhism, for instance, suffers relatively little from a lack of epistemic humility, Hinduism has traditionally exhibited a comparatively high degree of hospitality toward the truth of other religions, giving it the reputation of being a particularly tolerant religion. That said, there can be no doubt that dialogue will require some degree of hermeneutical effort and religious creativity from every religious tradition. Some of the same hermeneutical principles may apply to various religious traditions. But the way in which these principles are worked out in the context of particular worldviews and teachings will of course differ from one religion to the next. In the process of dialogue, religions may also learn from and be inspired by the ways in which other religions have overcome their own respective barriers to dialogue. Moreover, such dialogue may itself lead to mutual critique and to a sharper realization of some of the religious beliefs and attitudes that inhibit an open and constructive exchange with other religions.

The conditions for dialogue developed in this book do not present fixed and absolute principles that must be fully operative in a tradition for dialogue of any kind to be possible. They represent what I consider to be the ideal conditions or ultimate horizon of any fruitful and constructive dialogue. It is almost certainly the case that they are never fully satisfied in the dialogue between religions. But any degree of fulfillment of these conditions may already allow for some form of constructive exchange. Rather than a matter of possibility or impossibility, the capacity for dialogue is thus itself a process, involving, indeed calling for, continuous critical self-examination and a creative retrieval of resources that may open the tradition to the religious other and to growth in the truth.

NOTES

Acknowledgments

1. The original seed for this work was published in the volume *The Concept of God in Global Dialogue,* ed. Werner Jeanrond and Aasluv Lande (Maryknoll, N.Y.: Orbis Books, 2005), 3–18. Some of the ideas contained in later chapters were presented at conferences or as invited lectures in Antwerp, Seattle, Tokyo, Washington, Melbourne, Bilbao, and Boston.

Introduction

1. See the articles by Leonard Swidler, John Cobb, Paul Knitter, and Monika Hellwig in Leonard Swidler et al., *Death or Dialogue? From the Age of Monologue to the Age of Dialogue* (London: SCM Press, and Philadelphia: Trinity Press International, 1990); Jacques Dupuis, *Toward a Christian Theology of Religious Pluralism* (Maryknoll, N.Y.: Orbis Books, 1997); Raimon Panikkar, *The Intra-Religious Dialogue* (New York: Paulist Press, 1999); and most recently the majority of articles collected in the volume *How to Conquer the Barriers to Intercultural Dialogue,* ed. Christine Timmerman and Barbara Segaert (Berlin: Peter Lang, 2005).

2. For some more recent discussion of these methodological issues, see Russell T. McCutcheon, ed., *The Insider-Outsider Problem in the Study of Religion: A Reader* (London: Cassell, 1999); Kimberly Patton and Benjamin Ray, eds., *A Magic Still Dwells: Comparative Religion in the Postmodern Age* (Berkeley: University of California Press, 2000); Jonathan Smith, *Relating Religion* (Chicago:

University of Chicago Press, 2004); Jeppe Jensen, *The Study of Religion in a New Key* (Aarhus, Denmark: Aarhus University Press, 2003).

Chapter One / Humility

1. "Human Personality," 1942–1943, in *Simone Weil: An Anthology,* ed. Sian Miles (New York: Weidenfeld & Nicolson, 1986), 67.

2. This radical understanding is implied in the original Latin root of "humility" in the term *humus,* earth, which also has etymological associations with the word "human."

3. This is evident in religions based on universal claims to truth. But it also manifests itself in religions with claims limited to a particular people or to particular ritual functions. Within its own area of religious expertise, each religious belief and practice lays claim, implicitly or explicitly, to ultimacy and superiority over all rival forms of religious expression.

4. Raimon Panikkar, *The Intra-religious Dialogue* (New York: Paulist Press, 1999), 37.

5. *The Philokalia,* vol. 1, trans. G. E. H. Palmer, P. Sherrard, and K. Ware (London: Faber and Faber, 1979), 341.

6. *Sermon 142* (Commentary on John 14:16), par. 11, in *The Works of Saint Augustine,* a Translation for the 21st Century Series, vol. 3/4, trans. E. Hill (Brooklyn, N.Y.: New City Press, 1990), 421. When asked about the Christian way or discipline, Augustine also writes: "This way is in the first place, humility; in the second place, humility; in the third place, humility.... As often as you ask me about the Christian religion's norm of conduct, I choose to give no other answer than: humility." See *Letter* 118, 3, 22, quoted in *The Rule of Saint Augustine with Introduction and Commentary,* ed. T. J. Van Bavel (Kalamazoo, Mich.: Cistercian Publications, 1996), 56.

7. Bernard of Clairvaux, *The Steps of Humility,* trans. G. B. Burch (Cambridge, Mass.: Harvard University Press, 1940).

8. *The Rule of St. Benedict,* trans. J. McCann (Westminster, Md.: Newman Press, 1952), chap. 7, p. 45.

9. *The Steps of Humility,* chap. 4, 14, p. 149.

10. "Gravity and Grace" in *Simone Weil: An Anthology,* 83.

11. Saint Augustine, *City of God,* preface to Book I.

12. Brian Daley, *To Be More Like Christ: The Background and Implications of the "Three Kinds of Humility"* (St. Louis: Seminar on Jesuit Spirituality, 1995), 35. C. S. Lewis points to the virtue of humility as the very basis for the distinctiveness of Christian morals. In *Mere Christianity* (London: HarperCollins Publishers, 2001; original 1942), 121.

13. It has been noted that this is the only beatitude that promises the blessing in the present, rather than the future, perhaps reflecting the fact that humility brings with it its own reward. See Jean-Louis Chrétien, *Le regard de l'amour* (Paris: Desclée, 2000), 26. Chrétien himself also quotes Bernard in *In advantu Domini, Sermo 4, Opera,* ed. J. Leclercq (Rome, 1966), 4:185.

14. *The Rule of Saint Benedict,* 39. His twelve steps of humility are: guarding against evil desires, surrender to the will of God, obedience, patient endurance, humble confession, contentment, self-humiliation, submission to the Rule, silence, self-control, humility in speech, and humility in posture.

15. Gregory the Great, *Regula Pastoralis,* Part III, chap. 17.

16. In "The Talks of Instruction," 23, *Meister Eckhart,* trans. R. Blackney (New York: Harper & Row, 1941), 37.

17. *The Cloud of Unknowing,* ed. James Walsh (New York: Paulist Press, 1981), 151.

18. Chrétien, *Le regard de l'amour,* 50.

19. In *The Imitation of Christ,* book 2, ed. C. L. Fitzpatrick (New York: Catholic Book Publishing, 1993), chap. 2.

20. In *The Life of Saint Teresa of Avila by Herself,* trans. J. M. Cohen (New York: Penguin Books, 1957), chap. 15, 108.

21. In *The Ascent of Mount Carmel,* book II, chap. 24, 7. In *The Collected Works of St. John of the Cross,* trans. K. Kavanaugh and O. Rodriguez (Washington: Institute for Carmelite Studies, 1979), 191.

22. *Summa Theologica* II-II, q. 161, art. 5.

23. Ibid., II-II, q. 161, art. 6.

24. Sebastian Carlson, *The Virtue of Humility* (Dubuque: W. C. Brown, 1952), 100. Carlson attributes this understanding of the extent of humility to Thomas Aquinas.

25. Thomas à Kempis places the following words in the mouth of Jesus: "I became the lowliest and the least of human beings, so that you might overcome your pride through My humility. You who are but ashes, learn to obey; you who are but the dust of the earth, learn to humble yourself and to bow beneath the feet of others for My sake. Learn to break your own will and to give yourself to all subjection." *The Imitation of Christ,* book 3, chap. 13, 127–28.

26. G. Ganss, S.J. *The Spiritual Exercises of St. Ignatius* (Chicago: Loyola Press, 1992), n. 167.

27. Chrétien, *Le regard de l'amour,* 17.

28. Ibid., 18.

29. Rémi Brague, "L'anthropologie de l'humilité" in *Saint Bernard et la Philosophie,* ed. R. Brague (Paris: Presses Universitaires de France, 1993), 140.

30. *The Steps of Humility,* chap. 4, 15.

31. Ibid., chap. 1.

32. *The Cloud of Unknowing,* 181.

33. Book 1, chapter 2, 4 (p. 18).

34. Chrétien, *Le regard de l'amour,* 14.

35. *The Steps of Humility,* chap. 4, 14.

36. Thomas à Kempis, *The Imitation of Christ,* book 1, chaps. 2, 4.

37. That said, it may fairly be asked whether in the present context of religious pluralism, other religions are not sometimes overtly, and as it were a priori, idealized, as if to compensate for the negative distortions of the past. This sort of distortion no less than the other, except perhaps less painfully, inhibits genuine dialogue. After all, most religions contain a complex mixture of good and evil, holiness and corruption.

38. *The Steps of Humility,* 205.

39. Ibid., chap 2, 5.

40. *Sermon* 142, par. 12, in *The Works of Saint Augustine.*

41. *The Steps of Humility,* chap. 3, 16.

42. James Fodor, *Christian Hermeneutics: Paul Ricoeur and the Refiguring of Theology* (Oxford: Clarendon Press, 1995), 20.

43. *The Steps of Humility,* chap. 6, 19.

44. "He who is caught up, supported by someone else's strength, not his own, not knowing whither he is being borne, cannot be proud of himself either wholly or partly, since he does nothing, either by himself or with assistance." In *The Steps of Humility,* chap. 8, 22.

45. *The Steps of Humility,* chap. 7, 21.

46. Ibid., chap. 8, 23.

47. *Opera* 3193, quoted in *The Steps of Humility,* 112.

48. The role of monastic hospitality in the dialogue between religions is developed by Pierre de Béthune, one of the pivotal figures in the inter-monastic dialogue, in his book *Par la foi et l'hospitalité* (Clerlande: Publications de Saint-André, 1997).

49. In the 1993 document evaluating the history of inter-monastic dialogue, humility is indeed mentioned as one of the monastic virtues (besides discernment, hospitality, and simplicity) relevant to dialogue with other religions. *Contemplation et Dialogue Interreligieux: Repere et perspectives dans l'expérience des moines* (1993).

50. Bede Griffiths, *The Marriage of East and West* (Springfield, Ill.: Templegate Publishers, 1982), 43.

51. Abhishiktananda, *Saccidananda: A Christian Approach to Advaitic Experience* (Delhi: ISPCK, 1974), 19.

52. "Quod ubique, quod semper, quod ad omnibus," expression attributed to Vincent of Lérins (434).

53. J. H. Newman, *An Essay on the Development of Christian Doctrine* (Notre Dame, Ind.: Notre Dame University Press, 1989; original text 1878).

54. Vatican II document *Unitatis Redintegratio,* 11. In A. Flannery, ed., *Vatican Council II* (Northport, N.Y.: Costello Publishing Company, 1975), 462.

55. Vatican II document *Lumen Gentium,* 25. In ibid., 380. The notion of infallibility was introduced in the Vatican I document *Pastor Aeternum* (1870). It is said to apply to the Roman Pontiff, "when as supreme pastor of and teacher of all the faithful he proclaims in an absolute decision a doctrine pertaining to faith and morals" and

by the body of bishops "when, together with Peter's successor, they exercise the supreme teaching office." *Lumen Gentium*, 25.

56. This is Francis Sullivan's rendering of the expression *obsequium religiosum* in *Magisterium: Teaching Authority in the Catholic Church* (New York: Paulist Press, 1983), 164.

57. St. Augustine, *Of True Religion*, xxv, 47, trans. J. H. S. Burleigh (Chicago: Henry Regnery, 1959), 43.

58. Bernard Lonergan, *Method in Theology* (New York: Herder and Herder, 1972), 299.

59. It bears remembering that Bernard of Clairvaux, author of *The Steps of Humility*, was also one of the most vocal and forceful advocates of the Crusades.

60. Lonergan, *Method in Theology*, 325. This does not deprive doctrines of their absolute status and authority, since, as Lonergan puts it, "they are not just data but expressions of truths and, indeed, of truths that, were they not revealed by God, could not be known by man." Lonergan refers here to the Vatican I document *Dei Filius*, which speaks of the *causa cognoscendi*: what God has revealed and the church has infallibly declared is true; and the *causa essendi*, implying that the meaning of a dogma is not a datum but a truth.

61. In *Magisterium*, 81.

62. Hans Urs von Balthasar, *Truth Is Symphonic: Aspects of Christian Pluralism* (San Francisco: Ignatius Press, 1987), 55.

63. I have attempted such an engagement between Christianity and Hinduism in C. Cornille, *The Guru in Indian Catholicism: Ambiguity or Opportunity of Inculturation?* (Leuven: Peeters Press, 1991).

64. George Lindbeck, *The Nature of Doctrine, Religion, and Theology in a Postliberal Age* (Philadelphia: Westminster Press, 1984), 18.

65. Ibid., 80.

66. Ibid., 59.

67. Ibid., 61.

68. *Redemptoris Missio*, 18.

69. Ibid., 20.

70. Ibid., 56.

71. Jacques Dupuis, *Toward a Christian Theology of Religious Pluralism* (Maryknoll, N.Y.: Orbis Books, 1997), 346.

72. Paul Knitter, *Jesus and the Other Names* (Maryknoll, N.Y.: Orbis Books, 1996), 113.

73. Afraid that it may lead to radical relativism, some church documents have come to reject this position, insisting that "the kingdom of God cannot be separated from Christ and from the Church." See *Redemptoris Missio*, 18, *Dominus Iesus*, 18.

74. Gavin D'Costa, *The Meeting of Religions and the Trinity* (Maryknoll, N.Y.: Orbis Books, 2000), 130.

75. Nicholas of Cusa, *On Learned Ignorance*, 245, in *Nicholas of Cusa: Selected Spiritual Writings*, trans. Hugh Lawrence Bond (New York: Paulist Press, 1997), 197.

76. See Dupuis, *Toward a Christian Theology of Religious Pluralism*, 105–7.

77. *De Pace Fidei* I, 4. Roger Johnson argues that Cusanus in fact borrowed these conceptions of religious diversity from the Qur'an. In "The Beginnings of a Modern Theology of Religions: Nicholas of Cusa (1401–1464)," unpublished paper, read at the Boston Theological Institute, 2003.

78. John Hick, *God Has Many Names* (Philadelphia: Westminster Press, 1982), 94.

79. Michael Barnes, *Theology and the Dialogue of Religions* (Cambridge: Cambridge University Press, 2002), 245.

80. Karl Rahner, *Theological Investigations*, vol. 5 (London: Darton, Longman & Todd, 1966), 134.

81. Contrary to some, such as Albert von Ruville, who argued that it constitutes a uniquely Christian virtue. In his *Humility, the True Talisman* (London: Simpkin, Marshall, Hamilton, Kent & Co., 1913) he suggests that humility represents "another Christian Jewel which has endowed Christianity from the beginning with a degree of sublimity which no other religious organization on earth has ever attained" (xiv–xv).

82. B. Sot 1:1–2 V. 13ff./5A, quoted in Jacob Neusner, "Virtue in Formative Judaism," in *The Encyclopedia of Judaism*, ed.

J. Neusner, A. Avery-Peck, and W. Green (Leiden: Brill, 2000), 3:1467.

83. B. Pes 50A 3:7–8 II:4 B. Ibid., 1476.

84. Some therefore presume that the virtue of humility is distinctive to theistic traditions. Dietrich von Hildebrand, for example, argues that "it is only in our encounter with a personal God that we become fully aware of our condition as creatures, and fling from us the last particles of self-glory. The idealists who cherish ethical autonomy, the pantheists, the theosophists: these all are bent on escaping from subordination to an almighty Lord, and, consequently, from relinquishing a certain minimum sovereignty which flatters their pride." In *Humility, Wellspring of Virtue* (Manchester: Sophia Institute Press, 1949; reprint 1997), 24–25.

85. Further explicit references to humility may be found in chapters VII, XXVIII, LXI, LXVI, LXX, and LXXVIII.

86. See, for example, Valerie Saivings's famous critique of Niebuhr's discussion of the sin of pride in "The Human Situation: A Feminist View," in *Womanspirit Rising,* ed. Carol Christ and Judith Plaskow (San Francisco: Harper & Row), 1979.

87. F. Nietzsche, *The Genealogy of Morals,* first essay, xiv, trans. F. Golffing (New York: Doubleday, 1956), 180.

88. *The Dhammapada,* chapter 5, 14–15.

89. *Samyutta-nikaya* iii, 66.

90. Dalai Lama, *A Flash of Lightning in the Dark: A Guide to the Bodhisattva's Way of Life* (Boston: Shambala, 1994), 4.

91. Buddhaghosa, *The Visuddhimagga* III, 105. *The Path of Purification,* trans. Bhikkhu Nanamoli (Seattle: BPS Pariyatti Editions, 1991), 110.

92. In *The Bodhicaryavatara* 8, 140, trans. K. Crosby and A. Skilton (Oxford: Oxford University Press, 1995).

93. Dalai Lama, *A Flash of Lightning in the Dark,* 107.

94. *Madhyamikakārikāh,* chapter 13, stanza 8.

95. For a thorough discussion of this, see J. Garfield, *Empty Words: Buddhist Philosophy and Cross-Cultural Interpretation* (Oxford: Oxford University Press, 2002).

96. Shantideva, *The Bodhicaryavatara* 10, 2. "It is agreed that there are these two truths: the conventional and the ultimate. Reality is beyond the scope of intellection. Intellection is said to be conventional."

97. This very exercise is based on an awareness of the historical and cultural conditioning of all doctrinal language and on the attempt to expand one's own self-understanding through the use of philosophical frameworks other than the Greek or Hellenistic one in which the Christian doctrines were originally formulated.

98. John Keenan, *The Meaning of Christ: A Mahāyāna Theology* (Maryknoll, N.Y.: Orbis Books, 1989), 177.

99. Ibid., 203.

100. Joseph O'Leary, *Religious Pluralism and Christian Truth* (Edinburgh: Edinburgh University Press, 1996), 7.

101. Ibid., 127. See also his "Ultimacy and Conventionality in Religious Language" in *Religious Experience and the End of Metaphysics,* ed. J. Bloechl (Indianapolis: Indiana University Press, 2003).

102. Ibid., 251.

Chapter Two / Commitment

1. One of the most famous among these is *The Secret Doctrine,* published in 1889. It represents a highly idiosyncratic synthesis of teachings from various religious traditions.

2. For an in-depth study of New Age, see Christoph Bochinger, *"New Age" und moderne Religion: Religionswissenschaftlicher Perspektiven* (Gütersloh: Kaiser/Gütersloher Verlaghaus, 1994) and Wouter J. Hanegraaff, *New Age Religion and Western Culture* (Leiden: E. J. Brill, 1996).

3. Paul Heelas, *The New Age Movement* (Oxford: Blackwell Publishers, 1996), 155.

4. This expression was coined by the British sociologist Gracie Davie in her book *Religion in Britain since 1945: Believing without Belonging* (Oxford: Blackwell, 1994).

5. In his *Autobiography (The Story of My Experiments with Truth* [Boston: Beacon Press, 1957]) Gandhi criticizes various Hindu

ritual practices such as animal slaughter in service of the gods (235) and the veneration of Sadhus during the Kumbha Mela (389) as well as the various caste restrictions and prescriptions (393).

6. Ibid., 137.

7. Ibid., 452.

8. For some this is a temporary journey. There are many stories of individuals who, disgruntled with certain aspects of their own religion, have immersed themselves in other religious traditions, only to eventually find their way back to a single, final tradition — perhaps even the one where they began — enriched with new experiences and insight.

9. Lowell Streiker, *New Age Comes to Mainstreet* (Nashville: Abingdon Press, 1990), 46.

10. Peter Lemesurier, *This New Age Business* (Forres, Scotland: Findhorn Press, 1990), 185.

11. For a more in-depth analysis and discussion of multiple religious belonging, see Catherine Cornille, ed., *Many Mansions: Multiple Religious Belonging and Christian Identity* (Maryknoll, N.Y.: Orbis Books, 2002).

12. Jürgen Moltmann, "Is 'Pluralistic Theology' Useful?" in *Christian Uniqueness Reconsidered,* ed. Gavin D'Costa (Maryknoll, N.Y.: Orbis Books, 1990), 154.

13. In *Monopoly on Salvation?* (New York: Continuum, 2005), Jeannine Hill Fletcher rightly criticizes the way in which religious traditions have come to be hypostasized in discussions on religious plurality and dialogue. Fletcher uses feminist theory to argue for the recognition of difference within religions, and for the reality of "hybrid identities" determined not only by religion, but also by race, gender, economic status, etc. In her estimation, this more complex understanding of personal identity "allows for the partial identification of overlapping identities where a variety of identity features hold the potential for making connections" (91).

14. *Redemptoris Missio,* 55. The later document *Dialogue and Proclamation* reiterates the same notion that dialogue and proclamation are "intimately related but not interchangeable" (77).

15. *Redemptoris Missio,* 56.

16. *Dialogue and Proclamation*, 81.

17. Ibid., 82.

18. John Hick, "Christian Belief and Interfaith Dialogue" in John Hick, *God Has Many Names* (Philadelphia: Westminster Press, 1982), 117.

19. Raimon Panikkar, *The Intra-Religious Dialogue* (New York: Paulist Press, 1999), 62.

20. *An Apology for Apologetics*, 3.

21. See Sita Ram Goel, *Catholic Ashrams* (New Delhi: Voice of India, 1988), 3.

22. This term was coined and developed by Victor Turner in *The Forest of Symbols: Aspects of Ndembu Ritual* (Ithaca, N.Y.: Cornell University Press, 1967), 96ff.

23. Here, the concept has been developed primarily by Arnold van Gennep, who in his book *The Rites of Passage* (Chicago: University of Chicago Press, 1960) refers to rites of separation as "preliminal rites," those executed during the transitional stage as "liminal rites" and ceremonies of reintegration as "postliminal rites" (21).

24. Michael Amaladoss uses the term in the context of double religious belonging to refer to individuals who remain on the border between different religious communities and their distinctive symbolic universes, and who feel equally at ease in both religious communities. In "Le double appartenance religieuse" in *Vivre de plusieurs religions: Promesse ou illusion?* ed. D. Gira and J. Scheuer (Paris: Les Editions de l'Atelier, 2000), 52.

25. He became a priest in the Melkite Greek Catholic tradition in order to remain close to both Arab Christians and Muslims.

26. Panikkar's work *Christophany: The Fullness of Man* (Maryknoll, N.Y.: Orbis Books, 2004) is a case in point. Here, traditional Christian symbols and beliefs are reinterpreted mainly from the perspective of *Advaita Vedānta*.

27. This comes to the fore in his book *Love Meets Wisdom* (Maryknoll, N.Y.: Orbis Books, 1988) and is even more pronounced in his *Fire and Water* (Maryknoll, N.Y.: Orbis Books, 1996).

28. James Stuart, ed., *Swami Abhishiktananda: His Life Told through His Letters* (Delhi: ISPCK, 1989), 204–5.

29. *La montée au fond du Coeur: Le journal intime du moine chrétien-sannyasi hindou* (Paris: OEIL, 1986).

30. In this context, Lesslie Newbigin's distinction between "committed pluralism" and "agnostic pluralism" is especially helpful. While the latter refers to the belief that "truth is unknowable and that there are therefore no criteria by which different beliefs and different patterns of behavior may be judged," the former implies "the belief that truth can be known, not fully and completely, but in part and with increasing depth and range and coherence." Lesslie Newbigin, *A Word in Season: Perspectives on Christian World Mission* (Grand Rapids: Wm. Eerdmans, 1994), 168.

31. Leonard Swidler et al., *Death or Dialogue? From the Age of Monologue to the Age of Dialogue* (London: SCM Press, and Philadelphia: Trinity Press International, 1990), 64.

32. Francis Clooney, *Seeing through Texts: Doing Theology among the Srivaisnavas of South India* (Albany: SUNY Press, 1996), 296–311.

33. The controversy focused on whether these rites were purely civic in nature or whether they contained superstitious elements. The success of the Christian mission in China was seen to depend on the possibility of Chinese Christians to continue to practice some of their traditional rites. The controversy lasted for some two hundred years, and was finally settled in the 1742 Bull by Benedict XIV, *Ex Quo Singulari,* which severely limited the continued practice of the Chinese rites. For a history of the Chinese Rites controversy see George Minamiki, *The Chinese Rites Controversy* (Chicago: Loyola University Press, 1985).

34. To mention only some theologians involved in the dialogue with Hinduism: Michael Amaladoss, Felix Wilfred, and Jacques Dupuis.

35. Terrence Tilley, *The Wisdom of Religious Commitment* (Washington, D.C.: Georgetown University Press, 1995), 146.

36. Leonard Swidler, *After the Absolute: The Dialogical Future of Religious Reflection* (Minneapolis: Fortress Press, 1990), 44. The

use of the Vatican II expression *par cum pari* is here somewhat out of place. It was used during Vatican II to refer to the relationship of the pope or the bishop of Rome to other bishops, rather than to the relationship between religions.

37. Jean-Claude Basset, *Le dialogue interreligieux* (Paris: Les Editions du Cerf, 1996), 298.

38. Langdon Gilkey, "Plurality and Its Theological Implications" in *The Myth of Christian Uniqueness,* ed. J. Hick and P. Knitter (Maryknoll, N.Y.: Orbis Books, 1987), 37.

39. Swidler et al., *Death or Dialogue,* 32.

40. Gilkey, "Plurality and Its Theological Implications," 48.

41. He states that "when one knows that Jesus is truly savior, one does *not* know that he is the *only* savior. One's experience is limited and has not been able to take in the experiences and messages of all other so-called saviors or religious figures. But if Christians do not or cannot know that Jesus is the *only* savior, neither do they *have* to know this in order to be committed to this Jesus. The experience of Jesus that enabled them to say "truly" enables them to keep following him." In Paul Knitter, *Jesus and the Other Names* (Maryknoll, N.Y.: Orbis Books, 1996), 72–73.

42. Ibid., 107. The marital metaphor is a clever, but misleading one. While commitment to the truth of one's own religion creates not only openness to others, but also the desire to share one's own experience with others and bring them to the same, such is generally not the case in a marital relation.

43. This has been a constant theme in many of Paul Knitter's works, e.g., *Jesus and the Other Names* and *One Earth, Many Religions* (Maryknoll, N.Y.: Orbis Books, 1995) and even in his *Introducing Theologies of Religions* (Maryknoll, N.Y.: Orbis Books, 2002).

44. In *Problems of Religious Diversity* (Oxford: Blackwell Publishers, 2001), Paul Griffiths points to different kinds of incompatibility: contradictoriness (statements formulated in direct opposition to one another), contrariety (absolute statements that logically exclude one another), and noncompossibility (demands that cannot coexist) (32–36).

45. Moltmann, "Is 'Pluralistic Theology' Useful?" 155.

46. Pieris, *Love Meets Wisdom.*

47. Jacques Dupuis, *Christianity and the Religions: From Confrontation to Dialogue* (Maryknoll, N.Y.: Orbis Books, 2001), 135.

48. Jacques Dupuis, "Christianity and Religions: Complementarity and Convergence" in *Many Mansions? Multiple Religious Belonging and Christian Identity,* ed. C. Cornille (Maryknoll, N.Y.: Orbis Books, 2002), 66.

49. In "Plurality and Its Theological Implications" in *The Myth of Christian Uniqueness,* ed. J. Hick and P. Knitter (Maryknoll, N.Y.: Orbis Books, 1987), 45.

50. Ibid., 47.

51. Dupuis, *Christianity and the Religions,* 229.

52. Panikkar, *The Intra-Religious Dialogue,* 74

53. Swidler et al., *Death or Dialogue,* 31.

54. David Tracy, *Dialogue with the Other* (Leuven: Peeters Press, 1990), 73.

55. Paul Griffiths, *Problems of Religious Diversity* (Oxford: Blackwell Publishers, 2001), 27.

56. Lesslie Newbigin, *Signs amid the Rubble: The Purposes of God in Human History* (Grand Rapids: Wm. Eerdmans, 2003), 76.

57. In Jacques Dupuis, *Catholicism: Christ and the Common Destiny of Man* (San Francisco: Ignatius Press, 1988; original 1947), 289.

58. Hans-Georg Gadamer, *Truth and Method* (New York: Continuum, 1995), 385.

59. Tracy, *Dialogue with the Other,* 41.

60. Ibid., 42.

Chapter Three / Interconnection

1. Timothy Fitzgerald, "A Critique of Religion as a Cross-Cultural Category," *Method and Theory in the Study of Religion* 9, no. 2 (1997): 91–110. Most of the critiques of the concept of religion are based on Wilfred Cantwell Smith's groundbreaking work *The Meaning and End of Religion* (New York: Macmillan, 1963).

2. Masao Abe, "Buddhism and Christianity as a Problem of Today," *Japanese Religions* 3, no. 2 (1963): 15.

3. In John Cobb and Christopher Ives, eds., *The Emptying God: A Buddhist-Jewish-Christian Conversation* (Maryknoll, N.Y.: Orbis Books, 1990).

4. Between 1975 and 2000 the book was published in forty-three editions in twenty-three languages. Another book in this same vein is Jeremy Hayward's *Shifting Worlds, Changing Minds: Where Science and Buddhism Meet* (Boston: New Science Library, 1987).

5. Martin Marty and Scott Appleby, eds., *Fundamentalisms Observed, Fundamentalisms and Society, Fundamentalisms and the State, Accounting for Fundamentalisms, Fundamentalisms Comprehended.* These five volumes were published between 1993 and 2004 by the University of Chicago Press.

6. From this perspective, one can applaud John Paul II's "We Remember: A Reflection on the Shoah" (1998), in which the pope expressed toward the Jewish people "deep sorrow for the failure of her sons and daughters in every age."

7. Hans Küng, *Global Responsibility: In Search of a New World Ethic* (New York: Crossroad, 1991), 105.

8. Paul Knitter, *One Earth, Many Religions* (Maryknoll, N.Y.: Orbis Books, 1995), 57.

9. In uncharacteristically pessimistic terms, John Cobb warns that "some of the existing common ground [between religions] may reflect little more than shared participation in assumptions whose outworking is destroying our earth." In John Cobb, *Transforming Christianity and the World* (Maryknoll, N.Y.: Orbis Books, 1999), 84.

10. Evelyn Tucker and John Grim, eds., *Religions of the World and Ecology* (Cambridge, Mass.: Harvard University Press, 2000), xxiii. Other works that focus on ecology from an interreligious and dialogical perspective are Charlene Spretnak, *States of Grace: The Recovery of Meaning in the Post-Modern Age* (San Francisco: Harper, 1991); Baird Callicott, *Earth's Insights* (Albany: State University of New York Press, 1994); and David Kinsley, *Ecology and Religion: Ecological Spirituality in a Cross-Cultural Perspective* (Englewood Cliffs, N.J.: Prentice Hall, 1995).

11. Knitter, *One World, Many Religions,* 58. For more on the particular religious perspectives on the global economy, see Paul Knitter and Chandra Muzaffar, eds., *Subverting Greed* (Maryknoll, N.Y.: Orbis Books, 2002).

12. Paul Knitter, *Jesus and the Other Names* (Maryknoll, N.Y.: Orbis, 1996), 19.

13. Originally published in 1902. I will use the edition published in 1907 by Longmans and Green, London.

14. William James, *The Varieties of Religious Experience* (London: Longmans and Green, 1907), 266.

15. Ibid., 220.

16. Ibid., 410.

17. Nishida Kitaro, *An Inquiry into the Good,* trans. Masao Abe and Christopher Ives (New Haven: Yale University Press, 1990; original publication in Japanese in 1921), 156.

18. Sarvepalli Radhakrishnan and Charles Moore, eds., *A Source Book in Indian Philosophy* (Princeton, N.J.: Princeton University Press, 1957), 637.

19. For a critique of the so-called neutrality of this position, see Gavin D'Costa, *The Meaning of Religions and the Trinity* (Maryknoll, N.Y.: Orbis Books, 2000), 53–71.

20. Frithjof Schuon, *The Transcendent Unity of Religions* (New York: Harper & Row, 1975).

21. Aldous Huxley, *The Perennial Philosophy* (New York: Harper and Brothers, 1945), vii.

22. For example, the difference between introvertive and extrovertive mysticism (W. T. Stace) or between nature-mysticism, monastic mysticism, and theistic mysticism (R. C. Zaehner).

23. In their book *Mysticism, Buddhist and Christian* (New York: Crossroad, 1995), Paul Mommaers and Jan Van Bragt compare the two mystical traditions in order to investigate whether the term "natural contemplation" used by the Flemish mystic Jan Van Ruusbroec might coincide with Buddhist accounts of the ultimate experience. In their conclusion, the authors reject the idea that Buddhist meditation leads to a form of natural contemplation, thereby

rescuing the Buddhist experience from being an inferior form of the Christian one.

24. Steven Katz, ed., *Mysticism and Philosophical Analysis* (New York: Oxford University Press, 1978), *Mysticism and Religious Traditions* (New York: Oxford University Press, 1983), *Mysticism and Language* (New York: Oxford University Press, 1993), *Mysticism and Sacred Scripture* (New York: Oxford University Press, 2000).

25. Naomi Burton, Brother Patrick Hart, and James Laughlin, eds., *The Asian Journal of Thomas Merton* (New York: New Directions, 1973), 308.

26. A.I.M., *Bulletin of the A.I.M.* no. 29 (1980): 25.

27. In Donald Mitchell and James Wiseman, eds., *The Gethsemani Encounter: A Dialogue on the Spiritual Life by Buddhist and Christian Monastics* (New York: Continuum, 1998), xv. This meeting was convened at the suggestion of the Dalai Lama in Gethsemani and gathered twenty-five Christians and Buddhists from various denominations. It focused on the sense of communion between different religions in the pursuit of the spiritual path.

28. These practices have also extended beyond strictly monastic discipline to inform the practice of lay Christians eager to expand or deepen their spiritual life, leading to what James Arraj has called the *koanization* or *keshoization* of Christianity. In *Christianity in the Crucible of East-West Dialogue* (Chiloquin, Ore.: Inner Growth Books, 2001), 45.

29. Abhishiktananda, *Souvenirs d'Arunachala* (Paris: Epi, 1978), 27.

30. William Johnston, *The Still Point: Reflections on Zen and Christian Mysticism* (New York: Fordham University Press, 1970), 77.

31. Heinrich Dumoulin, *Zen Buddhism in the 20th Century,* trans. J. O'Leary (New York: Weatherhill, 1992), 120.

32. Dumoulin states that "Christians and Buddhists are involved in similar behavior during objectless mediation, despite the different motivational contexts" (ibid.). And Johnston offers a more elaborate account of these similarities: "The silence, the rejection of words and thoughts, the obscurity or darkness of the mind, the thinking of

nothing, the emptiness or the void — all point to a similar psychological state of mind in these two forms of concentration. Then there is the 'going down' of descent, the breaking through various levels of consciousness to the center of the soul, the seeing into one's own nature, the loss of the empirical ego, the enlightenment experience beyond subject and object provoked by a period of intense anxiety — whether it be the dark night of the senses or the great doubt and death. Again, there is in both an attitude of suspicion toward voices and visions and psychic anomalities" (*The Still Point,* 76).

33. Most religions recognize different types of religious experience: theistic or nontheistic, unitive or relational. Each religion may presume a different hierarchy or sense of superiority of one kind of experience over the other. But other religions may still point to dimensions of a particular type of experience or to ways of attaining this experience hitherto undeveloped or underdeveloped within one's own religious tradition.

34. Monika Hellwig, "The Trust and Tenor of our Conversations" in *Death or Dialogue: From the Age of Monologue to the Age of Dialogue* (London: SCM Press, 1990), 51.

35. For a sociological discussion of the relationship between monotheism and violence, see Rodney Stark, *One True God: Historical Consequences of Monotheism* (Princeton, N.J.: Princeton University Press, 2001).

36. John Hick, *God Has Many Names* (London: Macmillan, 1980). One may also find it in the work of Leonard Swidler, who calls for an "ecumenical Esperanto," which would involve "speaking not of Christ, Buddha or God when referring to the Final as dealt with by all the religions and ideologies, but rather by speaking of *Ultimate Reality,* or some such variant." In *After the Absolute: The Dialogical Future of Religious Reflection* (Minneapolis: Fortress Press, 1990), 211. He goes on to state that "hence, the body of reflection on *Ultimate Reality* might well be called *Realitology.*"

37. John Hick, *An Interpretation of Religion* (New Haven: Yale University Press, 1989), 235–36.

38. Hick, *God Has Many Names,* 94.

39. John Hick, *Philosophy of Religion* (Englewood Cliffs, N.J.: Prentice Hall, 1989), 119.

40. John Hick, "On Grading Religions," *Religious Studies* 17 (1981): 463.

41. Mark Heim, *Salvations: Truth and Difference in Religion* (Maryknoll, N.Y.: Orbis Books, 1999), 28.

42. Gavin D'Costa, *The Meeting of Religions and the Trinity* (Maryknoll, N.Y.: Orbis Books, 2000), 26. It is worth noting that this amounts to charging Hick with having begun with Kant's first *Critique,* which he can hardly deny, only to arrive at conclusions recognizably close to what one finds in the second *Critique* — and with presuming neutrality for the entire venture.

43. Ibid., 30.

44. Masao Abe, *Buddhism and Interfaith Dialogue* (Honolulu: University of Hawaii Press, 1995), 46. This might indeed be deduced from the fact that Hick speaks of "a shift from the dogma that Christianity is at the centre to the realisation that it is *God* who is at the centre, and that all the religions of mankind, including our own, serve and revolve around him." In *God and the Universe of Faiths* (London: Macmillan, 1973), 131.

45. Abe, *Buddhism and Interfaith Dialogue,* 47.

46. Ibid.

47. John Cobb, *Transforming Christianity and the World* (Maryknoll, N.Y.: Orbis Books, 1999), 90.

48. Ibid., 147.

49. Ibid., 105.

50. John Cobb, "Dialogue" in *Death or Dialogue* (London: SCM Press, 1990), 4.

51. Mark Heim, *The Depth of the Riches: A Trinitarian Theology of Religious Ends* (Grand Rapids: Wm. Eerdmans, 2001), 42.

52. Mark Heim, *Salvations,* 145.

53. Here, Heim adopts a more apologetic stance, arguing with Jerome Gellman that "the best accounts of the varied reports of religious ends will be those that preserve the highest degree of concrete validity in the largest number of them." In *The Depth of the Riches,* 42.

54. John Makransky, "Buddha and Christ as Mediators of of the Transcendent: A Buddhist Perspective," in *Buddhism and Christianity in Dialogue,* ed. Perry Schmidt-Leukel (London: SCM Press, 2005), 176–99.

55. Ibid., 199.

56. Ibid., 194.

57. Heim, *The Depth of the Riches,* 32–34.

58. Makransky, "Buddha and Christ as Mediators of the Transcendent," 194.

59. Heim, *The Depth of the Riches,* 292.

60. Makransky, "Buddha and Christ as Mediators of the Transcendent," 198.

61. Raimon Panikkar, *Christophany: The Fullness of Man* (Maryknoll, N.Y.: Orbis Books, 2004).

62. Ibid., 156.

63. Raimon Panikkar, *The Intra-Religious Dialogue* (New York: Paulist Press, 1999), 71.

64. In *Christophany* he states that "every being is a christophany, a manifestation of the christic adventure of the whole of reality on its way to the infinite mystery" (146). Against possible misunderstanding, he insists that his concept of christophany "is a question not of converting the whole world to Christianity but of recognizing that the very nature of reality shows the nondualist polarity between the transcendent and the immanent in its every manifestation." *Christophany,* 15.

65. John Cobb, "Dialogue" in *Death or Dialogue,* 82.

Chapter Four / Empathy

1. In Lesslie Newbigin, *A Word in Season: Perspectives on Christian World Mission* (Grand Rapids: Wm. Eerdmans, 1994), 18.

2. From *Waiting for God,* trans. Emma Craufurd (New York: HarperCollins Books, 2001; first published in 1951), 118–19.

3. Gerardus van der Leeuw, *Religion in Essence and Manifestation* (Princeton, N.J.: Princeton University Press, 1986), 674. Van

der Leeuw is actually somewhat reticent about using the term "empathy" because, as he puts it, it "overstresses the feeling aspect of the process, although not without some justification."

4. See Russell T. McCutcheon, ed., *The Insider-Outsider Problem in the Study of Religion* (London: Cassell, 1999).

5. See Jeppe Jensen, *The Study of Religion in a New Key* (Aarhus, Denmark: Aarhus University Press, 2003), 94.

6. One of the latest critiques of empathy may be found in Gavin Flood's *Beyond Phenomenology: Rethinking the Study of Religion* (London: Cassell, 1999), 162.

7. In Jacques Dupuis, *Christianity and the Religions: From Confrontation to Dialogue* (Maryknoll, N.Y.: Orbis Books, 2002), 230.

8. John Dunne, *The Way of All the Earth* (New York: Macmillan, 1972), ix.

9. Already in the eighteenth century, David Hume defined sympathy as "the propensity that one has to receive emotional communications from others, however different they may be from our own." In *A Treatise on Human Nature,* 3rd. ed., ed. H. A. Selby-Bigge (Oxford: Clarendon Press, 1968; original in 1739), 316.

10. The term "empathy" appears to have received this technical assignment first from Robert Vischer in 1873. Theodore Lipps in "Einfuhlung, inner Nachahmung und Organempfindaungen" in *Archiv für die Gesamte Psychologie* 2 (1903): 185–204. Translated and reprinted as "Empathy, Inner Imitation, and Sense-Feelings," *A Modern Book of Esthetics,* ed. Melvin Rader (New York: Holt, Rinehart and Winston, 1979), 374–82.

11. See Karsten Stueber, *Rediscovering Empathy: Agency, Folk Psychology and the Human Sciences* (Cambridge, Mass.: MIT Press, 2006).

12. Edith Stein, *On the Problem of Empathy* (The Hague: Martinus Nijhoff, 1964), 11.

13. Ibid., 83, 107.

14. *Issues in Husserl's Ideas II,* ed. T. Nenon and L. Embree (The Hague: Kluwer Academic, 1996), 287.

15. E. Titchener, *Elementary Psychology of the Thought Process* (New York: Macmillan, 1909), 21.

16. Max Scheler, *The Nature of Sympathy* (London: Routledge & Kegan Paul, 1954), 8.

17. Lauren Wispé, *The Psychology of Sympathy* (New York: Plenum Press, 1991), 318.

18. Hans-Georg Gadamer, *Truth and Method* (New York: Continuum, 1995), 385.

19. In Hume, *A Treatise on Human Nature*, 318.

20. Van der Leeuw, *Religion in Essence and Manifestation*, 675.

21. Eduard Spranger, *Types of Men: The Psychology and Ethics of Personality* (Halle: Max Niemeyer Verlag, 1928), 373. Though he generally insisted on the purely formal or "legal" nature of these universal mental structures, Spranger also points to some concrete ways in which all humans are thought to relate to reality: "We believed that we were able to say of its total structure that beyond all temporal and spatial differences, cognition is always a value for man, that the economic value always controls him, that aesthetic experience and creation signify a necessary value direction in him and that his relations to society are always guided by the value tendencies of power and love. Above these different value directions we found the ethico-religious value as their normative synthesis. And we maintained, furthermore, that every value region has from the outset its own immanent constructive law and objective organisation which we considered only insofar as they are organised by the dominant value."

22. Van der Leeuw, *Religion in Essence and Manifestation*, 672.

23. Claude Lévi-Strauss, *The Savage Mind* (London: Weidenfeld and Nicolson, 1966), 10.

24. Georg Vielmetter, "The Theory of Holistic Simulation," in *Empathy and Agency*, ed. Kogler and Stueber (Boulder, Colo.: Westview Press, 2000), 87. In *Rediscovering Empathy*, Stueber calls attention to the existence of "mirror neurons" that facilitate the reading of the minds of other agents.

25. Wilhelm Dilthey, *Selective Writings*, ed. H. Rickman (Cambridge, Mass.: Cambridge University Press, 1976), 221. In specifying

the content of the universal features of the "objective mind," Dilthey states that "these common bonds are expressed in identity of reason, in sympathy on the emotional plane and in the mutual commitments of right and duty accompanied by consciousness of obligation." Ibid., 186.

26. Max Scheler, *The Nature of Sympathy* (London: Routledge & Kegan Paul, 1954; first published in 1913), xxxix.

27. M. Heidegger, *Being and Time,* trans. Joan Stambaugh (Albany: State University of New York Press, 1996), 124.

28. P. Ricoeur, *Oneself as Another* (Chicago: University of Chicago Press, 1992), 317.

29. *Issues in Husserl's Ideas II,* 168.

30. Gabriel Marcel, "The Ego and Its Relation to Others" in *Homo Viator: Introduction to a Metaphysic of Hope* (London: Harper & Row, 1965), 23.

31. Dilthey, *Selective Writings,* 227.

32. From an article on method published in 1926, translated and published by Jacques Waardenburg in his anthology *Classical Approaches to the Study of Religion* (New York: Walter de Gruyter, 1999), 403.

33. Van der Leeuw, *Religion in Essence and Manifestation,* 675.

34. Joachim Wach, *The Comparative Study of Religions* (New York: Columbia University Press, 1958), 12.

35. This renders all the more remarkable the work of certain missionaries who, albeit for the purpose of conversion, were able to gain exceptionally accurate information about — and at times even understanding of — the religions and the cultures in which they worked. An example of this may be found in the work of the French missionary J. A. Dubois, who worked as a missionary in South India from 1792 to 1823. Though not afraid of highly judgmental statements regarding the "silly beliefs in astrology" (379) or "the disgusting lingam" (173), Abbé Dubois also demonstrates a — for his time — impressive understanding of Hinduism in his famous tome *Hindu Manners, Customs and Ceremonies,* 3rd ed. (Oxford: Clarendon Press, 1906).

36. In Dilthey, *Selective Writings,* 226.

37. Ibid.

38. In Edmund Husserl, *Cartesian Meditations: An Introduction to Phenomenology* (The Hague: Martinus Nijhoff, 1960), 151.

39. In Wach, *The Comparative Study of Religions*, 12.

40. Perhaps Heidegger is an exception. In *Being and Time* he says that "of the two modes of self-temporalization, only recollection goes over into empathy, not expectation" (159).

41. In Dilthey, *Selective Writings*, 227.

42. In Scheler, *The Nature of Sympathy*, 47.

43. Ibid.

44. In Stein, *On the Problem of Empathy*, 104.

45. Ibid., 105.

46. *Issues in Husserl's Ideas II*, 274–75.

47. This is developed in detail much too elaborate for me to even sketch at this juncture in Husserl's *Cartesian Meditations*.

48. Spranger, *Types of Men*, 377.

49. Dilthey, *Selective Writings*, 227.

50. Theodore Lipps, "Einfuhlung, inner Nachahmung und Organempfindaungen" I, 1ff. The example he used was that of watching a person walking a tightrope and experiencing the anxiety and excitement of the other in the process of perception.

51. Yet it must be said that the particularities of unfamiliar cultural expressions often appeal to the imagination, rather than hinder it. Christians interested in Zen Buddhism, for example, may have often been enticed by the esthetic beauty of Japanese rock gardens or the serenity of tea ceremonies as much as by the particular content of Zen teachings. In the same way, the appeal of Christianity to Hindus at times derived precisely from its Western forms and associations.

52. Spranger, *Types of Men*, 370.

53. Husserl, *Cartesian Meditations*, 5, 119.

54. Ibid., 113.

55. Van der Leeuw, *Religion in Essence and Manifestation*, 671–72. For van der Leeuw, however, this applies as much to one's own experiences as to those of others, and, given the proper historical and religious knowledge, it would be no more difficult to reconstruct he

experience of the other than it would be to reconstruct one's own past experience.

56. It is of course possible that individuals belonging to one religion may develop a genuine assent to the truth or devotion to the God of the other religion. However, here we enter into the domain of religious conversion or multiple religious belonging.

57. It is not certain that this can be said of one who feels the joy of a friend in love, and even some of what it is to be in love, though not love for her beloved.

58. Wach, *The Comparative Study of Religions*, 13.

59. In Tvetan Todorov, *Mikhail Bhaktin: The Dialogical Principle*, trans. Wlas Godzich (Minneapolis: University of Minnesota Press, 1984), 109.

60. Quoted from Mikhail Bhaktin's *Toward a Philosophy of the Act* in Flood, *Beyond Phenomenology*, 163.

61. Spranger, *Types of Men*, 377.

62. Van der Leeuw, *Religion in Essence and Manifestation*, 398.

Chapter Five / Hospitality

1. The notion of "hospitality" has also become prominent in philosophical hermeneutics. For a discussion of this category in an interreligious context, see Paul Ricoeur, *On Translation* (London and New York: Routledge, 2006), 23–24; and Richard Kearney, *Anatheism: Returning to God after God* (New York: Columbia University Press, forthcoming), chaps. 1–2.

2. See Pierre-François de Béthune, *Par la foi et l'hospitalité* (Clerlande: Publications de Saint-André, 1997).

3. Stanislas Breton, *Unicité et monothéisme* (Paris: Les Editions du Cerf, 1981), 154.

4. Often, the terminological distinction between "religion" and "cult" is used to mark the difference between religions that are worthy of respect and dialogue and those that are not. However, most uses of such terminology tend to be highly arbitrary and reflective of certain religious or ethnic prejudices rather than of differences that are fundamental, or at least logical.

5. *The First Apology of Justin,* chap. 5. From L. Russ Bush, ed., *Classical Readings in Christian Apologetics* (Grand Rapids: Zondervan, 1983), 6.

6. Karl Barth, *Church Dogmatics* 2/1 (London and New York: T & T Clark, 1961), 307.

7. Ibid., 350. In other words, it is not dependence on grace as such that forms the basis for truth, but rather "the reality of grace itself by which one religion is adopted and distinguished as the true one before all others" (356).

8. Ibid., 356.

9. Ibid., 357.

10. Congregation for the Doctrine of the Faith, *Declaration "Dominus Iesus" on the Unicity and the Salvific Universality of Jesus Christ and the Church* (2000), 7.

11. Ibid., 8.

12. Ibid., 22.

13. See *Dominus Iesus,* 4, which states that "as a consequence, it is held that certain truths have been superseded; for example, the definitive and complete character of the revelation of Jesus Christ, the nature of Christian faith as compared with that of belief in other religions, the inspired nature of the books of Sacred Scripture, the personal unity between the Eternal Word and Jesus of Nazareth, the unity of the economy of the Incarnate Word and the Holy Spirit, the unity and salvific universality of the mystery of Jesus Christ, the universal salvific mediation of the Church, the inseparability — while recognizing the distinction — of the Kingdom of God, the Kingdom of Christ, and the Church, and the subsistence of the one Church of Christ in the Catholic Church."

14. Barth, *Church Dogmatics* 2/1, 357.

15. See our discussion of the relationship between dialogue and mission in Chapter 2.

16. Henri de Lubac, *Amida* (Paris: Editions du Seuil, 1955), 10 (my translation).

17. In Francis Clooney, *Hindu God, Christian God* (Oxford: Oxford University Press, 2001), 160.

18. George Lindbeck, *The Nature of Doctrine, Religion and Theology in a Postliberal Age* (Philadelphia: Westminster Press, 1984), 81.

19. Ibid., 61.

20. Ibid., 54.

21. In "The End of Dialogue" in Gavin D'Costa, ed., *Christian Uniqueness Reconsidered* (Maryknoll, N.Y.: Orbis Books, 1990), 190. It should be noted that unlike the confessionalist exclusivism of someone like Barth, Milbank's position is fundamentally philosophical, bearing the early stamp of Alasdair MacIntyre's theory of narrative.

22. In Paul Griffiths, *Problems of Religious Diversity* (Oxford: Blackwell Publishers, 2001), 54.

23. See, for example, Francis Clooney's books *Hindu God, Christian God* (New York: Oxford University Press, 2001), and *Divine Mother, Blessed Mother* (New York: Oxford University Press, 2005).

24. These religious prohibitions have become the starting point for Küng's formulation of a global ethic. Hans Küng and Karl-Josef Kuschel, *A Global Ethic: The Declaration of the Parliament of the World's Religions* (London: SCM Press, 1993), 24–36.

25. In *The Meeting of Religions and the Trinity* (Maryknoll, N.Y.: Orbis Books, 2000), Gavin D'Costa convincingly demonstrates that this is the case even for such seemingly open and pluralist thinkers and religious leaders as Sarvepalli Radhakrishnan and the Dalai Lama (53–95).

26. Karl Rahner, *Theological Investigations,* vol. 5 (New York: Crossroad, 1966), 125. Throughout history, Christianity has acknowledged the existence of "pagan saints," individuals who, while never having encountered the fullness of Christian truth, nonetheless did exhibit a life of unquestionably high spiritual and moral value, even by Christian standards. Yet until recently, these individuals were regarded as saintly not because of their own religious traditions, but in spite of them. Emphasizing the social and historical nature of individual life and religious awareness, Rahner argued that the presence

of truth in other religions was to be regarded as an indication of the fact that the religions themselves were "lawful."

27. Karl Rahner, *Foundations of Christian Faith*, trans. William Dych (New York: Herder & Herder, 1982), 316.

28. E.g., *Dominus Iesus*, 12, 21.

29. *Dominus Iesus*, 21.

30. *Theological Investigations* vol. 5, 121. This not merely implies a knowledge of the existence of Christianity, but rather a deep personal encounter with its truth.

31. I have tried to demonstrate this with regard to the use of the Hindu term *guru* in the inculturation of Christianity in India. See Catherine Cornille, *The Guru in Indian Catholicism: Ambiguity or Opportunity of Inculturation?* (Leuven: Peeters Press, 1991).

32. D'Costa, *The Meeting of Religions and the Trinity*, 22–23.

33. "Declaration on the Relation of the Church to Non-Christian Religions," art. 2, in *Vatican Council II: The Conciliar and Post Conciliar Documents*, ed. A. Flannery (Northport, N.Y.: Costello Publishing Company, 1975), 739. My emphasis.

34. Jacques Dupuis, *Christianity and the Religions: From Confrontation to Dialogue* (Maryknoll, N.Y.: Orbis Books, 2001), 144. The ambiguity regarding the relationship between the Spirit and Christ is one of the points noted in the Vatican *Notification* (2001), or call for clarification, of Dupuis's work. The Notification states that "the Church's faith teaches that the Holy Spirit, working after the resurrection of Jesus Christ, is always the Spirit of Christ sent by the Father, who works in a salvific way in Christians as well as non-Christians. It is therefore contrary to the Catholic faith to hold that the salvific action of the Holy Spirit extends beyond the one universal salvific economy of the Incarnate Word" (III).

35. Jacques Dupuis, *Toward a Christian Theology of Religious Pluralism* (Maryknoll, N.Y.: Orbis Books, 1997), 326.

36. D'Costa, *The Meeting of Religions and the Trinity*, 122.

37. Ibid., 114. D'Costa's notion of fulfillment thus departs from that of Rahner insofar as Christianity itself may come to be fulfilled in the other religion.

38. Mark Heim, *The Depth of the Riches: A Trinitarian Theology of Religious Ends* (Grand Rapids: Wm. Eerdmans, 2001), 179.

39. Ibid., 213.

40. Dupuis, *Christianity and the Religions,* 136. Dupuis's notion of "complementarity" not only evolves, but also changes location slightly. At times, it characterizes an implication of the seeds of "truth and grace" present in other religions while at other times it refers to sacred scriptures as a whole.

41. Heim, *The Depth of the Riches,* 128 and 289.

42. John Hick, "On Grading Religions" in *Religious Studies* 17 (1981): 463.

43. Paul Knitter, *Jesus and the Other Names* (Maryknoll, N.Y.: Orbis Books, 1996), 36.

44. Roger Haight, *Jesus, Symbol of God* (Maryknoll, N.Y.: Orbis Books, 2000), 395.

45. Ibid., 409.

46. Dupuis, *Toward a Christian Theology of Religious Pluralism,* 294.

47. This is particularly evident in John Keenan's work *The Meaning of Christ: A Mahāyāna Theology* (Maryknoll, N.Y.: Orbis Books, 1989), where he reinterprets the person of Jesus from the perspective of the Buddhist category of emptiness and the two truths.

48. Breton, *Unicité et monotheisme,* 153–54. For a more expanded discussion of Breton's contribution to the theology of religions, see my article "Stanislas Breton on Christian Uniqueness" in *Philosophy and Theology* 16, no. 2 (2004): 283–96.

49. An example of this may be found in *Mysticism, Buddhist and Christian* (New York: Crossroad, 1995), where Paul Mommaers and Jan Van Bragt develop a dialogue between Buddhist and Christian forms of mysticism, adapting Ruusbroec's critique of quietistic currents in Christianity to strands within the Buddhist tradition.

50. John Cobb, *Beyond Dialogue: Toward a Mutual Transformation of Christianity and Buddhism* (Philadelphia: Fortress Press, 1982), 113.

51. Frank de Graeve, "From O.T.S.O.G. to T.A.S.C.A.S., Eleven Theses toward a Christian Theology of Interreligious Encounter" in *Louvain Studies* 7 (1979): 314–25.

52. Quoted from various sources by Judson Trapnell, *Bede Griffiths: A Life in Dialogue* (Albany: State University of New York Press, 2001), 188.

53. De Graeve, "From O.T.S.O.G. to T.A.S.C.A.S.," 321.

BIBLIOGRAPHY

Abe, Masao. "Buddhism and Christianity as a Problem of Today." *Japanese Religions* 3, no. 2 (1963).

———. *Buddhism and Interfaith Dialogue.* Honolulu: University of Hawaii Press, 1995.

———. "Kenotic God and Dynamic Sunyata." In *The Emptying God: A Buddhist-Jewish-Christian Conversation,* ed. John Cobb and Christopher Ives. Maryknoll, N.Y.: Orbis Books, 1990.

Abhishiktananda. *La montée au fond du coeur: Le journal intime du moine chrétien-sannyasi hindou.* Paris: OEIL, 1986.

———. *Saccidananda: A Christian Approach to Advaitic Experience.* Delhi: ISPCK, 1974.

———. *Souvenirs d'Arunachala.* Paris: Epi, 1978.

Abu-Nimer, Mohammed. "The Miracles of Transformation." In *Interfaith Dialogue and Peacebuilding,* ed. David Smock. Washington: United States Institute of Peace Press, 2002.

Amaladoss, Michael. "La double appartenance religieuse." In *Vivre de plusieurs religions: Promesse ou illusion?* Ed. D. Gira and J. Scheuer. Paris: Les Editions de l'Atelier, 2000.

Amell, Katrin. *Contemplation et dialogue: Quelques exemples de dialogue entre spiritualités après le concile Vatican II.* Stockholm: Gotab, 1998.

Arraj, James. *Christianity in the Crucible of East-West Dialogue.* Chiloquin, Ore.: Inner Growth Books, 2001.

Balthasar, Hans Urs von. *Truth Is Symphonic: Aspects of Christian Pluralism.* San Francisco: Ignatius Press, 1987.

Barnes, Michael. *Theology and the Dialogue of Religions.* Cambridge: Cambridge University Press, 2002.

Barth, Karl. *Church Dogmatics.* London and New York: T & T Clark, 1961.

Basset, Jean-Claude. *Le dialogue interreligieux.* Paris: Les Editions du Cerf, 1996.

Bernard of Clairvaux. *The Steps of Humility and Pride.* Trans. G. B. Burch. Cambridge, Mass.: Harvard University Press, 1940.

Bernhardt, Reinhold. *Ende des Dialogs? Die Begegnung der Religionen und ihre theologische Reflexion.* Zurich: Theologischer Verlag, 2005.

Brague, Rémi. "L'anthropologie de l'humilité." In *Saint Bernard et la Philosophie,* ed. Rémi Brague. Paris: Presses Universitaires de France, 1993.

Breton, Stanislas. *Unicité et monothéisme.* Paris: Les Editions du Cerf, 1981.

———. *The Word and the Cross.* Trans. Jacqueline Porter. New York: Fordham University Press, 2002.

Buddhaghosa. *The Path of Purification.* Trans. Bhikkhu Nanamoli. Seattle: BPS Pariyatti Editions, 1991.

Carlson, Sebastian. *The Virtue of Humility.* Dubuque: Brown, 1952.

Chrétien, Jean-Louis. *Le regard de l'amour.* Paris: Desclée, 2000.

Clooney, Francis. *Divine Mother, Blessed Mother: Hindu Goddesses and the Virgin Mary.* New York: Oxford University Press, 2005.

———. *Hindu God, Christian God.* Oxford: Oxford University Press, 2001.

———. *Seeing through Texts: Doing Theology among the Srivaisnavas of South India.* Albany: SUNY Press, 1996.

Cobb, John B. *Beyond Dialogue: Toward a Mutual Transformation of Christianity and Buddhism.* Philadelphia: Fortress Press, 1982.

Cobb, John B., and Christopher Ives, eds. *The Emptying God: A Buddhist-Jewish-Christian Conversation.* Maryknoll, N.Y.: Orbis Books, 1990.

Cobb, John B., and Paul F. Knitter. *Transforming Christianity and the World*. Maryknoll, N.Y.: Orbis Books, 1999.

Cornille, Catherine, ed. *Many Mansions: Multiple Religious Belonging and Christian Identity*. Maryknoll, N.Y.: Orbis Books, 2002.

————, ed. *Song Divine: Christian Commentaries on the Bhagavadgita*. Leuven: Peeters Press, and Grand Rapids: Wm. Eerdmans, 2006.

————. "Women between Fundamentalism and Interreligious Dialogue." In *How to Conquer the Barriers to Intercultural Dialogue*, ed. Christine Timmerman and Barbara Segaert, 197–214. Brussels: Peter Lang, 2005.

Cracknell, Kenneth. *In Good and Generous Faith: Christian Responses to Religious Pluralism*. Cleveland: Pilgrim Press, 2006.

Dalai Lama. *A Flash of Lightning in the Dark: A Guide to the Bodhisattva's Way of Life*. Boston: Shambala, 1994.

Daley, Brian. *To Be More Like Christ: The Background and Implications of the "Three Kinds of Humility."* St. Louis: Seminar on Jesuit Spirituality, 1995.

D'Arcy May, John, ed. *Converging Ways? Conversion and Belonging in Buddhism and Christianity*. Sankt Ottilien: EOS Klosterverlag, 2007.

Davie, Gracie. *Religion in Britain since 1945: Believing without Belonging*. Oxford: Blackwell, 1994.

D'Costa, Gavin, ed. *Christian Uniqueness Reconsidered*. Maryknoll, N.Y.: Orbis Books, 1990.

————. *The Meeting of Religions and the Trinity*. Maryknoll, N.Y.: Orbis Books, 2000.

de Béthune, Pierre-François. *Par la foi et l'hospitalité*. Clerlande: Publications de Saint-André, 1997.

de Lubac, Henri. *Amida*. Paris: Editions du Seuil, 1955.

————. *Catholicism: Christ and the Common Destiny of Man*. Trans. Lancelot Sheppard and Elizabeth Englund, O.C.D. San Francisco: Ignatius Press, 1988.

Dilthey, Wilhelm. *Selective Writings*. Ed. H. Rickman. Cambridge: Cambridge University Press, 1976.

DiNoia, J. A. "Pluralist Theology of Religions: Pluralistic or Non-Pluralistic?" In *Christian Uniqueness Reconsidered,* ed. Gavin D'Costa. Maryknoll, N.Y.: Orbis Books, 1990.

Dumoulin, Heinrich. *Zen Buddhism in the 20th Century.* Trans. J. O'Leary. New York: Weatherhill, 1992.

Dunne, John. *The Way of All the Earth*. New York: Macmillan, 1972.

Dupré, Wilhelm. *Patterns in Meaning: Reflections on Meaning and Truth in Cultural Reality, Religious Traditions, and Dialogical Encounters*. Kampen: Pharos, 1994.

Dupuis, Jacques. "Christianity and Religions: Complementarity and Convergence." In *Many Mansions? Multiple Religious Belonging and Christian Identity,* ed. C. Cornille, 61–75. Maryknoll, N.Y.: Orbis Books, 2002.

———. *Christianity and the Religions: From Confrontation to Dialogue.* Maryknoll, N.Y.: Orbis Books, 2001.

———. *Toward a Christian Theology of Religious Pluralism.* Maryknoll, N.Y.: Orbis Books, 1997.

Fitzgerald, M., and M. Borelli. *Interfaith Dialogue: A Catholic View.* Maryknoll, N.Y.: Orbis Books, 2006.

Fitzgerald, Timothy. "A Critique of Religion as a Cross-Cultural Category." *Method and Theory in the Study of Religion* 9, no. 2 (1997): 91–110.

Fletcher, Jeannine Hill. *Monopoly on Salvation? A Feminist Approach to Religious Pluralism.* New York: Continuum, 2005.

Flood, Gavin. *Beyond Phenomenology: Rethinking the Study of Religion.* London: Cassell, 1999.

Fodor, James. *Christian Hermeneutics: Paul Ricoeur and the Refiguring of Theology.* Oxford: Clarendon Press, 1995.

Fredericks, James. *Buddhists and Christians: Through Comparative Theology to Solidarity.* Maryknoll, N.Y.: Orbis Books, 2004.

————. *Faith among Faiths: Christianity and Non-Christian Religions.* New York: Paulist Press, 1999.

Gadamer, Hans-Georg. *Truth and Method.* New York: Continuum, 1995.

Gandhi, Mahatma. *Gandhi, An Autobiography: The Story of My Experiments with Truth.* Boston: Beacon Press, 1957.

Geffré, Claude. *The Risk of Interpretation: On Being Faithful to the Christian Tradition in a Non-Christian Age.* Trans. D. Smith. New York: Paulist Press, 1978.

Gennep, Arnold van. *The Rites of Passage.* Chicago: University of Chicago Press, 1960.

Gilkey, Langdon. "Plurality and Its Theological Implications." In *The Myth of Christian Uniqueness,* ed. J. Hick and P. Knitter, 37–52. Maryknoll, N.Y.: Orbis Books, 1987.

Gira, Denis, and Jacques Scheuer. *Vivre de plusieurs religions: Promesse ou illusion?* Paris: Les Editions de l'Atelier, 2000.

Gopin, Marc. "The Use of the Word and Its Limits." In *Interfaith Dialogue and Peacebuilding,* ed. David Smock, 33–46. Washington, D.C.: United States Institute of Peace Press, 2002.

Graeve, Frank de. "From O.T.S.O.G. to T.A.S.C.A.S., Eleven Theses toward a Christian Theology of Interreligious Encounter." *Louvain Studies* 7 (1979).

Griffiths, Bede. *The Marriage of East and West.* Springfield, Ill.: Templegate Publishers, 1982.

————. *Vedanta and Christian Faith.* Middletown, Calif.: Dawn Horse Press, 1973.

Griffiths, Paul. *An Apology for Apologetics.* Maryknoll, N.Y.: Orbis Books, 1991.

————. *Problems of Religious Diversity.* Oxford: Blackwell Publishers, 2001.

Haight, Roger. *Jesus, Symbol of God.* Maryknoll, N.Y.: Orbis Books, 1999.

Hanegraaff, Wouter J. *New Age Religion and Western Culture.* Leiden: E. J. Brill, 1996.

Heelas, Paul. *The New Age Movement*. Oxford: Blackwell Publishers, 1996.

Heidegger, Martin. *Being and Time*. Trans. Joan Stambaugh. Albany: State University of New York Press, 1996.

Heim, Mark. *The Depth of the Riches: A Trinitarian Theology of Religious Ends*. Grand Rapids: Wm. Eerdmans, 2001.

———. *Salvations: Truth and Difference in Religion*. Maryknoll, N.Y.: Orbis Books, 1999.

Heisig, James. *Dialogues at One Inch above the Ground*. New York: Crossroad, 2003.

Hick, John. *God and the Universe of Faiths*. London: Macmillan, 1973.

———. *God Has Many Names*. London: Macmillan, 1980.

———. "On Grading Religions." *Religious Studies* 17 (1981): 451–67.

———. *An Interpretation of Religion*. New Haven: Yale University Press, 1989.

———. *Philosophy of Religion*. Englewood Cliffs, N.J.: Prentice Hall, 1989.

———, ed. *Truth and Dialogue*. London: Sheldon Press, 1974.

Hick, John, and Paul Knitter, eds. *The Myth of Christian Uniqueness*. Maryknoll, N.Y.: Orbis Books, 1987.

Hildebrand, Dietrich von. *Humility, Wellspring of Virtue*. Manchester: Sophia Institute Press, 1997.

Hume, David. *A Treatise on Human Nature,* ed. H. A. Selby-Bigge. Oxford: Clarendon Press, 1968.

Husserl, Edmund. *Carthesian Meditations*. Trans. Dorian Cairns. Dordrecht: Marinus Nijhoff, 1960.

———. *Ideas Pertaining to a Pure Phenomenology and to a Phenomenological Philosophy*. Second Book: *Studies in the Phenomenology of Constitution*. Trans. R. Rojcewicz and A. Schuwer. The Hague: Kluwer Academic, 1989.

Huxley, Aldous. *The Perennial Philosophy*. New York: Harper and Brothers, 1945.

Ignatius of Loyola. *The Spiritual Exercises of St. Ignatius,* ed. G. Ganss, S.J. Chicago: Loyola Press, 1992.

James, William. *The Varieties of Religious Experience.* London: Longmans and Green, 1907.

Jeanrond, Werner, and Aasluv Lande, eds. *The Concept of God in Global Dialogue.* Maryknoll, N.Y.: Orbis Books, 2005.

Jensen, Jeppe. *The Study of Religion in a New Key.* Arhus, Denmark: Aarhus University Press, 2003.

John of the Cross. *The Collected Works of St. John of the Cross.* Trans. K. Kavanaugh and O. Rodriguez. Washington: Institute for Carmelite Studies, 1979.

Johnston, William. *The Still Point: Reflections on Zen and Christian Mysticism.* New York: Fordham University Press, 1970.

Katz, Steven, ed. *Mysticism and Language.* New York: Oxford University Press, 1993.

————, ed. *Mysticism and Philosophical Analysis.* New York: Oxford University Press, 1978.

————, ed. *Mysticism and Religious Traditions.* New York: Oxford University Press, 1983.

————, ed. *Mysticism and Sacred Scripture.* New York: Oxford University Press, 2000.

Kearney, Richard. *The Wake of Imagination.* Minneapolis: University of Minnesota Press, 1988.

Keenan, John. *The Gospel of Mark: A Mahāyāna Reading.* Maryknoll, N.Y.: Orbis Books, 1995.

————. *The Meaning of Christ: A Mahāyāna Theology.* Maryknoll, N.Y.: Orbis Books, 1989.

Kitaro, Nishida. *An Inquiry into the Good.* Trans. Masao Abe and Christopher Ives. New Haven, Conn.: Yale University Press, 1990.

Knitter, Paul F. *Jesus and the Other Names: Christian Mission and Global Responsibility.* Maryknoll, N.Y.: Orbis Books, 1996.

————. *One Earth, Many Religions.* Maryknoll, N.Y.: Orbis Books, 1995.

Kögler, H., and K. Stueber, eds. *Empathy and Agency: The Problem of Understanding in the Human Sciences.* Boulder, Colo.: Westview Press, 2000.

Küng, Hans. *Global Responsibility: In Search of a New World Ethic.* New York: Crossroad, 1991.

Leeuw, Gerardus van der. *Religion in Essence and Manifestation.* Trans. J. E. Turner. Princeton, N.J.: Princeton University Press, 1986.

Lemesurier, Peter. *This New Age Business.* Forres: Findhorn Press, 1990.

Le Saux, Henri. "A Benedictine Ashram." In *Saccidananda Ashram: A Garland of Letters.* India: Tiruchchirappali, 1989.

Lévi-Strauss, Claude. *The Savage Mind.* London: Weidenfeld and Nicolson, 1966.

Lewis, C. S. *Mere Christianity.* London: HarperCollins, 2001.

Liechty, Joseph. "Mitigation in Northern Ireland." In *Interfaith Dialogue and Peacebuilding,* ed. David Smock, 89–102. Washington, D.C.: United States Institute of Peace Press, 2002.

Lindbeck, George. *The Nature of Doctrine, Religion and Theology in a Postliberal Age.* Philadelphia: Westminster Press, 1984.

Lipps, Theodore. "Empathy, Inner Imitation and Sense-Feelings." In *A Modern Book of Esthetics,* ed. Melvin Rader, 374–82. New York: Holt, Rinehart and Winston, 1979.

Lonergan, Bernard. *Method in Theology.* New York: Herder and Herder, 1972.

Lubac, Henri de. *Amida.* Paris: Editions du Seuil, 1955.

———. *Catholicism: Christ and the Common Destiny of Man.* San Francisco: Ignatius Press, 1988.

Makransky, John. "Buddha and Christ as Mediators of the Transcendent: A Buddhist Perspective." In *Buddhism and Christianity in Dialogue,* ed. Perry Schmidt-Leukel, 176–99. Norwich: SCM Press, 2005.

Makreel, Rudolph. "How Is Empathy Related to Understanding?" In *Issues in Husserl's Ideas II*, ed. T. Nenon and L. Embree, 199–212. The Hague: Kluwer Academic, 1996.

Marty, Martin, and Scott Appleby, eds. *Fundamentalisms and Society*. Chicago: University of Chicago Press, 1993.

———, eds. *Fundamentalisms Observed*. Chicago: University of Chicago Press, 1994.

———, eds. *Fundamentalisms Comprehended*. Chicago: University of Chicago Press, 1995.

———, eds. *Fundamentalisms and the State*. Chicago: University of Chicago Press, 1996.

———, eds. *Accounting for Fundamentalisms*. Chicago: University of Chicago Press, 2004.

Masuzawa, Tomoko. *The Invention of World Religions*. Chicago: University of Chicago Press, 2005.

McCutcheon, Russell T., ed. *The Insider-Outsider Problem in the Study of Religion*. London: Cassell, 1999.

Merton, Thomas. *The Asian Journal of Thomas Merton*, ed. Naomi Burton, Patrick Hart, and James Laughlin. New York: New Directions, 1973.

Milbank, John. "The End of Dialogue." In *Christian Uniqueness Reconsidered*, ed. Gavin D'Costa, 174–91. Maryknoll, N.Y.: Orbis Books, 1990.

Mitchell, Donald, and James Wiseman, eds. *The Gethsemani Encounter: A Dialogue on the Spiritual Life by Buddhist and Christian Monastics*. New York: Continuum, 1998.

Moltmann, Jürgen. "Is 'Pluralistic Theology' Useful?" In *Christian Uniqueness Reconsidered*, ed. Gavin D'Costa, 149–56. Maryknoll, N.Y.: Orbis Books, 1990.

Mommaers, Paul, and Jan Van Bragt. *Mysticism, Buddhist and Christian*. New York: Crossroad, 1995.

Neckebrouck, Valeer. *Gij alleen de Allerhoogste: Christus en de andere godsdiensten*. Leuven: Davidsfonds, 2001.

Newbigin, Lesslie. *Signs Amid the Rubble: The Purposes of God in Human History.* Grand Rapids: Wm. Eerdmans, 2003.

———. *A Word in Season: Perspectives on Christian World Mission.* Grand Rapids: Wm. Eerdmans, 1994.

Newman, John Henry. *An Essay on the Development of Christian Doctrine.* Notre Dame, Ind.: University of Notre Dame Press, 1989.

Nicholas of Cusa. *Selected Spiritual Writings.* Trans. Hugh Lawrence Bond. New York: Paulist Press, 1997.

Nietzsche, Friedrich. *The Genealogy of Morals.* Trans. Francis Golffing. New York: Doubleday, 1956.

O'Leary, Joseph. *Religious Pluralism and Christian Truth.* Edinburgh: Edinburgh University Press, 1996.

Panikkar, Raimon. *Christophany: The Fullness of Man.* Maryknoll, N.Y.: Orbis Books, 2004.

———. *The Intra-Religious Dialogue.* New York: Paulist Press, 1999.

Phan, Peter. *Being Religious Interreligiously: Asian Perspectives on Interfaith Dialogue.* Maryknoll, N.Y.: Orbis Books, 2004.

Pieris, Aloysius. *Fire and Water: Basic Issues in Asian Buddhism and Christianity.* Maryknoll, N.Y.: Orbis Books, 1996.

———. *Love Meets Wisdom: A Christian Experience of Buddhism.* Maryknoll, N.Y.: Orbis Books, 1989.

Proudfoot, Wayne. *Religious Experience.* Berkeley: University of California Press, 1985.

Rahner, Karl. *Foundations of Christian Faith.* Trans. William Dych. New York: Herder & Herder, 1982.

———. *Theological Investigations.* Vol. 5. London: Darton, Longman & Todd, 1966.

Ratzinger, Joseph Cardinal. *Truth and Tolerance: Christian Belief and World Religions.* San Francisco: Ignatius Press, 2004.

Ricoeur, Paul. *Oneself as Another.* Chicago: University of Chicago Press, 1992.

———. *On Translation.* London and New York: Routledge, 2006.

Ruville, Albert von. *Humility: The True Talisman.* London: Simpkin, Marshall, Hamilton, Kent, 1913.

Scheler, Max. *The Nature of Sympathy.* London: Routledge & Kegan Paul, 1954; first published in 1913.

Schmidt-Leukel, Perry, ed. *Buddhism and Christianity in Dialogue.* Norwich: SCM Press, 2005.

Schuon, Frithjof. *The Transcendent Unity of Religions.* New York: Harper & Row, 1984.

Shantideva. *The Bodhicaryavatara.* Trans. K. Crosby and A. Skilton. London: Windhorse Publishers, 2003.

Smith, Wilfred Cantwell. *The Meaning and End of Religion.* New York: Macmillan, 1963.

———. *Questions of Religious Truth.* New York: Charles Scribner's Sons, 1967.

Spranger, E. *Types of Men: The Psychology and Ethics of Personality.* Halle: Max Niemeyer Verlag, 1928.

Standaert, Nicolas. *L' "autre" dans la mission.* Brussels: Editions Lessius, 2003.

Stark, Rodney. *One True God: Historical Consequences of Monotheism.* Princeton, N.J.: Princeton University Press, 2001.

Stein, Edith. *On the Problem of Empathy.* The Hague: Martinus Nijhoff, 1964.

Streiker, Lowell. *New Age Comes to Mainstreet.* Nashville: Abingdon Press, 1990.

Stuart, James, ed. *Swami Abhishiktananda: His Life Told through His Letters.* Delhi: ISPCK, 1989.

Stueber, Karsten. *Rediscovering Empathy: Agency, Folk Psychology and the Human Sciences.* Cambridge, Mass.: MIT Press, 2006.

Sullivan, Francis. *Magisterium: Teaching Authority in the Catholic Church.* New York: Paulist Press, 1983.

Swidler, Leonard. *After the Absolute: The Dialogical Future of Religious Reflection.* Minneapolis: Fortress Press, 1990.

Swidler, Leonard, John Cobb, Paul Knitter, and Monika Hellwig, eds. *Death or Dialogue: From the Age of Monologue to the Age of Dialogue.* London: SCM Press, 1990.

Teasdale, Wayne. *Catholicism in Dialogue: Conversations across Traditions.* Lanham, Md.: Rowman & Littlefield Publishers, 2004.

Teresa of Avila. *The Life of Saint Teresa of Avila by Herself.* Trans. J. M. Cohen. New York: Penguin Books, 1957.

Thomas à Kempis. *The Imitation of Christ,* ed. C. L. Fitzpatrick. New York: Catholic Book Publishing, 1993.

Tilley, Terrence. *The Wisdom of Religious Commitment.* Washington, D.C.: Georgetown University Press, 1995.

Timmerman, Christine, and Barbara Segaert, eds. *How to Conquer the Barriers to Intercultural Dialogue: Christianity, Islam and Judaism.* Brussels: Peter Lang, 2005.

Titchener, E. *Elementary Psychology of the Thought Process.* New York: Macmillan, 1909.

Todorov, Tzvetan. *Mikhail Bhaktin: The Dialogical Principle.* Trans. Wlad Godzich. Minneapolis: University of Minnesota Press, 1984.

Tracy, David. *Dialogue with the Other.* Leuven: Peeters Press, 1990.

———. *Plurality and Ambiguity: Hermeneutics, Religion, Hope.* San Francisco: Harper & Row, 1987.

Trapnell, Judson. *Bede Griffiths: A Life in Dialogue.* Albany: State University of New York Press, 2001.

Tucker, Evelyn, and John Grim, eds. *Religions of the World and Ecology.* Cambridge, Mass.: Harvard University Press, 2000.

Turner, Victor. *The Forest of Symbols: Aspects of Ndembu Ritual.* Ithaca, N.Y.: Cornell University Press, 1967.

Van Bavel, Tarcisius J. *The Rule of Saint Augustine with Introduction and Commentary.* Kalamazoo, Mich.: Cistercian Publications, 1996.

Vielmetter, Georg. "The Theory of Holistic Simulation." In *Empathy and Agency,* ed. Hans-Herbert Kögler and Karsten R. Stueber. Boulder, Colo.: Westview Press, 2000.

Von Bruck, Michael, and Whalen Lai. *Christianity and Buddhism: A Multicultural History of Their Dialogue.* Maryknoll, N.Y.: Orbis Books, 2001.

Wach, Joachim. *The Comparative Study of Religions.* New York: Columbia University Press, 1958.

Weil, Simone. "Human Personality." In *An Anthology,* ed. Sian Miles. New York: Weidenfeld & Nicolson, 1986.

———. *Waiting for God.* Trans. Emma Craufurd. New York: HarperCollins Books, 2001.

Wispé, Lauren. *The Psychology of Sympathy.* New York and London: Plenum Press, 1991.

INDEX

Index

Of Related Interest

Robert P. Imbelli, ed.
HANDING ON THE FAITH
The Church's Mission and Challenge

Catholic Press Award Winner!

What is the substance of Catholic faith and hope?
What are the best means for conveying the faith,
particularly in North America?

The Crossroad Publishing Company presents the first
volume of The Church in the 21st Century series spon-
sored by Boston College. In *Handing on the Faith*
Robert P. Imbelli, a renowned theologian and teacher,
introduces the work of leading Catholic theologians,
writers, and scholars to discuss the challenges of
handing on the faith and the opportunity it creates for
Catholics to rethink the essential core of their identity.
This volume includes original contributions by figures
such as Robert P. Imbelli, Mary Johnson, William D.
Dinges, Paul J. Griffiths, Luke Timothy Johnson,
Robert Barron, Robert Louis Wilken, Michael J.
Himes, Christopher and Deborah Ruddy, Terrence W.
Tilley, Thomas Groome, Bishop Blase Cupich, and
John C. Cavadini.

0-8245-2409-8, paperback

crossroad

Of Related Interest

James Heisig
DIALOGUES AT ONE INCH
ABOVE THE GROUND
Reclamations of Belief in an Interreligious Age

James Heisig has spent his life traveling along many roads, living in Tokyo, Madrid, and the Unites States, and listening to other religious traditions while remaining a Roman Catholic. Heisig is the storyteller and wise elder that every gathering needs, one who keenly observes details and brings the reader into the realm of religion encountering religion.

Topics in this engaging book include: ~ The Recovery of the Senses ~ Six Sutras on Dialogue ~ What Time Is It for Christianity? ~ Make-Believe Nature ~ Sufficiency and Satisfaction ~ Converting Buddhism to Christianity, Christianity to Buddhism

978-0-8245-2114-1, paperback

Check your local bookstore for availability.
To order directly from the publisher,
please call 1-800-707-0670 for Customer Service
or visit our Web site at *www.cpcbooks.com.*
For catalog orders, please send your request to the address below.

THE CROSSROAD PUBLISHING COMPANY
16 Penn Plaza, Suite 1550
New York, NY 10001

crossroad